Building a PC

FOR

DUMMIES®

5TH EDITION

Building a PC
FOR
DUMMIES®
5TH EDITION

by Mark L. Chambers

WILEY

Wiley Publishing, Inc.

Building a PC For Dummies®, 5th Edition

Published by
Wiley Publishing, Inc.
111 River Street
Hoboken, NJ 07030-5774

www.wiley.com

Copyright © 2006 by Wiley Publishing, Inc., Indianapolis, Indiana

Published by Wiley Publishing, Inc., Indianapolis, Indiana

Published simultaneously in Canada

For general information on our other products and services, please contact our Customer Care Department within the U.S. at 800-762-2974, outside the U.S. at 317-572-3993, or fax 317-572-4002.

For technical support, please visit www.wiley.com/techsupport.

Wiley also publishes its books in a variety of electronic formats. Some content that appears in print may not be available in electronic books.

Library of Congress Control Number: 2005932591

ISBN-13: 978-0-471-76772-5

ISBN-10: 0-471-76772-7

Manufactured in the United States of America

10 9 8 7 6 5 4 3 2

5B/RT/RQ/QV/IN

WILEY

About the Author

Mark L. Chambers has been an author, a computer consultant, a BBS sysop, a programmer, and a hardware technician for more than twenty years — pushing computers and their uses far beyond normal performance limits for decades now. His first love affair with a computer peripheral blossomed in 1984 when he bought his lightning-fast 300bps modem for his Atari 400. Now he spends entirely too much time on the Internet and drinks far too much caffeine-laden soda.

With a degree in journalism and creative writing from Louisiana State University, Mark took the logical career choice: programming computers. However, after five years as a COBOL programmer for a hospital system, he decided there must be a better way to earn a living, and he became the Documentation Manager for Datastorm Technologies, a well-known communications software developer. Somewhere in between writing software manuals, Mark began writing computer how-to books. His first book, *Running a Perfect BBS*, was published in 1994 — and after a short decade or so of fun (disguised as hard work), Mark is one of the most productive and best-selling technology authors on the planet.

Along with writing several books a year and editing whatever his publishers throw at him, Mark has also branched out into Web-based education, designing and teaching a number of online classes — called *WebClinics* — for Hewlett-Packard.

His favorite pastimes include collecting gargoyles, watching St. Louis Cardinals baseball, playing his three pinball machines and the latest computer games, supercharging computers, and rendering 3-D flights of fancy with TrueSpace — and during all that, he listens to just about every type of music imaginable. Mark's worldwide Internet radio station, *MLC Radio* (at www.mlcbooks.com), plays only CD-quality classics from 1970 to 1979, including everything from Rush to Billy Joel to *The Rocky Horror Picture Show*.

Mark's rapidly expanding list of books includes *iMac For Dummies,* 4th Edition; *Mac OS X Tiger All-in-One Desk Reference For Dummies; Scanners For Dummies,* 2nd Edition; *CD & DVD Recording For Dummies,* 2nd Edition; *PCs All-in-One Desk Reference For Dummies,* 2nd Edition; *Mac OS X Tiger: Top 100 Simplified Tips & Tricks; Microsoft Office v. X Power User's Guide; BURN IT! Creating Your Own Great DVDs and CDs; The Hewlett-Packard Official Printer Handbook; The Hewlett-Packard Official Recordable CD Handbook; The Hewlett-Packard Official*

Digital Photography Handbook; Computer Gamer's Bible; Recordable CD Bible; Teach Yourself the iMac Visually; Running a Perfect BBS; Official Netscape Guide to Web Animation; and the *Windows 98 Troubleshooting and Optimizing Little Black Book.*

His books have been translated into fourteen languages so far — his favorites are German, Polish, Dutch, and French. Although he can't read them, he enjoys the pictures a great deal.

Mark welcomes all comments and questions about his books. You can reach him at mark@mlcbooks.com, or visit MLC Books Online, his Web site, at www.mlcbooks.com.

Dedication

This book is posthumously dedicated to my friend and teacher, LSU journalism professor Jim Featherston. Jim taught me everything I need to know — now I can put ideas to paper.

Author's Acknowledgments

I find that writing the acknowledgments is always the easiest part of any book because there's never a shortage of material. I always have a big group to praise.

First, a well-earned round of thanks to my knowledgeable technical editor, Colin Banfield, who checked every word for accuracy (while enduring every bad joke and pun).

I'd like to thank my old friend Jody Cooper for his excellent color photography — a picture is worth a thousand words, so I figure the brand-new 16-page color insert in this edition ought to roughly double our page count!

As with every book I've written, I'd like to thank my wife, Anne, and my children, Erin, Chelsea, and Rose, for their support and love — and for letting me follow my dream!

Finally, I send my heartfelt appreciation to the hard-working editors at Wiley Publishing, Inc., who were responsible for the launch and completion of this long-lived fifth revision: my project editor and copy editor, Susan Pink, and my acquisitions editor, Bob Woerner. They're talented, dedicated people, and I count myself very lucky that I had their assistance for this project — and many to come, I hope!

Publisher's Acknowledgments

We're proud of this book; please send us your comments through our online registration form located at www.dummies.com/register/.

Some of the people who helped bring this book to market include the following:

Acquisitions, Editorial, and Media Development

Project Editor: Susan Pink

Acquisitions Editor: Bob Woerner

Copy Editor: Susan Pink

Technical Editor: Colin Banfield

Editorial Manager: Jodi Jensen

Media Development Supervisor: Richard Graves

Editorial Assistant: Amanda Foxworth

Cartoons: Rich Tennant (www.the5thwave.com)

Composition Services

Project Coordinator: Adrienne Martinez

Layout and Graphics: Jonelle Burns, Carl Byers, Andrea Dahl, Stephanie D. Jumper, Barbara Moore, Ron Terry

Proofreaders: Leeann Harney, Jessica Kramer, Dwight Ramsey, Shannon Ramsey

Indexer: TECHBOOKS Production Services

Publishing and Editorial for Technology Dummies

> **Richard Swadley,** Vice President and Executive Group Publisher
>
> **Andy Cummings,** Vice President and Publisher
>
> **Mary Bednarek,** Executive Acquisitions Director
>
> **Mary C. Corder,** Editorial Director

Publishing for Consumer Dummies

> **Diane Graves Steele,** Vice President and Publisher
>
> **Joyce Pepple,** Acquisitions Director

Composition Services

> **Gerry Fahey,** Vice President of Production Services
>
> **Debbie Stailey,** Director of Composition Services

Contents at a Glance

Table of Contents

Part II: Building Your PC 41

Chapter 3: Building the Foundation: The Case and Motherboard ...43

Chapter 4: A Bag of Chips: Adding RAM and a CPU 61

Chapter 5: The Three PC Senses: Ports, Mouse, and Keyboard 73

Introduction

Y ou've decided to build your own computer. Congratulations! That statement might seem a little like "You've decided to fly a 747" or "You've decided to teach yourself accounting" — but I'm here to tell you that this book was especially written to make it both *easy* and (believe it or not) *fun* to build your own multimedia computer with an Intel Pentium or AMD processor. (Oh, and don't forget that you're likely to save a significant chunk of cash as well, especially if you're building a powerful PC for applications such as gaming and video editing.)

To sum up, I explain the mysterious parts in the box in honest-to-goodness English, with a little humor and without the jargon — and then help you build the PC that's perfect for you!

About This Book

You'll find that each chapter in this book acts as a reference for each type of computer hardware that you can add to your computer; some are required components, and others are optional devices that add extra functionality to your PC. You can start at any point — each chapter is self-contained — although the chapters are arranged in a somewhat linear order that I recommend that you follow. The book also includes a glossary of computer terms and an appendix with information about the various operating systems available for the PC, which comes in handy if you haven't decided on an operating system to run.

Each chapter also provides the general information you need to make a buying decision between different flavors of the same component. For example, in Chapter 9, I discuss both bare-bones and advanced sound cards (without resorting to engineer-speak).

Conventions Used in This Book

From time to time, I might ask you to type a command within Windows (or whatever operating system you're using). That text often appears in bold like this: **Type me**. Press the Enter key to process the command.

I list menu commands with this format: File⇨Open. For example, this shorthand indicates that you should click the File menu and then choose the Open menu item.

From time to time, I mention messages you should see displayed onscreen by an application or the operating system. Those messages look like this: `This is a message displayed by an application`.

Although you don't really need to know a great deal of technical information to build a computer, you might be curious about the technical details that surround computers and the components that you're using. This technical information is usually formatted as a sidebar (in a separate box) to separate it from the stuff that you really *have* to know.

What You're Not to Read

If you're interested in buying and installing a particular component, such as a DVD drive or a video adapter card, you can jump directly to the chapter that describes the device and start reading. Most chapters end with general installation instructions that familiarize you with the installation process. (They don't replace the specific documentation that accompanies each component, although the generic steps that I provide give you an idea of what's involved.)

On the other hand, if you're interested in building a computer from scratch, start with Chapter 1 and follow the chapters in order; you can also skip to other chapters whenever necessary for information that you might need.

Foolish Assumptions

Here's a friendly warning: You might run across one or two doubting Thomases when you announce that you're building your own PC. Those folks probably make lots of foolish assumptions about what's involved in building a PC, and you just might want to burst their bubble by telling them the following truths:

✔ You *don't* have to be a computer technician with years of training, and you don't need a workshop full of expensive tools. In this book, no assumptions are made about your previous knowledge of computers, the Internet, programming your DVD player, or long division.

✔ No experience? Don't let that stop you! I introduce you to each of the systems in your computer, what they do, and how you install them, including advanced technology that would make a technoid green with envy. (I can't fix spaghetti by myself, so you know that building a PC must be easier than it first appears!)

✔ Some people still think that you don't save a dime by building your own PC. If that's the case, why is it still such a booming business? By assembling your own computer, you can save hundreds of dollars (and take advantage of used parts from an older computer).

✔ Finally, some people might ask you what you plan to learn by building your own PC — and that's an easy one! By the time that you're finished, you'll be ready to add and upgrade parts yourself so that you'll save money in the future — and computer-repair techs will growl when you meet them.

Now that I've put those myths to rest, it's time for the good stuff!

How This Book Is Organized

I've divided this book into six major parts. The first five are made up of a number of chapters, and each chapter is further divided into sections. You'll find all the nasty acronyms and abbreviations, part names, and relevant items in the index; important topics and information that appear elsewhere in the book are cross referenced to make them easier to find. The book also has a spiffy full-color photo shoot of a PC assembly that would please even the pickiest supermodel.

Part 1: Can 1 Really Do This?

In Part I, I introduce you to the tool (yes, only one tool) of the PC assembly trade (a screwdriver, which tells you how complex the hardware *really* is), what components make up a PC, and how they work together within your computer. You also determine what type of computer you should build by examining your current and future needs.

Part II: Building Your PC

In Part II, you assemble the required components to build a bare-bones PC —
it won't play the latest 3-D shoot-'em-up game with all the visual bells and
whistles, but it will have all the basic features that you need. You'll be able to
load your choice of operating system after you've finished this part.

Part III: Adding the Fun Stuff

In Part III, I cover the addition of hardware that makes a multimedia PC fun to
use — such as a digital stereo sound card, a DVD drive, and a dial-up modem.
After you've completed this part, you can use your new PC to access the Internet or watch a DVD movie while you work. Or you can finally play that latest
3-D shoot-'em-up game with every last visual bell and whistle turned on.

Part IV: Adding the Advanced Stuff

In Part IV, I introduce you to advanced hardware that pumps up the performance of your PC, including home networking (both the wired and the wireless type), cable and DSL Internet connections, digital scanners, and SCSI
devices. (If the acronyms sound like Egyptian hieroglyphics, read all about
them here.) Not every computer owner needs the technology found in this
part, but after you've read these chapters, you'll be familiar with the
enhancements that you can add to create a power user's PC.

Part V: The Part of Tens

The five chapters in Part V are a quick reference of tips and advice on several
topics related to the assembly of PCs. For example, you'll find a chapter
devoted to potential problems and a chapter to help you speed up your new
computer.

Part VI: Appendixes

The first appendix features a comparison of the different operating systems
typically used on today's PCs. If you haven't considered what type of operating system that you'll use, this information can be very helpful to you. The
second appendix is a glossary of computer components, terms, abbreviations, and acronyms.

Icons Used in This Book

Some things that you encounter while building your PC are just too important to miss. To make sure that you see certain paragraphs, they're marked with one of the following icons.

This icon marks the hardware you're likely to find in a power user or gamer's PC: the latest, the fastest, or the most powerful components at the time this book was written. You may have to pay more for hot hardware, but the performance you'll get is usually worth the extra coinage.

These are important. Consider my maxims to be the stuff you'd highlight in a college textbook — these facts and recommendations that would make a good tattoo, because they're universal and timeless in scope. (You'll see!)

Information marked with this icon is the printed equivalent of those sticky notes that decorate the front of some PCs. You might already know this stuff, but a reminder never hurts.

Are you thinking of adding hardware from an older computer or used hardware that you've bought or been given? If so, stay on the lookout for the Scavenger icon; it highlights information and recommendations on using older hardware. (Remember, though, that scavenged parts won't have a warranty like new components — or perform as well as new hardware, either.)

The Tip icon makes it easy to spot information that will save you time and trouble (and sometimes even money).

If you're like me and you're curious about what's happening behind the scenes — you know, if you're the kind of person who disassembled alarm clocks as a kid — this icon is for you. The Technical Stuff icon highlights information that you don't really need for assembling your PC but which you might find interesting. This information can also be blissfully ignored.

As you can imagine, the Warning icon steers you clear of potential disaster. Always read the information under this icon first!

Where to Go from Here

Before you turn the page, grab yourself a pencil and some scratch paper for taking notes — or throw caution to the wind and write directly in the book. If you need help on a particular component, jump to the right chapter; if you need to start from the beginning, start with Part I.

Enjoy yourself and *take your time*. Remember Mark's First Maxim of PC Assembly:

You're not running a race!

(I told you that maxims were universal and timeless, didn't I?) Although the process of building your own PC might seem a little daunting now, it *really is* easy. Plus, nothing is more satisfying than using a computer that you built yourself or answering PC questions from friends and relatives because "you're the computer expert!"

Part I
Can I Really Do This?

The 5th Wave   By Rich Tennant

"It's all here, Warden. Routers, hubs, switches, all pieced together from scraps found in the machine shop. I guess the prospect of unregulated telecommunications was just too sweet to pass up."

In this part . . .

1 introduce you to the various components used to build a computer, and you find out what task each part performs. I also cover some of the basic rules of computer assembly, and I explain how you can use scavenged parts from an older computer to help cut the cost of your new PC. Finally, you act as your own consultant and determine which type of custom computer you should build to fit your needs.

Chapter 1

What's in a Computer, Anyway?

Ask most people what they know about computers, and they'll tell you that a PC is a complex, sealed box full of confusing parts that you need an engineering degree to understand — something like a cross between an unopened Egyptian pyramid and a rocket engine. Ask those same people whether they want to try their hand at actually *building* a computer, and they'll probably laugh out loud. Even if you did buy all the mysterious electronic parts (which techno-types affectionately refer to as computer *components*), where would you start? Where do you buy everything? How do you fit the components together? Nobody but an honest-to-goodness computer nerd could possibly put a computer together!

Well, ladies and gentlemen, I have great news: If you can handle the tool shown in Figure 1-1 — yes, the humble Phillips screwdriver — you can safely assemble your own computer (and even enjoy doing it!). After you discover how to build your own computer and start to use it, you'll probably agree with me: Building a computer is easier than figuring out how to use some of the complicated software that the computer can run. The idea that building a computer is as difficult as building or repairing a car is just a myth (probably encouraged by computer salespeople).

Figure 1-1:
The tool of choice for computer builders.

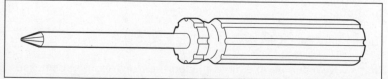

In this chapter, I introduce you to the standard electronics and peripherals that you can use to build your computer, and then I show you how they fit together. (And after you've successfully built your first computer, drop me an e-mail at `mark@mlcbooks.com`, and I can congratulate you personally!)

Anyone Can Assemble a PC

You might have heard a horror story or two about someone who tried to upgrade a PC and ended up being sucked through a black hole into another dimension. When you announce to the world that you're going to build your own computer, you're likely to face a number of common myths:

- ✔ **"Why, you have to be practically psychic about how machinery works to stick your hands inside a computer!"** Wrong. In fact, you don't have to know how any of the components work, so you don't have to be an expert in laser optics, magnetism, or electronic theory. You just need to connect the parts together correctly and attach them to the motherboard and computer case.

- ✔ **"You can't build a computer on a card table, you know. You're going to need an airstrip, a complete toolkit, and a warehouse full of parts."** Nope. You can not only assemble a computer on your dining room table but also do so with no special tools. Find your favorite screwdriver, and you're a lean, mean, computer-assembling machine.

- ✔ **"It's going to take you years to put together a computer. Heck, by the time you're finished, your computer will already be out of date."** Depends on how long it takes. No, no — just kidding! This myth is *definitely* false. If you have all your components ready to go, assembling a PC is a first-time project that you can easily finish during a long weekend.

- ✔ **"Something's not going to work with something else. You'll see."** Wrong again. (Geez, who *are* these people? They probably still think that airplanes will never get off the ground.) Today's computer components are designed to work with each other. Regardless of what brand name you buy or how much you spend, if you buy a standard computer device, it should join in that big cooperative team effort that makes a working computer.

What's the secret to building a PC? Time for the first Mark's Maxim for this book:

There really isn't a secret to building a PC.

That's why many people have started their own home businesses building custom computers in their spare time — and why thousands of my readers have built their own computers using this book. Building a computer is fun — that is, after you conquer your initial fear. Plus, you get a big ego boost after people find out that you built your own computer. Suddenly, you're a genuine PC guru to your family and friends, so be prepared to handle those technical support questions at your next party.

Building a better mousetrap (or computer)

Over the past few years, I've developed a simple rule for myself, which applies perfectly to building anything from a mousetrap to a computer. I call this rule *CA* — or, for those who can't stand abbreviations, *commonsense assembly.* The idea is a simple one: You can prevent most mistakes while assembling a PC by using a little common sense.

Keep the following CA rules in mind when handling and connecting computer components:

- **Give yourself plenty of empty space and adequate lighting.** If you're building a computer on the dining table, make sure that your work area is covered with newspaper to avoid scratches. I also recommend keeping an adjustable desk lamp handy to shine light where you need it.

- **Don't start without all the necessary components.** If you don't have everything that you need to follow a project from beginning to end, don't start yet (only to find you have to stop halfway through). It's too easy to miss a step or forget something if you leave your computer's bedside and come back the next day.

- **Treat your components carefully.** This commonsense rule doesn't mean that you need to wear gloves when handling cables or that you need to refrigerate your adapter cards. Just don't drop a part on the floor or toss it to a friend. Keep components in their antistatic packaging until you're ready to install them.

- **Follow the Three Absolutes of Component Care and Feeding.**

    1. *Never* bend a circuit board or an adapter card.

    2. *Always* make sure the cables that connect your parts aren't pinched.

    3. *Never* try to make something fit. Take the component out, check the instructions again, and try it a different way if possible.

Installing adapter cards on your motherboard can sometimes take a little longer or require a little more force than plugging a game cartridge into a video game. But determining whether a card is aligned correctly with the slot is usually easy because the slot is keyed to the shape of the corresponding card.

✔ **Read any documentation that comes with each computer component.** Although I provide step-by-step assembly instructions throughout this book, one of your components might require special switch settings or some other unique treatment.

✔ **Keep all your parts manuals together for easy reference.** After your computer is running, you can refer to your manuals quickly if you need to change any settings. In the future, if you want to sell the old device and upgrade, it's considered good manners to provide the original manual with the component. (*Complete with manual* makes a better impression on eBay.)

✔ **Save your boxes and receipts.** Although it's rare, you might find yourself stuck with a brand-new defective item, and you'll need the original packaging to return it.

✔ **Use bowls to hold small parts.** Loose screws, jumpers, and wires have a habit of wandering off if left on their own. If you end up with extra screws or doodads after successfully assembling a PC, put these parts in a bowl and start your own spare-parts warehouse. Trust me: They'll come in handy in the future. If you're a true techno-nerd, get thee hence to a hardware store and buy one of those wall racks with all the little compartments — they're perfect for organizing everything from screws to wires and jumpers.

✔ **Keep a magnetic screwdriver handy.** It *never* fails. Sooner or later, you end up dropping a screw inside your computer case. If no loose components are in the case, feel free to pick up the case, turn it upside down, and let gravity do its thing. However, if you've installed a component that's not screwed down yet, I recommend using a magnetic screwdriver for picking up wayward screws.

✔ **Check *all* connections after you install a component.** I can't explain this phenomenon (other than to invoke Murphy's Law), but you'll often connect a new component firmly only to discover later that you somehow disconnected some other connector accidentally.

✔ **Never forget the common foe: static electricity.** I'll show you how you can easily ground yourself before you touch any circuitry or adapter cards — *grounding* sounds painful, but it's not! Unless you ground yourself, you run the risk of damaging a component from the static electricity that might be lurking on your body.

✔ **Leave the computer cover off during assembly.** There's no reason to replace the case's cover immediately after installing a part — what if you connected a cable upside down? Instead, test your newly installed device first, if possible. As long as you don't touch any of the circuit boards inside the case, you'll be fine.

By the way, nothing inside your machine will explode or spew nasty radiation, so you don't have to step behind a lead screen when you fire it up. Simply make sure that you don't touch any circuit boards inside while the machine is running. Personally, I replace the case's cover on a work-in-progress only at the end of the day (to fend off dust, felines, and small fingers).

The primary, number-one, all-important, absolutely necessary, required rule

Do not panic!

There's very little chance that you can destroy a component simply by connecting it the wrong way. Take your time while you build your computer and move at your own pace — you can avoid mistakes that way. Here's an important Mark's Maxim:

Building a computer is not a contest, and there is no time limit.

After you've gained experience and built a few machines, you can work on speed records; for now, just try to schedule as much uninterrupted time as possible. For example, I know several supertechs who can assemble a complete PC in a single hour. Of course, people often laugh at them at dinner parties — being a techno-nerd does have its dark side, I guess.

The other primary, number-one, all-important, absolutely necessary, required rule

Liquids are taboo!

If you even so much as think of parking your soda or mineral water next to your computer (even just for a *second*), you might remind yourself of Chernobyl or Three Mile Island. If you spill beverages or other liquids on your computer components, that liquid will ruin everything that it touches — period.

PCs Are Built with Standard Parts

When the first personal computers appeared way back in the late 1970s, you had to be good with electronics — and a soldering iron — to build one. Everything was soldered by hand to circuit boards, and you even had to build the computer's case yourself. A *hacker* (as applied to computers) was a person who "hacked together" a computer from bits and pieces of hardware. (Today, unfortunately, the word carries a darker connotation.)

Computers have advanced a few light-years since then; now they're more like appliances, in that one computer is put together pretty much like another. Ever since IBM introduced the IBM PC, computers have been built using standard components with the same connectors and dimensions, so you no longer need the experience of an electronics engineer to assemble one. And the parts are self-contained, so you don't need to worry about soldering (or gears and springs, either). Everyone uses the same building blocks that fit together the same way.

In fact, assembling standardized computer components is how popular mail-order and direct-sale computer manufacturers build their machines. Like you, they order standard computer components and peripherals and then follow a procedure (much like the ones that I describe in this book) to assemble the computer according to your specifications.

The process that you follow to build your own computer is much like following a recipe. Like baking a cake, you add certain parts to your mixture in a certain order. Before you know it, you're taking a big bite — or, in this case, using the Internet, writing the great American novel, or blasting your favorite aliens from the planet Quark.

Understanding Your Computer's Components

Before you find out more about where to buy the parts that make up a computer (or, if you're lucky, where to scavenge them), allow me to introduce you to each of the major components of your computer. I describe each component in general, although you can find out all the details about each computer part in other chapters of this book.

By the way, *scavenging* parts is more wholesome than it sounds; I use the term to refer to components that you've removed from an older computer, used components that you've bought, or used parts that someone has given you. Check out Chapter 2 for some good tips and hints on where to scavenge computer components.

The metal mansion

Your computer's *case* is its home, complete with a power supply, the various buttons and lights on the front, and the all-important fan that keeps the inside of your computer cool. Today's high-power gaming machines have three or four fans, depending on how many devices inside are generating heat — heck, the fastest PCs that gamers build these days are liquid-cooled, just like your car!

You might notice several large, rectangular cutouts on the front of your case. Don't worry — your computer case isn't defective; it's supposed to have them. These holes, called *drive bays,* enable you to add components, such as a tape backup drive or a DVD-ROM drive. An unused drive bay is usually covered by a plastic insert. Or the front of your case might have a door that swings open for access to the bays.

You can get computer cases in various sizes. The size that you choose depends on how many toys (usually called *peripherals*) you want to add to your computer. See Chapter 3 for a more detailed discussion of your computer's case.

The big kahuna

A number of different circuit boards are inside a computer, but only one is big enough, complicated enough, and important enough to be called your computer's *motherboard.* Your computer motherboard holds

- ✔ **The CPU chip:** This acts as the brain of your PC.
- ✔ **The RAM modules:** These act as your computer's memory while it's turned on.
- ✔ **All sorts of connectors:** You connect lots of things to your motherboard, such as hard drives, a DVD drive, and power cables.

In fact, the motherboard holds just about everything, as you can see in Figure 1-2. (PCI slots are covered in Chapter 4, and your motherboard's BIOS makes an appearance in Chapters 3 and 7.)

If you enjoy acronyms and abbreviations, you'll be happy to know that CPU stands for *central processing unit,* and RAM stands for *random access memory.*

Computer CPUs come in different speeds, measured in gigahertz (GHz), such as 3 GHz. Older processors used to be measured in megahertz (MHz), such as 350 MHz. Sometimes, the CPU speed is mentioned after the processor name, such as Pentium 4 3.06 GHz. In general, the faster the CPU speed, the faster your computer.

The most popular brand of CPU these days is the Intel Pentium series, which includes the Pentium 4 and Pentium Extreme Edition, but you can also find processors from Advanced Micro Devices, which everyone calls *AMD.* AMD's alternative CPUs are usually less expensive and often run faster and more efficiently than the Pentium 4. I discuss the most popular processors and their advantages later in Chapter 4.

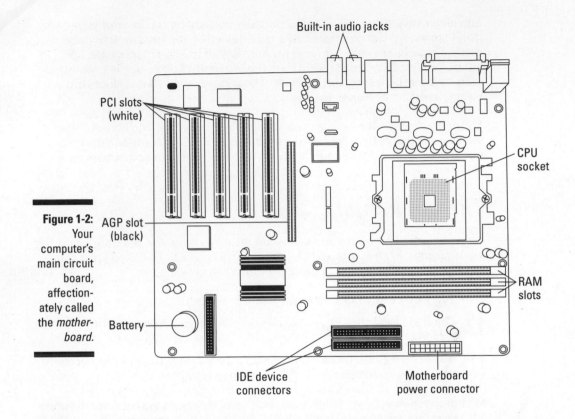

Built-in audio jacks

PCI slots
(white)

CPU
socket

Figure 1-2:
Your
computer's
main circuit
board,
affection-
ately called
the *mother-
board.*

AGP slot
(black)

RAM
slots

Battery

IDE device
connectors

Motherboard
power connector

Your motherboard is probably one of the more expensive parts that you need to buy. If you can find a used motherboard in good shape with a Pentium 4 class CPU already installed, you should consider it if the price is right. What price is right? Motherboard prices fluctuate every month (usually downward), so check the price on a new motherboard that has a similar Pentium-series chip to determine whether you're getting a good deal on the used board. I find Newegg (www.newegg.com), eBay (www.ebay.com), and PriceWatch (www.pricewatch.com) to be the best resources for checking prices.

For all the details on your motherboard, see Chapter 3. I discuss CPU chips and RAM modules in Chapter 4.

The eye candy

Next on your list are the *video card* and *monitor.* Together, these two parts display everything from your e-mail to your latest financial figures to all those killer Web pages (and don't forget those flashy enemy Quarkians you need to disintegrate).

All video cards have their own special, onboard RAM modules; the more RAM, the more colors and detail the card can display. Today's state-of-the-art video cards also help speed up your computer while it displays 3-D graphics or digital video. The video card performs most of the display work itself, giving your CPU a well-deserved rest. (Note that many of today's motherboards have a built-in video card, so you may not need a separate card if you're not interested in playing the latest games.)

Monitors have screen areas that typically range from 15 inches to 21 inches (measured diagonally across the case). You can go even larger if you crave that much space, or you can put two monitors side-by-side for a larger virtual desktop. Naturally, the larger the monitor, the more expensive it is. The latest liquid crystal display (LCD) monitors, which use less electricity and emit very little radiation, are more expensive than CRT (or tube) monitors of the same size.

Chapter 6 contains just about everything that you ever (or never) wanted to know about video cards and PC monitors.

The places for plugs

Your power cord isn't the only connection that you need on the outside of your computer. For example, you also need to attach a mouse and a keyboard (unless you've gone wireless), and you might also want to add a portable MP3 player, a gamepad, a digital camera, and a printer. These days, virtually all the *ports* (the connectors so proudly displayed on the back of your PC) are built into the motherboard, but you can install new ports for external devices separately.

You can point and click with things other than a mouse, such as a trackball, a touchpad, or a drawing tablet. A mouse is practically a requirement for Windows (although you can still navigate strictly from the keyboard if necessary).

Even the traditional keyboard has changed. Ergonomically shaped keyboards are designed to make typing easier on your hands, wrists, and forearms. And Windows XP recognizes two or three new keys to activate the Start button and display menus in an application. (Thank goodness Bill Gates can't add new letters to the alphabet.) However, if you can scavenge a standard PC keyboard, it should still work just fine.

Your computer also needs at least one universal serial bus (USB) and one parallel port to use many external devices. For example, most digital cameras are connected with USB ports, and your printer can use either a parallel port or a USB port. Other proprietary, specialized ports (such as a FireWire port for digital video) might end up sticking out the back of your new computer, depending on what components you add. (Need the complete rundown on ports? Jump to Chapter 5.)

Oh, and don't forget your Ethernet network port. Many motherboards now have built-in Ethernet cards, or you can add an Ethernet network adapter card separately. For all the details on building your own network (or connecting your new PC to an existing network), swing by Chapter 12.

The data warehouse

Earlier in this chapter, I mention that your RAM modules act as your computer's memory while the computer is running. However, when you switch off your computer, it forgets the data in RAM, so you need a permanent place to store Uncle Milton's Web page address or your latest stock report. This permanent storage comes in three forms: hard drive, removable storage drive (for example, a CD/DVD recorder or a Zip drive), and floppy disk drive (with its accompanying floppy disk).

Your computer includes at least one hard drive and one floppy drive; the standard PC floppy drive still uses a 3½-inch disk that holds 1.44MB. Hard drives, on the other hand, have much greater storage capacities. Older drives can store hundreds of megabytes (MB), but newer hard drives hold gigabytes (GB) of data (that's 1000 megabytes). At the time of this writing, typical hard drives range in capacity from 40GB to more than 300 or 400GB — and those figures are constantly rising, while costs are constantly dropping. (You've gotta love that free-market competitive model!)

Newer hard drives are typically faster than old drives, too. The new ones can deliver more data to your computer in less time than drives made as little as two or three years ago.

If you're buying a new hard drive, buy as much data territory as possible. Chapter 7 is your guide to both hard drives and floppy drives.

The bells and whistles

Today's multimedia PCs have almost more extras, add-ons, and fun doodads than any mere mortal can afford — well, except for Bill Gates, that is. If you want to be able to install and run today's software, though, you need at least a CD-ROM drive. Multimedia applications and games also need a sound card (or built-in audio hardware on your motherboard), along with a set of speakers. In Chapter 8, I tell you more about CD-ROM and DVD drives, and Chapter 9 has the skinny on PC sound cards.

Another common addition to a PC is a printer. If you need the lowdown on today's printer technology, jump to Chapter 14. And don't forget a dial-up modem for connecting your computer to other computers across telephone lines, especially if you're an Internet junkie. (I cover modems in Chapter 10.) If a high-speed cable or DSL Internet connection is available in your area and you can afford it, you can jump on the Internet broadbandwagon. (That's so bad it doesn't even qualify as a pun.)

In later chapters, I also discuss advanced stuff for power users, such as network hardware and scanners. You don't have to read those chapters, and you won't be tested on them. But they're there in case you feel adventurous (or you really need them).

Connecting Your Computer Components

You might be wondering how to connect all the various components that make up a computer. "What happens if I connect something wrong? Am I going to light up like a Christmas tree? Will I burn up an expensive part?"

I admit that when I built my first computer in the early 90s, I had these same concerns. To reassure you, consider these facts:

- ✔ **Most connectors for computer components are marked to help you plug them in correctly.** In fact, some connectors are designed so that you can install them in only one direction.

- ✔ **Ruining a computer component simply by plugging it in the wrong way is almost impossible.** At the worst, the device simply won't work. Just connect the component properly, and it should work just fine.

- ✔ **Although you connect your computer to a wall socket, unless you disassemble the power supply or monitor (which you are *not* going to do), you won't be exposed to dangerous voltage.** Of course, it pays to take basic precautions — such as unplugging your PC each time you add or remove a component.

Most components within a computer are connected with cables. For example, Figures 1-3 and 1-4 show a floppy drive cable and a power cable, respectively. I give you instructions on how to make sure that you're connecting cables properly.

You'll also be adding *adapter cards.* These circuit boards plug into your computer, much like how a game cartridge plugs into a video game. Adapter cards provide your computer with additional features — for example, you can add a sound card (see Chapter 9) and an internal modem (see Chapter 10) to provide better audio and a dial-up Internet connection, respectively. Adapter cards are arranged in rows at one end of a computer, as shown in Figure 1-5.

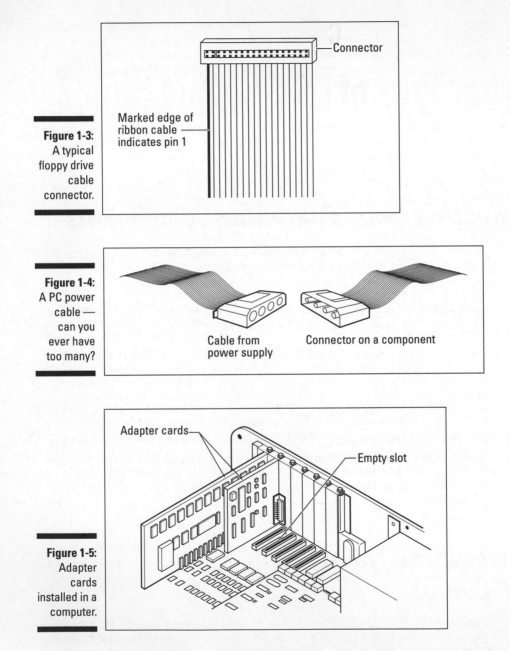

Figure 1-3: A typical floppy drive cable connector.

Connector

Marked edge of ribbon cable indicates pin 1

Figure 1-4: A PC power cable — can you ever have too many?

Cable from power supply

Connector on a component

Figure 1-5: Adapter cards installed in a computer.

Adapter cards

Empty slot

Depending on the type of motherboard that you install, you'll use PCI, PCI-Express, or AGP adapter cards. In Chapter 3, I explain how to select the right type of adapter card as well as what all those NASA-inspired abbreviations mean. Make sure that you get the right kind of adapter card because the wrong type of card won't fit.

Chapter 2

What Type of PC Should I Build?

*W*hen you walk into an oh-so-hip retail electronics store these days to buy a computer, the salesperson is supposed to help you choose the right one for your needs. If you build your own computer, however, you need to figure out *for yourself* what type of computer is best for you. Take it from me — you're likely to come up with something far better than many so-called experts who sell computers. Remember that they're interested primarily in making money, so it's in their best interest to talk you into a more expensive model than you really need.

In this chapter, I show you how to figure out what type of computer fits your needs, and I suggest three basic configurations. I tell you what parts you need to buy. I also fill you in on the different sources for buying computer parts — especially used parts, which can cut the cost of building your new machine even further.

Interrogating Yourself on Your Computer Needs

If every computer owner had the same needs, only a single model would be available. But because today's computers are used at home *and* at the office, for business *and* for pleasure, what works well for one person might not fit for another. Although most computers sold at the time of this writing are Pentium 4 computers, they're about as different from each other as the thirty-odd flavors at your local ice cream parlor — or at least they *should* be.

To custom-build the computer that *you* need, you have to design it around who you are and what you plan to do. The easiest way to determine what type of computer you need is to ask yourself a series of questions. For those who enjoy TV shows about lawyers, here's a chance to cross-examine yourself. Grab a pen and a notebook and write your answers to the questions on this checklist:

✔ **Primary application:** What will be the main function of your computer? In other words, what will you be doing with it about 75 percent of the time that you're using it? For example, do you plan to use the computer for word processing, drafting, or Internet e-mail and Web surfing? Are you a big-time game player who likes to play the latest and hottest 3-D game releases? Jot down the main function of your computer under the heading "Primary application."

If you're not quite sure what your primary application will be, just write a general term such as *office work, home use,* or *very expensive paperweight.*

✔ **Secondary application:** What will be the secondary function of your computer? In other words, what will you typically use it for if you're not performing the main function? Do you play games during the evening, or does your family use the computer for education or those hot eBay bargains? Write the secondary use for your computer under the "Secondary application" heading.

✔ **Family computer:** Will children be using your computer for education or games? If so, write that use under the "Family computer" heading.

✔ **High-quality video:** Will you be using your computer for heavy-duty graphics, such as the latest cutting-edge 3-D games, professional desktop publishing, home DVD theater, video editing with a program such as Adobe Premiere Pro, or advanced image editing with a program such as Jasc Paint Shop Pro? If so, write *required* under the "High-quality video" heading.

✔ **Power user:** Are you going to run an entire suite of computer programs such as Microsoft Office or Macromedia's Studio MX? Will you be running sophisticated, expensive applications such as Adobe Creative Suite 2? If you're planning on using complex programs, write *yes* under the "Power User" heading.

Some people want the fastest possible computer. They hate waiting, and they're willing to pay extra to get the Cadillac of computers that's ready for anything. If you fit this description and you don't mind paying extra for many of your computer components, go ahead and write *yes* under the "Power User" heading. You'll spend more money than the typical person because you're buying more powerful and expensive parts, but you'll probably end up with the nicest computer on your block.

✔ **Network user:** Will you connect your computer to other computers over a wired or wireless LAN? (That's techno-babble gibberish for *local area network* — or, if you have a life, just *the network*.) If your answer to this question is *yes,* write that down under the "Network user" heading (and prepare yourself for an extra headache or two later, in Chapter 12, where I discuss networks).

✔ **One last question:** Where were you on the night of the 15th? (Too bad Perry Mason didn't have a computer to keep track of all those details!)

See, that didn't hurt! You've now eliminated the salesperson and built a list of your computer tasks and activities. From this list, you can build your own description of your computer needs. Pat yourself on the back and pour yourself another cup of coffee or grab another soda. In the following section, you use this list to determine what type of components you need to build into your computer.

Answering Your Computer-Needs Questions

If you were buying a computer through a retail store, the salesperson's next move after inquiring about your computer needs would be to saunter over to one particular model and say something reassuring, like "Based on what you've told me, I'd recommend this as the perfect PC for you. Will that be cash, check, or charge?"

Whoa, Nellie! Chances are that the salesperson's choice *might* meet your needs, but when you're building your own computer, *you* get to decide which parts are more important than others. Are you looking for speed? Storage space? The best sound or the best 3-D graphics?

In this section, you use the description of your computer needs (which you created in the preceding section) to choose between three standard computer designs. I've created each of these basic designs to fit a particular type of computer owner. Later in this chapter, you find out whether you need to add special stuff to your base model. (You might recognize this method as the same one used by savvy car buyers to get exactly the car they want at the lowest possible price.)

Look through the descriptions of each of the three designs that follow and then select one that can best serve as the base model for your computer. Of course, you can add or subtract parts, select more expensive parts for any of these designs, or just jot down extra parts that you want to add after your computer is up and running. The following computer designs aren't hard-and-fast specifications, just suggestions.

I include in each of the following designs a final entry (the *Optional* field) that names one or more extras that most people find useful for one reason or another. They're not required to run programs, but they make life a heck of a lot easier! Some optional items that I suggest might be upgrades to an existing part in that design. For example, if you're willing to spend extra for a faster processor, I recommend the type of processor that you should look for.

Because the standards for CPU speeds, requirements for random access memory (RAM), and hard drive capacities change often in today's PC industry, you'll find my absolute latest and greatest recommendations for all three designs — as well as links to my favorite Web stores and resource sites — on my Web site, www.mlcbooks.com.

Design 1: The Jack Benny economy-class

One of the reasons why you might want to build a computer is to save money. My first design is tailored for those who want to build a basic, no-frills computer for the least amount of money. (Fans of old-time radio, think about the penny-pinching Jack Benny.) You won't be piloting the latest flight simulator on this computer . . . but then again, life doesn't begin and end with games. However, you can skip only certain pieces of hardware; for example, avoid asking, "Do I really need a keyboard?" (Hey, even a Maxwell needs wheels.)

This type of computer is suitable if the checklist description that you compiled in the preceding section fits this profile:

- ✔ Both your primary and secondary applications are word processing, home finance, keeping track of household records, Internet e-mail, or similar simple applications that don't require the fastest computer or a large amount of memory.

- ✔ According to your checklist, you have no entry under "Family computer," you do not require high-quality video, and you are not a power user.

In Table 2-1, I list the appropriate details about the computer components that you need to build this bare-bones, basic computer design. Although it has no bells and only a few whistles, it still qualifies as an entry-level PC — and it's also representative of what you can build from used parts. (Find more details on all these components in upcoming chapters.) This PC will run its best using Windows XP Home.

Table 2-1 Requirements for a Bare-Bones Pentium-Class Computer

Computer Component	What to Look For
Case	Standard "pizza-box," ATX minitower, or desktop model; single fan
CPU/motherboard	Celeron, Pentium 4, Sempron or Athlon XP; peripheral component interconnect (PCI) slots
System RAM	256MB
Hard drive	One enhanced integrated drive electronics (EIDE) drive with at least 40GB of storage capacity
Floppy drive	One 3½-inch, 1.44MB disk drive
CD-ROM	48x internal drive
Video card	Standard 32MB or 64MB PCI/AGP super video graphics array (SVGA) adapter
Monitor	15-inch SVGA
Ports	At least two universal serial bus (USB) ports and one parallel port
Input	Standard 101-keyboard; mouse
Optional	A modem for connecting to the Internet; a DVD recorder for creating data and audio CDs and DVD-video discs; inkjet printer

Design 2: The Cunningham standard edition

Remember Richie Cunningham and his family from *Happy Days*? If home computers had been around in the 1950s, Richie and crew would have used this standard edition design. (Think of this model as the family sedan.) It's typical in every way, including the moderate amount of money that you'll spend building it. This computer has standard multimedia capabilities, and it can handle Adobe Photoshop Elements without blinking.

This type of computer is suitable if your checklist description fits this profile:

- ✔ Your primary application involves browsing the Web, using Internet e-mail, working with more advanced productivity programs (such as spreadsheets and scheduling applications), using simple desktop-publishing software, or creating computer artwork.

- ✔ Your secondary application involves computer games, multimedia, or educational software on CD or DVD.

- ✔ You do not require high-quality video, and you are not a power user.

Table 2-2 lists the requirements for the most important parts that you need for building this midrange design.

Table 2-2	Requirements for a Middle-Range Pentium-Class Computer
Computer Component	*What to Look For*
Case	ATX minitower model; single fan
CPU/motherboard	Pentium 4 or AMD Athlon XP; AGP and PCI slots
System RAM	512MB
Hard drive	One EIDE or SATA drive with at least 80GB of storage capacity
Floppy drive	One 3½-inch, 1.44MB disk drive
Video card	Standard 64MB accelerated graphics port (AGP) 3-D video adapter with NVIDIA or ATI graphics chipset
Modem	56 Kbps v.90 internal data/fax
CD-ROM	16x internal DVD recorder
Sound card	PCI audio card (64 voices)
Monitor	17-inch SVGA
Ports	Four USB ports and one parallel port
Input	Standard 101-keyboard; mouse
Optional	Inkjet or monochrome laser printer; scanner; 19-inch monitor; FireWire port for a digital camcorder; wired or wireless Ethernet adapter; cable/digital subscriber line (DSL) modem

Design 3: The Wayne Manor Batcomputer

"Holy microchips, Batman!" Design 3 is the power user's dream — everything is first class. This system can handle even the toughest jobs, such as creating 3-D artwork, putting games such as Half-Life 2 through their paces, and editing images with Adobe Photoshop CS2. The Batcomputer that you build can be as good as any top-of-the-line computer that you can buy at That Big Store That Sells PCs — except, of course, that you'll spend hundreds of dollars less.

This type of computer is suitable if your checklist description fits this profile:

- ✔ Your primary application involves advanced or heavy computational work, such as computer-aided drafting, video editing, or 3-D animation. If your primary application is playing the latest and greatest computer games in all their glory, you should consider the Batcomputer, too.

- ✔ According to your checklist, you require high-quality video, and you are a power user.

- ✔ You simply want the best possible computer, which will last the longest time before it requires upgrading. (Speaking of upgrading, in the sidebar "Finding bargains in so-called obsolete computers" elsewhere in this chapter, I show you how to take advantage of *other people* upgrading their computers.)

Table 2-3 lists the requirements for the most important components that you need for this design.

Table 2-3	Requirements for a Top-of-the-Line Pentium-Class Computer
Computer Component	*What to Look For*
Case	Full-tower model; dual fan
CPU/motherboard	The fastest doggone Pentium Extreme Edition or Athlon 64 processor available; AGP or PCI-Express video slot, PCI and PCI-Express slots
System RAM	At least 1GB
Hard drive	One EIDE, SATA, or SCSI drive with at least 120GB of storage capacity
Floppy drive	One 3½-inch, 1.44MB disk drive

(continued)

Table 2-3 *(continued)*

Computer Component	What to Look For
Video card	AGP or PCI-Express 3-D SVGA adapter with at least 128MB of video memory; NVIDIA or ATI graphics chipset
Modem	56 Kbps v.90 internal data/fax
CD-ROM	16x dual-layer DVD recorder
Sound card	PCI audio card (64 voices, 3-D positional sound, hardware MP3 encoding)
Monitor	19-inch SVGA or 17-inch liquid crystal display (LCD) flat-screen display
Ports	Four to six USB ports, two FireWire ports, and one parallel port
Input	Ergonomic keyboard with extra Windows keys, trackball
Optional	Scanner; inkjet or laser printer; wired or wireless Ethernet adapter; 21-inch monitor; cable/digital subscriber line (DSL) modem; videoconferencing (Webcam) camera; TV tuner card

After you select the best base-model computer that meets your needs, you're ready to identify any special add-ons (or, in the language of the techno-wizards, *peripherals*) you need to use your applications.

Getting Your Hands on the Special Stuff

If you plan to use your new computer almost exclusively for a particular purpose (composing music or drafting, for example), you might already know what special stuff you need. In case you're a newcomer to your particular application, however, the following sections outline some of the special stuff that you might need.

Drafting, graphics, and pretty pictures

If you're an artist or you're interested in computer graphics, you might want to get your hands on some of the equipment in this list. The first two are peripherals, and the second two are upgrades to standard components:

✔ **Drawing tablet:** This computer peripheral is something like an electronic piece of paper — now there's a real technological advancement, right? You can draw on the surface of the tablet, as shown in Figure 2-1, which in turn sends your drawing directly to the screen. Many freehand artists and drafting gurus prefer drawing with natural movements of the hand rather than trying to draw a line by using a mouse cursor. (For more information on the drawing tablet, jump to Chapter 5.)

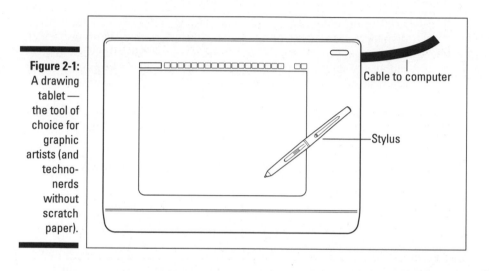

Figure 2-1: A drawing tablet — the tool of choice for graphic artists (and techno-nerds without scratch paper).

Cable to computer

Stylus

✔ **Scanner:** A scanner (as shown in Figure 2-2) enables you to "read" pictures from printed material directly into a graphics program. You can also use a scanner to read (or *acquire*) text from a magazine article or book directly into your word processing program. Some scanners use a feature named OCR — an abbreviation that's actually easier to use than the full phrase, *optical character recognition.* (For all the details on scanner technology, head to Chapter 14.)

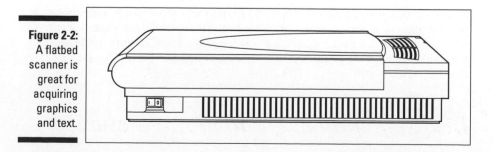

Figure 2-2: A flatbed scanner is great for acquiring graphics and text.

- ✔ **Upgrades:** If you wrote *required* under the "High-quality video" heading in your description, you need a faster, more expensive video card with these features:

  - **3-D accelerator chip:** This accelerator chip takes care of the video processing that would normally be handled by your CPU, so your Windows games and programs with high-resolution graphics run faster. The latest high-performance video cards from NVIDIA and ATI both feature 3-D acceleration onboard.

  - **Additional video RAM:** Extra video RAM enables your monitor to display more colors with higher resolutions within Windows (which is easier on your eyes). With extra RAM, your computer can display higher resolutions. For example, a professional desktop-publishing application can easily create layouts that require a minimum resolution of 1600 x 1200. And you can display larger pictures with more accurate colors.

Home-office and small-business stuff

Are you going to get all businesslike on me? No problem — a computer can help you organize a home office so that you can find the right information when you need it. (Imagine that!) Consider these extras as company money well spent:

- ✔ **Printer:** Most home office computers need an inkjet or a laser printer. Both these printers have distinct advantages, and I explain the differences in detail in Chapter 14.

- ✔ **Scanner:** If your PC came equipped with a data/fax modem, you might consider adding a scanner. Besides the advantages that I mention in the preceding section, a scanner provides the "missing link" for your modem's fax capabilities. Without a scanner, you can fax only electronic documents that you create on your computer — you're stuck if you want to fax something from a paper copy. With a scanner, however, you can scan in the pages from your hard copy and then fax the images.

- ✔ **Data/fax/voice modem:** Speaking of modems, how would you like your computer to answer the phone for you? If you pick up a data/fax/voice modem, you can set up separate voice mailboxes for you and your business. I talk more about voice modems in Chapter 10.

Mozart's musical computer

Too bad Wolfgang Amadeus never got to jam using a computer. If you're a musician, you might already know some of the cool stuff that you can do with a computer. Whether or not you're a musician, the following computer components can turn your PC into a miniature recording studio. Check out these toys:

- ✔ **MIDI:** No self-respecting computer musician would be without a sound card with MIDI support. With the Musical Instrument Digital Interface (MIDI) standard, you can play music directly into the computer from your instrument and then edit the music. Or your computer can take control of a MIDI-capable instrument that you've connected to the MIDI port and play it automatically. (For the complete description of MIDI, visit Chapter 9.)

- ✔ **MP3:** Are you interested in riding the recent wave of MP3 popularity? These digital music files can be downloaded from the Internet and stored on your computer's hard drive, yet they sound exactly like you're listening to an audio CD. You can also transfer these files to one of the new generation of handheld MP3 personal players (like my favorite, the iPod from Apple) and listen while you're walking or working. A sound card with MP3 hardware support can create superb MP3 files or allow a slower computer to play MP3 files without distortion. (I serve up the MP3 details in Chapter 9.)

- ✔ **CDs:** One of my favorite extras enables you to record your own audio CDs. Musicians and audiophiles can burn MP3 files to create custom CDs — and your home-brewed CDs can sound as good as the music CDs you buy in a store. Figure 2-3 illustrates a typical external DVD recorder. (For all the details on CD and DVD drives, skip to Chapter 8.)

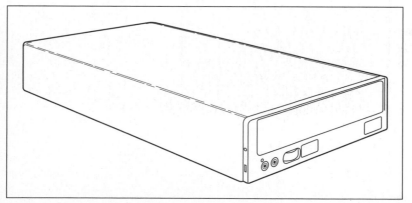

Figure 2-3:
Tape is dead — now you have a CD or DVD recorder for creating your own audio CDs!

The ultimate bad-guy blasting box

Now, you might have to pretend with your friends and family, but you can relax around here: I know the *real* reason why you need a computer. If you haven't played some of today's best action, strategy, and simulation computer games, you're missing out on the chance to fly an Apache helicopter, play 18 holes with Arnold Palmer, or take over the entire galaxy, planet by planet! Here's the special stuff that you need to create your ultimate game machine:

✔ **Joystick:** When you mention that you're ready to play games, most people think of a computer joystick (or its close relative, the PC gamepad) first. The traditional favorite for flight games, joysticks come in a wide range of styles: Some have two buttons and sell for less than $10, and others have twenty buttons that are programmable for every game and sell for more than $100. Joysticks aren't the only controller choice, though. You can find steering wheels and pedals for car racing, video-game-style gamepads, and even 3-D controllers for games such as Doom 3 and Half-Life 2.

If you're willing to spend the extra cash, you can even get a *force feed-back* joystick (as shown in Figure 2-4) that shakes and rumbles when your F-16 or Spitfire gets hit. Thank goodness no one's developed a missile that you can launch from your computer! (Set your sights on Chapter 15 to find out more about this hot joystick.)

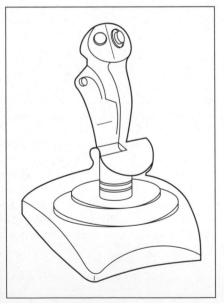

Figure 2-4:
An advanced programma-ble force-feedback joystick for those *Top Gun* wannabes.

✔ **3-D video card:** If you prefer 3-D games, you need an advanced 3-D video card that can help speed up the action. This type of card takes care of the complex math necessary for realistic 3-D effects, leaving your computer free to concentrate on running the program. A 3-D video card fits the bill also if you're looking for extra video RAM. Today's 3-D video cards use one of two slots on your motherboard: PCI-Express or AGP. (Chapter 6 includes more info about video cards.)

✔ **Audiophile sound card:** A great game machine needs the same high-quality sound card demanded by computer musicians. Most games released these days have spectacular soundtracks, and the Dolby Digital sound from a good sound card enhances gameplay. Some games even use a technique called *stereo positioning* (which the more expensive sound cards can take advantage of). If a racecar passes you on the right, for example, you hear the sound of its engine through your right speaker. (If you're interested in sound cards, check out Chapter 9.)

✔ **Subwoofer speaker:** Speaking of speakers, if you want to feel like you're inside your game, consider a more expensive PC speaker system that includes a subwoofer. Audiophiles know that a *subwoofer* speaker provides the richest, deepest bass (even down to subsonics that you can't actually hear), and game players enjoy the rumble that it adds to special effects such as laser blasts, machine guns, and afterburners. (Chapter 9 has more details on speaker systems and subwoofers.)

Picking Up the Parts

"Okay, Mark, now I know what parts I need, but where am I going to find them?" As little as ten years ago, you would have had a hard time locating all the individual components for a computer. But now that a personal computer has practically become a household necessity (and more people are building their own computers), you have several sources for the parts that you need.

In general, I recommend that you buy brand-new components for your computer whenever possible. Why? Some components in a computer (for example, the hard drives, which are complex and have a large number of moving parts) can fail after a few years of use. In addition, prices for the fastest and most powerful components are constantly dropping. Consider the example of a used hard drive: Why install an older, slower, used hard drive that holds only 40GB for $25 when you can add a newer, faster drive that holds a whopping 250GB (for about $100)?

In this section, I compare new versus used parts and tell you several likely sources for each.

Researching before you buy

From time to time during your computer shopping, you might feel as though you're alone and that there's no one to help you decide between brands or make decisions on features. Not so! ("Everybody's a critic," as they say in show business.) If you feel that you need more information before deciding on parts to buy or scavenge, consider these sources:

- **Computer magazines:** You need look no further than your local newsstand to find a half-dozen excellent magazines that specialize in product reviews, tips, and tricks for the novice computer owner and coverage of the newest and hottest computer technology. I recommend *PC Magazine* and *Maximum PC* for their hardware reviews.

  Some magazines hand out awards for the hardware and software that they rate most highly. If the computer component that you're considering carries two or three of these awards on its box, you probably have a winner. For example, I personally rate the *PC Magazine* Editor's Choice Award as an indicator of a high-quality product.

- **The Web:** Most publishers of computer magazines also offer online versions of their printed material, and you can search through an entire site for product information, reviews, and product comparisons. Some good examples are PC Magazine (at www.pcmag.com), PC World (www.pcworld.com), Tom's Hardware (www.tomshardware.com), IDG.net (www.idg.net), ZDNet (www.zdnet.com), and other sites, such as CNET.com (www.cnet.com) and Price Watch (www.pricewatch.com). Many online stores also offer reviews and ratings submitted by customers, like www.newegg.com.

- **Internet newsgroups:** Although you need an Internet connection to read messages, newsgroups such as alt.comp.hardware.homebuilt and comp.hardware are chock-full of interesting reviews, hints, and tips. If you need to ask something specific, you can simply post a message to the newsgroup and receive an answer by e-mail or in a reply posting on the newsgroup. Visit Google Groups at http://groups.google.com to read these newsgroups using your Web browser.

- **Computer user groups:** Computer user groups come in handy! You'll likely find someone who has already traveled down the same road and bought a similar computer component. You can learn from that person's mistakes or success without spending a dollar.

I live for mail order

What's that you say, Bunkie? You need to buy some new parts, like a motherboard, hard drive, and video card? You say that you want to save money and don't want to pay the inflated prices at your local Maze O' Wires computer store? Or perhaps you live in a small town without a local computer store? Never fear — use mail order, and let the postal service (or, more likely, FedEx or UPS) leap to the rescue.

When you order parts from a reputable mail-order company, you can choose from a huge selection of computer parts, and you always save money over buying them from a retail computer store. Depending on where you live, you might also save money by avoiding local sales tax on your purchase.

If you've never ordered parts through the mail and you're not sure whether you're working with a reputable company, keep these guidelines in mind:

✔ **Check the specs:** Ask the salesperson for a detailed description of the part before you complete the order, just to make certain that you're buying the right item. Feel free to ask questions — for example, "Is that an AGP or a PCI video card?" If you like things in writing, ask the salesperson to mail or fax you the specifications and the price.

✔ **Research refunds:** Make sure that the company allows you to return a part for a full refund if it doesn't turn out to be what you need. If you return a component, some companies charge you a *restocking fee,* which is basically a charge that you pay the company for the hard work involved in sticking a returned box back on a shelf. (I wish I had a piece of *that* action!)

✔ **Choose COD or charge:** Some people are wary of using a credit card over the phone or over the Internet. If you prefer, ask for COD shipment instead. Ordering COD will cost you extra, but it's better than mailing a personal check and then waiting for it to clear. Personally, I always use a credit card, which provides me with additional leverage if there's a problem.

✔ **Buy only what you want:** If you can't get exactly the part that you need from one company, you can *always* get it elsewhere. Beware of salespeople and online stores that tell you that they're out of the particular part that you're looking for but can sell you a better model of the same part for a higher price.

✔ **Keep your shipment grounded:** Some companies tack on an additional shipment charge, or they automatically charge you for next-day shipment unless you request regular shipment. Unless you really *do* need that part tomorrow, you can probably save ten dollars or more by choosing regular ground shipment.

After you build your first computer, you'll develop a good relationship with at least one or two mail-order companies. I have several favorite companies, each of which is my first stop for a particular type of part. (It's always a good idea to find a monitor locally, though, because you can evaluate it with your own eyes and you won't pay a fortune on shipping.) For an updated list of my favorites in the world of mail-order companies, visit my Web site, MLC Books Online, at www.mlcbooks.com.

Ordering parts online

If you have access to the Internet at work, at school, or at a neighbor's house, you can travel through the limitless world of cyberspace looking for computer parts.

If you need a start in online shopping, visit three of my favorite online computer stores: the Shopper.com site (www.computershopper.com), Newegg (www.newegg.com), and Price Watch (www.pricewatch.com).

All three of these Web sites enable you to search for computer goodies from many different manufacturers, and each offers specials on overstocked parts. You can display side-by-side comparison charts of different parts so that you can compare features and performance online. Then check for the site with the current lowest price — without leaving the comfort of that swivel chair you bought for the computer room.

If the computer you're using has a printer, you can use your browser to print full descriptions of the parts you're researching. These descriptions can come in handy later when you have to make a final decision on which brand to buy.

Most of these Web sites accept only credit cards, although they offer secure connections if you're using Mozilla Firefox or Microsoft Internet Explorer — you can tell your connection is secure if a padlock icon appears in the browser's status line. The guidelines that I mention for mail-order purchases apply to online ordering, too.

Scavenging can be fun!

For a computer techno-nerd, nothing is more exciting than rooting around in an older computer and looking for spare parts. There's no telling what treasures you might uncover! RAM modules, a tape backup unit, or perhaps just a hard drive cable: All these components can go into your parts box for that next project or for a quick repair if a component fails on your new computer.

For your scavenging pleasure, here are a number of possible sources for used parts:

✔ **Computer stores:** Each time that I visit my favorite local computer store and repair shop — hi, guys! — I always ask whether they have any "new" (recently removed) used parts. Because these techies are always upgrading computers, they often hang on to older parts, which they might be more than happy to sell to you at a reduced price. This technique won't work with the MegaMultiMillion Computer Mall — they don't sell used

SCAVENGER

Finding bargains in so-called obsolete computers

Most computers now being replaced or scrapped work just fine. For most of us, a computer generally doesn't become obsolete until it no longer has the performance to run the programs that you want to use. I have several friends who are still quite pleased with their Pentium-III-based computers — they're not technical wizards, and they don't use their computers very often. Besides, if they can still run WordPerfect and Windows Explorer under Windows 98SE, their older computers suit them just fine.

You won't find any single answer to why a computer is deemed obsolete, but the answer doesn't matter all that much. The important point is that lots of people are upgrading their computers, which gives you a great opportunity to scavenge perfectly functional, used equipment for your own computer. (Of course, if you're building a new system designed for high-performance applications, you should avoid any scavenged parts that would slow down the performance of your new PC. In that case, I'd recommend only keyboards, pointing devices, and internal modems as used parts.)

Here are some reasons why people replace their "outdated" computer equipment:

✔ For some techno-wizards, a computer becomes outdated the moment a faster CPU hits the scene. Because these people are always on the leading edge of technology, they upgrade continually — and continually

get rid of older, yet functional, equipment. It's a great opportunity to get your hands on some good used gear.

✔ Although you might not believe it at first, it's not network computers or office PCs that wear out their welcome the quickest. That dubious honor goes to the PCs used by the computer gaming crowd. Computer games demand much more horsepower and advanced hardware than the average office suite of programs; therefore, computer gamers are a good source of used, high-performance equipment.

✔ The Internet is also a major reason why people are replacing their older computers. Connecting to the Web using a fast cable modem or DSL line takes more PC horsepower, and the plug-ins and multimedia animation offered by the Web don't run well on older hardware. Some people think, "New Web technology? Time to upgrade!" (and time for you to scam on their "older" equipment).

Look at the classified ads in your local newspaper (or check some of the resources mentioned in the section "Picking Up the Parts," elsewhere in this chapter). You're likely to find hundreds of people looking to unload their computer equipment — often at bargain-basement prices. (Oh, and don't forget eBay.)

parts. In fact, you might get stuck with that used-car computer salesperson again.

✔ **Computer user groups:** If you're a member of a local computer user group, ask around at the next meeting to see whether anyone has a spare video card or DVD-ROM to sell. If you're lucky, you might even get an offer of help with installing it. Some user groups can get special pricing on hardware and software through arrangements with manufacturers, too.

✔ **The Web:** A number of online companies specialize in selling used computer hardware on the Web. Many of these sites let you buy your components with a credit card over a secure Web connection, too. Try eBay (www.ebay.com) or the OnSale Online Auction Supersite (www.onsale.com); both sites offer new and used components through a real-time auction. Or try Web sites like Newegg (www.newegg.com) or The Used Computer Mall (www.usedcomputer.com) for super deals.

✔ **Computer bulletin board systems (BBSes):** In the Grand Old Days before the arrival of the Internet, computer bulletin board systems were the kings of cyberspace. Even today, tens of thousands of bulletin boards are still operating online throughout the country (including mine, at http://batboard.mlcbooks.com). If you live in just about any middle- to large-sized town, at least one bulletin board system is likely to carry advertisements selling used computer equipment.

✔ **Friends and family:** Is Uncle Milton using that old original Pentium to hold up the garage wall? After you're known in your family as a computer guru, you'll likely be presented with all sorts of older equipment. Friends will approach you for your opinion on how much they can get for their older computer (which is the perfect opportunity to make an offer of your own).

✔ **Garage sales:** I've found hundreds of dollars worth of good parts at local garage sales and bought them for pennies! Typically, you have to buy the entire computer, but as long as everything is working, you can get a really great deal. Just make sure that you plug the computer in and check it out before handing over the cash.

✔ **Classified ads:** Here's another source for used parts. Unfortunately, though, most owners who advertise in the classifieds think that their computers are worth far more than they actually are, so it might take some haggling to get a good price.

What's the deal with used parts?

Why do I continue to jabber away about used parts . . . after all, you're building a new computer, so why the heck should you add old parts to it? One reason is obvious: A used part can cost half as much as a new part — an important consideration if you're trying to save money. You might even find someone willing to give you an older computer, from which you can scavenge components for your new computer.

Again, don't forget this important maxim: You should consider adding used parts only when doing so won't hamper the performance of your PC!

If you're building your first computer, you might be surprised to discover that most computer parts can last for many years. For example, keyboards and mice can operate just as well on your new Pentium 4 computer as they did on that older Pentium III computer. Circuit boards and solid-state electrical components are surprisingly strong and hardy, and they have a long operational life.

You can find an increasing number of older computers out there, which you can buy for peanuts. Their CPUs just can't keep up with today's software, but most of the other parts work fine and can continue to work fine in your new computer. The modular design of today's computers enables you to yank a circuit board from an older computer and pretty safely assume that it will work on your new machine. For example, you can easily remove a Sound Blaster AWE64 sound card from a Pentium III computer and plug it right into your new computer; Windows XP can recognize and use a tremendous number of older hardware devices. If you're not interested in the highest-quality audiophile sound from your PC, you've just saved yourself some cash!

Yes, I'm going to preach again: If you decide to add used parts to your computer, make sure they are working fine and are not too old for your computer. In my discussion of computer components in other chapters, I provide a description of which types of used items are suitable for Athlon XP, Athlon 64, and Pentium 4 computers.

In general, you can scavenge used parts from a Pentium III computer to build Design 1 (which I discuss in the section "Answering Your Computer-Needs Questions," earlier in this chapter). You can even scavenge some components (such as a floppy drive, mouse, or keyboard) from an older Pentium II computer. Design 2 can also benefit from a used floppy drive, computer case, mouse, and keyboard. However, if you are a power user and are building a computer based on Design 3, I suggest that you buy only the latest parts; older technology that wasn't designed for Pentium 4 and Athlon 64 speeds will just slow down your supercomputer.

Part II
Building Your PC

The 5th Wave   By Rich Tennant

©RICHTENNANT

"Ronnie made the body from what he learned in Metal Shop, Sissy and Darlene's Home Ec. class helped them in fixing up the inside, and then all that anti-gravity stuff we picked up off the Web."

In this part . . .

The real fun commences when you build a bare-bones PC from the ground up. You install the required stuff that every computer needs, such as RAM modules, a CPU, a hard drive, and a video card. If that sounds a little frightening, don't worry; I explain each part in detail, and each chapter ends with a general set of step-by-step installation instructions that give you a good idea of what you can expect. After you're finished with this part, you'll be able to boot your new computer. *Remember:* All you need is a screwdriver!

Chapter 3

Building the Foundation: The Case and Motherboard

*Y*ou don't have to be an architect or a construction foreman to know that a building is only as good as its foundation. Build a skyscraper on sand, and it doesn't matter how well you wallpaper the bathrooms or how fast the elevators run. Eventually, a building with a weak foundation will fall, and it's certain to take everything with it.

In this chapter, you discover the various components that are common to all computer cases. I show you how to construct a sturdy foundation for your computer by selecting the right size and type of computer case, which provides the framework that houses the internal computer components. I introduce you to the geography of your motherboard; then you find out how to install the motherboard and connect it to the computer's power supply.

In later chapters, you continue your assembly project by finding out how to add components, such as a hard drive and a DVD recorder, to this chassis.

A Case Is Not Just a Box

Why is selecting the proper case for your computer so important?

- **Your computer needs room to grow:** If you're a power user, you need room to expand. (A *power user* is someone with considerable computer experience or someone who needs a powerful computer for advanced applications; see Chapter 2 for more details.) Adding devices and other toys can easily lead you to outgrow a standard desktop case. Believe me, it's a royal pain to upgrade to a larger case — you basically have to disassemble your entire computer, remove the motherboard and other components, and move them all to a larger case. Keep this upgrade possibility in mind when you select your case and think about your future needs.

- **You need room on your desk:** If your desktop space is limited (by either the size of your desk or your work habits), you can save yourself some valuable real estate by selecting a tower (vertical) case and placing it under your desk.

Most cases have at least one or two rectangular cutouts in front of empty drive bays. You can use these open bays to hold components that need access to the outside world, such as a new hard drive, a DVD drive, or a tape backup. (After all, it's a little hard to load a DVD or a floppy disk into a drive if it's buried inside the case.) When an open bay is empty, it's covered with a rectangular plastic piece that blends in with the outside of the case. Other drive bays remain hidden inside the case, with no access to the outside; these bays are usually reserved for additional hard drives, which don't need to be handled during routine use.

If coordinating your computer with your room is important, I bet those cases in designer colors and shapes are calling your name. But before you pick up an aerodynamic case in canary yellow or neon green, keep in mind that you'll probably find it difficult to find other parts in such exotic colors later on. Most computer components with external faceplates — such as DVD and floppy drives — come in only almond, off-white, and black, which tend to stand out like a sore thumb in an orange case. That's why the main colors for computer cases are still almond, off-white, and black, and I recommend that you stick with them unless you want a computer that looks like you assembled it at the junkyard.

If you must have a case in an exotic color, consider one with a hinged door that covers the drive bays — you can close the door when you're not loading a CD or DVD disc into your almond-colored DVD drive, and no one can tell that you're (gasp!) fashion-impaired.

Most new cases come with the mounting hardware necessary to attach your motherboard, although it never hurts to ask when you order your case. You also need screws and plastic spacers, and they should be included with either the case or the motherboard.

Choosing a case style that suits your needs

You can choose from three standard types of cases: pizza- and shoe-box, desktop, and tower. Each gives you a certain amount of elbow room for upgrading.

Pizza-box and shoe-box cases

Figure 3-1 illustrates the *pizza-box case,* which is very thin — and before you ask, it's not made of cardboard nor does it contain Italian deliciousness inside. (Sigh. I get that one all the time.) This case has only one or two open drive bays. Although you might not be able to add any adapter cards, this case does take up the smallest amount of space of any standard computer case. In fact, your friends might speculate that your svelte computer has been working out nights at the gym.

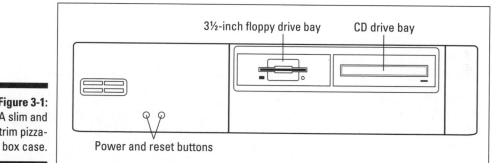

Figure 3-1: A slim and trim pizza-box case.

Pizza-box cases are typically used for network workstations or as simple terminals, so I don't recommend that you buy one of these for your home computer. However, if you're building an economy-class machine and want to save space as well as pizza money, the pizza-box case might be fine for your needs. (See Chapter 2 for details about what qualifies as an economy-class machine.)

Pizza-box cases don't offer much room for later upgrades.

A derivative of the pizza-box case is the shoe-box case, which is roughly square and a little taller than a shoe-box. These cases are favored by hard-core gamers who like to lug their PCs to a friend's house for multiplayer gaming — this type of case typically has a handle built into the top, and offers only one or two bays. (Again, not a champion for upgrading, but easily carried from one LAN gaming party to another.)

Desktop case

The next case in our fashion show is the traditional desktop case, as shown in Figure 3-2. This type of case usually sits horizontally on your desk, just like those ponderous PC XT and AT cases did back in the ancient 1980s. Today's desktop case has gone on a diet, however, and the days of those behemoths are long gone. The desktop case is not as compact as the pizza-box or shoe-box cases. Most desktop cases can switch between horizontal mode and vertical mode, depending on the orientation that you prefer.

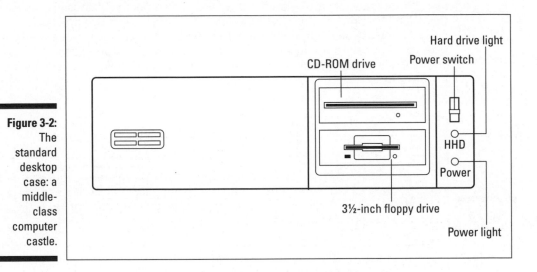

Figure 3-2:
The standard desktop case: a middle-class computer castle.

The desktop case usually provides two or three open drive bays on the front, with one or two hidden bays. This case typically has room for six or seven adapter cards in the back. This setup is usually par for the course for a home computer. Unless you're a power user, the desktop case is your case of choice.

Tower case

For the techno-nerd or power user who has everything, we have the Ferrari of cases — the brawny tower case, which sits vertically like an old mainframe computer. As shown in Figure 3-3, many tower cases have four, or even five, open drive bays. If you're planning on stuffing your computer full of extras, this is the case for you. Like the desktop case, the tower case has room for a standard six or seven adapter cards in back. Because of the weight and size of a fully outfitted tower case, it is designed to sit upright on the floor under your desk, where you can comfortably reach all the buttons and the CD-ROM drive.

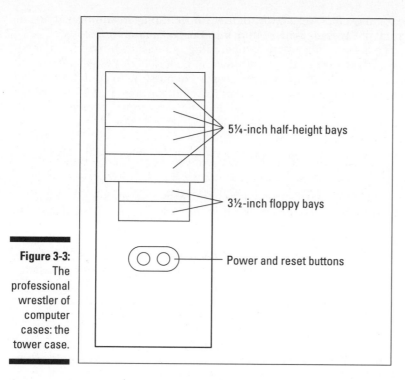

5¼-inch half-height bays

3½-inch floppy bays

Power and reset buttons

Figure 3-3:
The
professional
wrestler of
computer
cases: the
tower case.

Many manufacturers also produce a minitower case, which also sits vertically like a tower case but is designed to fit comfortably next to the monitor on top of your desk. An average minitower case has a drive bay capacity equal to that of a standard desktop case.

Feeding power to your computer

Your new computer will be hungry for power, and the power supply takes care of that need by reducing the voltage from your wall socket to something more easily handled by your computer. The power supply then pumps the juice to the computer's components through a number of individual power cables.

These cables end in a special connector that you can insert in only one direction, so it's well-nigh impossible to make a mistake and damage a hard drive or DVD drive because of an electrical short caused by a reversed connection. An ATX motherboard has only one power connector, and older AT motherboards require two power connectors. I show you how to connect both types later in this chapter.

Most cases are now sold with the power supply already installed (yea!); a preinstalled power supply not only eliminates a step in building your PC but also ensures that you get a power supply of the proper rating. In addition, you can be sure that all the holes for the switches and cables match up.

The more powerful the CPU, the more power it generally draws — and the more powerful the case fan and the processor fan must be to cool it. Also, power users tend to stuff their computers full of all sorts of neat hardware toys, each of which draws its own power. For these reasons, I *strongly* suggest that you invest in a case that includes at least a 400-watt power supply, especially if you're going to add a slew of internal extras, such as a DVD recorder and a tape backup drive. (In fact, AMD recommends at least a 400-watt power supply for the Athlon 64.)

If you buy a used case, make sure that it comes with a power supply and a working fan. You should also make sure that the power supply is UL listed — just check that it has a UL listed sticker.

A used power supply by itself isn't worth much, especially if it was built to fit a nonstandard case. *Never* open up a power supply to try to fix it or massage it to work in a particular case.

A Mark's Maxim to commit to memory: Live household voltage is not a welcome visitor within the human body.

Leave a malfunctioning or broken computer monitor alone for the same reason.

Keeping your computer cool

Because all the various devices and components in your computer produce lots of heat, your computer can actually shut down, lock up, or return errors if it gets too hot. Extended overheating reduces the operational life of your parts — especially your CPU — and leads to early failure. How does your computer keep its cool through this heat wave?

The answer is nothing elaborate or high-tech. In fact, it's just a fan! Your computer's power supply uses a fan to continually circulate air through the inside of the case. Pizza-box cases and standard-size desktop cases are small enough to require only one fan. However, if you're thinking of buying a tower case and your computer will use the latest Intel or AMD processor, I highly recommend that you buy a case with at least dual fans. Multiple fans — I've seen uber-PCs with *four* fans onboard — are a definite requirement if this type of computer is going to stay on for many hours at a time or if it's jammed full of parts and devices. Ball-bearing fans are preferred because they last longer.

CPU chips now run so hot that they come equipped with their own dedicated fan, which sits on top of or beside the processor. This fan is connected to one of the power cables leading to the power supply. If a CPU overheats, it generally locks up your computer or returns some strange results in your programs — and it will more than likely be permanently damaged. (Most motherboards now come with a CPU thermal-sensing feature that you can set in your PC's BIOS — if your CPU gets too hot, your system automatically shuts down!)

After your computer is running, it's also a good idea to place it where the fan exhaust isn't blocked by a wall or furniture. An open location provides better airflow.

Buttons, lights, and other foolishness

Most cases today have a power light and a hard drive activity light. Your motherboard runs these components. Some new cases also feature a *digital readout* of the computer's internal temperature (or, in some cases, the temperature of the CPU itself). If you're building a cutting-edge PC with a super-fast processor and plenty of internal devices, I heartily recommend one of these cases, which allow you to monitor your PC's cooling (and help prevent the China Syndrome from occurring on your motherboard).

Another favorite case *modding* (slang for modification) is the addition of neon lights inside your case that look simply delicious in low light — naturally, you'll need a case with transparent Plexiglas panels. (Remember the movie *The Fast and the Furious*?) I'm too old to need decals, special paint jobs, or neon finery on a case, but . . . kids today. Anyway, these lights typically need a standard internal power connector, so don't forget to reserve one if you're doing The Neon Thing.

Dust busting!

A computer needs at least one internal fan to keep its sensitive electronics cool. This circulating air has a drawback: All the internal parts within your new computer get dusty over time. *Hint:* Open your computer's case every year or so to blow the dust off your motherboard, power supply, and all the various devices that you've installed. Accumulated dust can act like an insulating blanket and cause chips and electrical parts to overheat. Consider it an anniversary of sorts. (Boy, I need to step away from the keyboard for a day or two.)

Before you open your case to upgrade or clear off the dust, head to your local computer store or photography shop and grab some *canned air* — one of those spray cans that shoots a compressed stream of air for dusting off cameras and computer parts. Techno-types swear by 'em. Take particular care when dusting off your motherboard and the fan intake on your power supply (which is likely to be filthy). Canned air is also handy for cleaning keyboards and adapter cards. Help out your planet by making sure that you choose a brand that doesn't deplete the ozone layer, and don't make the mistake of buying one of those air horns that the football types use at the game. (Take my word for it: They don't work, and they annoy the neighbors.)

As for buttons, your case will sport a power button and a reset button. If your case has a key lock — which I despise — I recommend that you ignore it.

Your case should also include a simple speaker, which looks just like the speaker in an inexpensive transistor radio. Although you'll definitely want to add a multimedia sound card and external speakers to your computer to take full advantage of today's software (see Chapter 9 for more about multimedia sound), this little internal speaker still performs an important task: If something is wrong when you start your computer, the speaker alerts you with a number of beeps.

Other than these standard items, your case can be as plain or as elegantly sculpted as you want. Naturally, designer cases from Gucci cost more, but you can subtly boast about your computer's good taste at parties, editors will want your picture in their fashion magazines, and you could become one of the in crowd. It could happen.

How about those slots?

Your case has a number of holes on the back, which are meant for adapter cards. Each of these slot openings enables you to screw in a bracket that attaches to an adapter card, holding the card firmly in place. If the card has any external ports, they are also visible through the back of the case.

Most cases have these slots open, although the slots need to be covered. Adding slot covers involves a little manual labor. If your slots are already covered, scoot to the next section; or, if you'll be installing at least one or two adapter cards (I show you how in later chapters), leave one or two slots uncovered to save yourself the trouble of removing them again.

Follow these instructions to close up the slot holes in the back of your case:

1. **Check the parts that came with your case to find the *slot covers,* which are thin, metal strips with a bend at the top.**

   You should also find a number of screws that fit into the screw holes at the top of each slot opening.

2. **Lay your open case down on top of your work surface.**

   You should be able to clearly see the screw holes and the slot openings at the back of your case.

3. **Slide a slot cover over one of the slot openings so that the screw hole lines up with the screw hole in the case, as shown in Figure 3-4.**

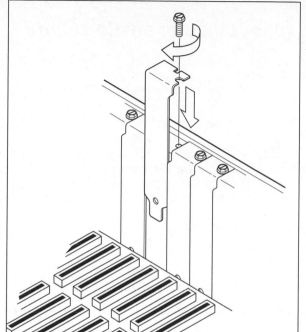

Figure 3-4:
Cover a
vacant slot
opening
with a slot
cover.

4. **Insert and tighten the screw to hold the cover over the opening.**

5. **Repeat Steps 3 and 4 until all the slot openings are covered.**

Your Motherboard Is Your Best Friend

The third color photo (see the color insert in the middle of the book) shows the main features of the heart and soul of your computer — its motherboard. The motherboard holds most of the electronics and circuits that your computer needs to follow your orders. Depending on the type of processor that you've chosen, the top of your motherboard has a big square or slot socket to hold your computer's CPU chip and several rows of small slots to hold your RAM (memory) modules.

Ten years ago, buying a motherboard by itself was much harder. However, with the constant acceleration of CPU speeds and the requirements of today's software, folks in the mall are selling motherboards rather than ice cream. Some companies that advertise in *Computer Shopper* magazine or operate Web-based parts stores sell nothing but motherboards. And you can generally buy a bare motherboard at your local computer store if it has a repair shop.

Keeping your computer castle secure

Even if security were a consideration, I *still* wouldn't use the key lock that comes on your computer case because it can be foiled by simply taking the cover off the computer and disconnecting the wire. Often, you find that cases manufactured by the same company have the same key pattern, so one nefarious jerk in an office could unlock half the computers in the building. Also, keys are easy to lose.

If you need to prevent access to your computer while you get a cup of java or a can of caffeine-laden soda, use a Windows screensaver with the password option turned on. If you need tighter security, use an encryption utility. Both options work through software, so you can forget about a silly metal key.

Another surefire security measure is to use a *boot password,* which prevents your computer from running unless you enter the correct password. Most motherboards can be configured to require a boot password through the BIOS menu.

Finally, you might decide to invest in one of the newest PC security technologies: a portable fingerprint scanner, which can replace passwords and protect both your PC's files and access to the Internet or your local network. Most fingerprint scanners connect to your PC through a universal serial bus (USB) port and retail for less than $100.

Motherboard sizes

Today's motherboards follow the ATX standard size guidelines — older computers used Baby AT or AT motherboards, but those are antiques now.

To ensure that you get a case that accepts your board, buying your motherboard first is a good idea. If you've found a used case or motherboard, make sure that whatever you buy fits your existing part. For example, an ATX motherboard requires an ATX case and an ATX power supply — (ahem) an AT-size motherboard doesn't fit in an ATX case. All of today's processors require an ATX case.

Motherboard features

While you're shopping for a motherboard, keep these guidelines in mind:

- ✔ **Stick with a minimum of a Pentium 4 or an Athlon XP.** You might have a strong temptation to jump on a great price for a Pentium III motherboard. No matter what the processor speed, however, you'll be buying yesterday's technology, and you won't have the Pentium 4 class power that you need for running many current (or future) programs and operating systems. Even if the advertisement reads "A Good Pick for Windows XP," say good-bye to the Pentium III (as readers of the first edition of this book said good-bye to the 486 and the original Pentium).

Okay, okay — so I guess if you were *given* a Pentium III motherboard by your next-door neighbor, you can use it — but don't expect it to keep up with the latest software, and (as they used to say in the TV show *Mission: Impossible*) "the Secretary will disavow all knowledge of your actions."

✔ **Consider an onboard drive controller.** As you might infer from the name, the *drive controller* sends and receives data to your hard drives and CD-ROM/DVD drive. (Think of a referee at a soccer match, and you get the idea.) Power users favor an onboard UltraDMA/133 controller, a serial ATA (SATA) controller, or a small computer system interface (SCSI) controller on a standard Pentium-series motherboard. Why UltraDMA/133, SATA, or SCSI? Because these standard controllers provide you with faster performance than the enhanced integrated drive electronics (EIDE) drive controller. (See Chapter 7 for more information on EIDE and SCSI drives.) A motherboard with an onboard controller doesn't need a separate hard drive/floppy drive controller. Therefore, you can save that adapter slot for another toy.

✔ **Spend extra for onboard ports.** Like an onboard drive controller, onboard USB and FireWire ports save an adapter slot. (Jump to Chapter 5 for the lowdown on port cards.) Many motherboards now carry onboard sound cards. In fact, some motherboards even have built-in video cards, although I prefer to add my own video adapter. An ATX motherboard should (by definition) already have serial and parallel ports onboard.

Don't give me any static!

Before you install the motherboard in your case, it's time for a warning about the dangers of static electricity. Static can damage electrical components in the blink of an eye, and not even Thomas Edison himself could fix them. I won't launch into a terribly interesting discussion of how static was discovered in 400 B.C. by somebody we don't know with a piece of silk and a glass rod. For all I care, the discovery of static electricity could have been made by prehistoric man shuffling across a bearskin rug.

Instead, just remember this simple rule while handling motherboards, adapter cards, circuit boards, and other computer parts: Before installing any circuit board, adapter card, or part on your computer (or before removing it from the case), discharge any static electricity that you might be harboring by touching something else made of metal. (You can discharge static also by touching your spouse on the earlobe, although I don't recommend this method.)

Typically, the metal chassis of your computer is a good choice, although you can also touch a metal table or chair. If your computer is plugged in with the cover off (which happens quite often when you're installing a hard drive or an adapter card), you can touch the metal housing of your power supply for a perfect ground.

Antistatic strips are available for keyboards and wrist rests that discharge static. However, the only time that I ever worry about static is when I'm handling parts and circuit boards, so I don't use this item.

✔ **Make sure that your new motherboard has at least two PCI slots and one AGP or PCI-Express slot.** Avoid any motherboard that includes more than a single industry standard architecture (ISA) slot; peripheral component interconnect (PCI) technology provides better performance for your adapter cards (for example, a PCI video capture card or a hard drive controller card). Your accelerated graphics port (AGP) or PCI-Express slot, on the other hand, is dedicated to your video card. (Chapter 4 explains more about these different slots.)

Every motherboard carries a set of chips called the *BIOS*. (This silly acronym stands for *basic input-output system*.) Your BIOS determines much of what your computer can do and also controls what happens for different types of input. For example, your BIOS keeps track of what hard drives and floppy drives you can use, what happens when you press a key on the keyboard, and how data is read and written to RAM. You can usually forget about your computer's BIOS and just let it do its work, but if your computer suffers a hardware failure or a serious error, it's your BIOS that displays the error message. Most computers today use one of five brand-name BIOS chipsets: Intel, Award, Phoenix, NVIDIA, or AMI.

✔ **Make sure that you update your flash BIOS.** Today's motherboards include *flash BIOS,* which sounds like the name of a hero from a science fiction film. This is actually a good feature; it enables you to update the capabilities of your computer with new features and bug fixes from the motherboard manufacturer. I check regularly for motherboard BIOS updates on the manufacturer's Web site.

✔ **Choose more random access memory.** All motherboards have a maximum amount of random access memory (RAM) that they can handle. Unless NASA has chosen you to control the next shuttle launch, a board that supports 2 to 3GB RAM should be sufficient. Real techno-nerds or ultra-power-users might demand support for up to 6GB RAM, although it's not likely that they'll ever use it all on a personal computer until the arrival of Windows Vista.

Grab Your Screwdriver and Install That Motherboard

It's showtime! Get ready to add your motherboard to your system case. Follow these steps:

1. **Protect your new motherboard from static electricity that you picked up from your lava lamp or from Trixie, the family Persian cat, and touch a metal surface beforehand.**

2. **Cover your work surface with newspaper and lay your open case down on top of the newspaper.**

   You should be able to clearly see the screw holes and the plastic spacer guides where the motherboard will sit. Check the documentation that came with your case for any special instructions.

3. **Hold the motherboard by the edges and lay it down inside the case to align it.**

   All the electrical components (such as the CPU socket, memory sockets, and adapter slots) should be on top; the underside of the circuit board should have no components. To align the case, make sure that the adapter card slots line up with the slots cut into the back of the case, as shown in Figure 3-5.

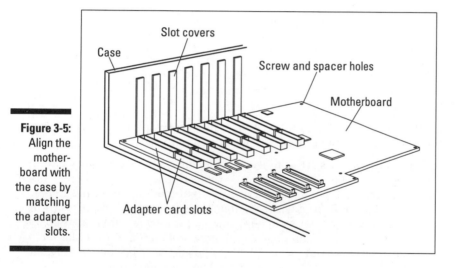

Figure 3-5: Align the mother-board with the case by matching the adapter slots.

Slot covers

Case

Screw and spacer holes

Motherboard

Adapter card slots

4. **Note which screw holes line up with the screw holes in your mother-board, and mark their position on a piece of paper.**

   Most cases use only two to four screws to hold the board, and the rest of the board is supported and held rigid by plastic spacers. These spac-ers usually slide under a metal tab or a metal guide — they serve to keep your motherboard away from any possible dangerous contact with the metal of your computer case. You might find additional help in your motherboard manual on locating these holes.

5. **Remove the motherboard from the case and add the plastic spacers to the holes (in your motherboard) that need them.**

   Figure 3-6 illustrates how you push the spacers through the holes from the bottom of the board. The spacers should snap firmly into place.

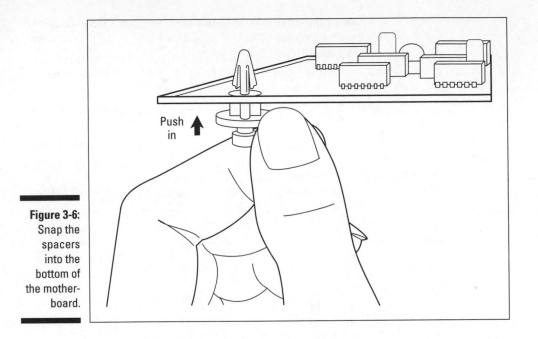

Push in

Figure 3-6:
Snap the
spacers
into the
bottom of
the mother-
board.

6. **Before you install the motherboard, take a few minutes to check for any switches or jumpers that might need to be set.**

Most motherboards are shipped with default settings that work fine, although it pays to check anyway — that's right, you have to crack open the motherboard manual and do a little light reading. Older mother-boards were configured with *dual inline packaging (DIP) switches* (little banks of slide or rocker switches) and *jumpers,* which are pins that you can connect with a small plastic-and-metal collar. (Pentium 4 class moth-erboards are designed for people like you and me who hate poking and moving tiny things, so they rarely need any configuration.)

If you need to set a DIP switch, use a pen to push the plastic sliders into the correct order, as shown in Figure 3-7, where switches 4 and 6 have been set to On.

Figure 3-7:
DIP
switches
might use
sliding
controls
(left) or
rockers
(right).

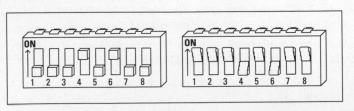

If you need to set a jumper, use your fingers or a set of tweezers to lift the plastic jumper and seat it into the correct position. Figure 3-8 shows a jumper on pins 1 and 2 of jumper J1.

Figure 3-8: A pair of tweezers comes in handy when setting a jumper.

7. **Pick up your motherboard by the edges and slide it into place, making sure that all the plastic spacers are correctly positioned.**

   Don't get upset if it takes a few tries, and don't bend or force anything. I've never installed a motherboard on my first attempt. Once again, make certain that the adapter slots line up with the slots in the case as before. After the motherboard is in, gently check each corner of the board to make sure that it's correctly seated and doesn't wobble.

8. **You're ready to lock it down. Put in the screws, but don't overtighten them — circuit boards tend to crack if you do.**

   Some boards come with thin, nonconductive washers for the screws, so don't forget to use them if they were included.

That's it! Congratulations! See, that wasn't that hard, was it?

You've completed your computer's basic chassis. In the next section, you connect the cables needed to provide power to the motherboard.

I Laugh at Pesky Wires!

The hard part of installing your motherboard is over, but the process isn't complete. You still need to connect the wires from the power supply as well as the wires to the buttons and lights on the front of your case. This is a good time to take care of these chores because your motherboard is easy to work with right now. You have unrestricted access to all the pins and connectors on your motherboard, with no adapter cards or cables hanging around to interfere with your work.

Pumping power to your motherboard

The first connection that you make is the most important — connecting your ATX motherboard to the power supply. To connect the two cables that supply power to the motherboard, follow these steps:

1. **If your case is plugged into a wall socket, unplug it first.**

2. **Locate the power connector on your motherboard.**

   Again, if you need help in finding the power connector, check your motherboard manual. Can you see why I recommend that you save all the documentation for your hardware? On an ATX motherboard, the two power cables are combined into one cable, and the plug is designed to connect only one way, so things are easier.

3. **Align the connector with the socket and press down gently until the connectors snap in place.**

Connecting the power cable might seem kind of scary the first time that you do it, but take heart: Thanks to the ATX standard, you can't go wrong!

Flashing lights, clicking switches, and a beeper to boot

Follow these steps to connect the motherboard to the various switches and lights (and your all-important PC speaker, if you have one) on your case:

1. **Check the documentation that came with your case to determine which wires lead to which lights and switches.**

   Typically, you get to play "match the colors." For example, the connector on the green and white wires might be for the power button, and the red and white wires might be the PC speaker. The connectors on the ends of the wires are also be marked with a word or two (such as *power* or *reset*) that identifies them.

   If you're using a secondhand case without any documentation, you can still determine what's connected to what with a bit of electrical detective work. Follow the wires back to their source, and jot down what switch or light each one is connected to — and don't forget to save that piece of paper for the next time you perform surgery on your computer.

2. **After you determine which connector is which, refer to your motherboard manual for the location of the following pins.**

   On most motherboards, these words (or an abbreviation) are also printed right next to the pins, making it easier to locate them if you don't have a copy of the manual:

- **Power light or power LED:** This is the power light on the front of the case.

- **HDD light or HD LED:** This is the hard-drive activity light on the front of the case. It lights whenever your computer accesses your hard drive, so it's flickering just about all the time.

- **Reset:** This is the reset switch on the front of the case; you press it when your computer is locked up.

- **Key lock:** This leads to the key lock on the front of your case. If your computer is locked with the key, your keyboard is disabled. Like the Turbo switch and Turbo light, the key lock is another anachronism from the ancient days of the 1980s and early 1990s, and thankfully most cases sold today have eliminated this irritating little feature. I've never used it, nor has anyone else I know. Unless you have some pressing need for this type of security, *don't spend extra money to get it* — if your case has a key lock, feel free to leave its wires disconnected.

- **Speaker or Spk:** This wire should lead to your computer's internal speaker. Even if you plan on adding a sound card later, you need to connect the speaker because it provides audio error messages that can help you diagnose problems with your computer. In fact, you use these audio error messages in Chapter 4.

3. **Attach each cable to its corresponding pins on the motherboard by pushing the connector onto the pins, as shown in Figure 3-9.**

Figure 3-9:
Connecting cables from your case to your mother-board.

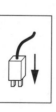

For the case cables that I mention in the preceding step, it doesn't matter which way the connector is facing. If a connector needs to be reversed, you can fix it in the next chapter, when you run your first tests. (The exceptions to this rule are the connectors from the power supply and power switch, as I discuss earlier.)

Chapter 4

A Bag of Chips: Adding RAM and a CPU

*A*fter you install the motherboard inside your computer's case, which I cover in Chapter 3, your PC might still be missing one or two very important parts: its brain (the central processing unit, or CPU) and its memory (random access memory, or RAM). When you run a computer program, your computer's CPU performs the calculations and executes the commands stored in that program. In tandem, your computer's RAM acts as a work area for the program: storing, changing, and retrieving data. As an example, if you run an address book program on your computer, your CPU can use the instructions within the program to search for names or print address labels, and your computer's RAM stores all those names and addresses until you exit the program.

I recommend buying a motherboard with the CPU and RAM modules preinstalled (commonly called a *populated* motherboard, for some strange socio-engineering reason). That way, you don't need to worry about compatibility problems or installation hassles. (Differences exist in socket types, voltage requirements, and physical measurements in both the Pentium and Athlon lines of CPU chips, so not every motherboard accepts every CPU.) If your motherboard comes with these chips preinstalled, you can skip most of this chapter and visit your local miniature golf course for a heady 18 holes. Don't forget, though — I need you back here to test the chassis in the last section of this chapter.

If you need to install your CPU or your memory — either before you install your motherboard inside your case or afterward — this chapter will attach itself to you like a suckerfish to the side of an aquarium. Just follow the appropriate steps and then test your chassis.

FYI about CPUs

You can choose from a number of CPU models these days, and you might be able to save a little money while shopping if you're faced with a decision between manufacturers and speeds (or if you're scavenging from an older PC). Therefore, review the general characteristics of the current crop of computer cranium components. I take them in order of price and power, starting with the low-end processors.

I mention this question elsewhere in this book, but the question bears repeating: What's the difference between a 2.4 GHz Pentium 4 CPU and a 2.8 GHz Pentium 4 CPU? No, it's not a trick question! Because the processors are the same type, it's the *speed,* which is expressed in megahertz (MHz) or gigahertz (GHz). When you're shopping for the processors that I describe in this section, make sure that you get at least the minimum speed for the type of computer you're building. (If you're not sure what that minimum speed or type is, see Chapter 2, or visit my Web site at www.mlcbooks.com for my latest recommendations.) However, you can also follow this simple Mark's Maxim:

Buy the fastest doggone possible processor you can afford!

Remember, adding plenty of RAM is just as important from a performance angle as buying the fastest CPU you can afford. With only 128MB of RAM, for example, Windows is still going to run slowly, even with a super-fast Pentium Extreme Edition processor. You'll find more details on how much RAM you should add later in this chapter.

Celeron and Sempron processors

Celeron and Sempron are two processors designed for the price-conscious consumer. In other words, although you get lots of bang for your buck from these CPUs, they aren't as advanced and don't have the extra punch of their more expensive brethren. Don't get me wrong, though: Either of these two processors is still more than speedy enough to power a typical family PC.

The Intel Celeron: The darling of the low-cost crowd

The Celeron, designed by Intel as a cheaper alternative to the Pentium since the days of the Pentium II, works quite well if you're building a midrange computer for use with an office suite or if you plan to explore the Internet. The Celeron has a lower amount of cache memory than the Pentium, so it's not as efficient as the Pentium 4, and its raw megahertz speed rating is typically slower than a full-blown Pentium 4.

Celeron processors are a little faster than the Sempron, which I discuss next. Celeron processors typically handle data at a faster bus speed than Sempron CPUs — the faster the bus speed, the faster the CPU can send and receive data to other system components, such as your video card and system RAM.

The AMD Sempron: A bare-bones hot rod

Because AMD designed the Sempron to compete directly with the Celeron, the Sempron is usually neck-and-neck in performance benchmarks. On the downside, because the Sempron is a stripped-down Athlon XP, it typically also runs hotter. I therefore recommend that you pick up a second fan for your case.

Pentium and Athlon processors

In this section, I cover the big CPU twosome dominating the current PC scene. The Pentium Extreme Edition and the Athlon 64 series are suitable for high-end power user systems. Either of these processors is my first recommendation for most folks playing the latest computer games, working with digital video or music, or using demanding business applications.

One step down the performance ladder, the Pentium 4 and the Athlon XP processors are perfect for a midrange PC for home or office. I cover them as well.

Today's Pentium 4 processors include *hyperthreading technology,* which allows a single CPU to perform like multiple CPUs. In fact, Windows XP and 2003 Server think that you're running a dual-processor motherboard! The adage "Two heads are better than one" is just as true when it comes to computer CPUs, and hyperthreading is a feature that you should ask for if you're buying a new CPU. A PC using one of these chips is more efficient and runs significantly faster when you're running more than one application at a time.

The Intel Pentium Extreme Edition: High-end horsepower

The Pentium Extreme Edition CPU is a super-fast processor that features Intel's hyperthreading technology, providing the best performance for today's games, 3-D applications, and video editing. The latest versions of the Extreme Edition CPU are dual-core processors, so they excel at multitasking and number crunching. At the time of this writing, the motherboard selection for Extreme Edition CPUs is sparse, but the market will continue to expand as time goes by. The Extreme Edition is a socket 478 or LGA 775 processor, depending on the version. (Remember, the type of socket your motherboard has — think "connector that the CPU plugs into" — determines what type of processor you can use.)

The Intel Pentium 4: Still king of the hill

The Pentium 4 is the most popular CPU on the market, and with good reason: It's a fantastic all-around CPU. Although it doesn't operate as efficiently as a standard Athlon 64 CPU — and doesn't offer 64-bit operation — the Pentium 4 is often faster in raw speed, and it runs with a wider range of motherboards. It's a great choice for just about any PC. The Pentium 4 is a socket 478 processor.

The AMD Athlon 64: The tyrannosaurus rex of processors

The Athlon 64 X2 is AMD's fastest, most efficient, and most advanced CPU. The Athlon 64 CPU X2 even outperforms the Pentium Extreme Edition dual-core processor line, and it's a particular favorite with the gaming community. But wait: Before you close this book and head to your Web browser, you should know that the Athlon 64 X2 is not the right choice for everyone. Like a sports car, the Athlon 64 X2 is far more expensive than a standard Athlon 64 processor. Plus, fewer motherboards are approved for use with the Athlon 64 X2. I would recommend it for techno-wizards who want absolutely the best performance available in a CPU or for those folks who want to look forward to three or four years of use before they plan to buy another motherboard or build another PC. AMD's other 64-bit processor is the Athlon 64 FX series, which delivers a level of performance between a standard single-core Athlon 64 and the Athlon 64 X2. Athlon 64 CPUs are socket 754 or socket 939, depending on the version.

By the way, that *64* in the Athlon 64 designation is no accident: All Athlon 64 processors support the latest 64-bit version of Windows, *Windows XP Professional x64 Edition*, as well as 64-bit Linux and the upcoming Windows Vista. The dynamic duo of one of these operating systems and any Athlon 64-bit processor results in faster performance, support for up to an unbelievable 128 gigabytes of RAM, and full support for dual-core CPUs. In the Intel corner, Extreme Edition processors with EM64T offer 64-bit support as well.

The AMD Athlon XP: A reliable workhorse

Like the aging Pentium 4, AMD's Athlon XP is no longer top dog, but it still offers respectable performance for a typical family or office PC, and again it provides more efficient operation than Pentium 4 models with similar speeds. The Athlon XP CPU is a socket A processor.

Your Monster Needs a Brain

Suppose that someone who upgraded a PC donated an Athlon 64 X2 CPU to your cause — hey, it could happen, right? Or, more likely, you found a CPU for sale online at a great price. Anyway, you need to install your CPU on your motherboard — after all, that's where your processor belongs (it won't work by itself), and the pins on a CPU can be damaged easily by small children, dogs, or a cat in an exceptionally bad mood.

For a novice, the CPU installation process is probably one of the scariest moments in the entire project. If you feel that you need professional help on this one, just bring your case (with motherboard installed) and CPU to your local computer repair shop or ask a computer guru whom you know to handle the CPU installation. Ask the expert to install the CPU, and watch the process closely. *Hint:* After you've seen it installed correctly, it's not a big deal at all.

As I outlined previously, motherboards made for today's processors, such as the Pentium 4 or Extreme Edition or the Athlon XP or 64, use a socket A, socket 370, socket 478, socket 754, socket 939, or LGA 775 CPU. In plain English, that means you're looking at a square socket that accepts a flat processor chip. Follow these steps to install your CPU chip:

1. **Don't handle anything until you touch a metal surface first.**

    I'll bet that you just finished pulling a load of fuzzy socks out of your clothes dryer, didn't you?

    Static electricity can damage sensitive computer components! Touching a metal surface, such as your computer's chassis, conducts static electricity away from your body.

2. **Haul your open computer chassis onto your work surface.**

    Don't plug the chassis in yet — nothing will happen. We'll plug in the power cord later in this chapter.

3. **Locate the CPU socket on your motherboard.**

    The CPU socket is a big square that looks like it could hold two or three thousand pins. If you need help finding the CPU socket, refer to the schematic in your motherboard's manual. Pentium and Athlon motherboards typically feature special sockets called zero insertion force (ZIF) sockets for the CPU. Unlike older motherboards that used 386 and 486 processors, ZIF sockets allow you to easily install or remove CPUs without requiring force.

Unfortunately, the CPU is not one of those parts that are cleverly designed to fit only one way, but at least the nice folks at the plant give you a marker to help during installation. Figure 4-1 shows two typical CPU chips and two different types of sockets. See the stubby corner on the chip? That corner should point in the same direction as the socket's marker. Depending on the motherboard, the matching corner on the socket might be stubby as well, or it could have a small dot or a tiny groove. If you're the least bit unsure about how to line up the CPU chip, check your motherboard manual.

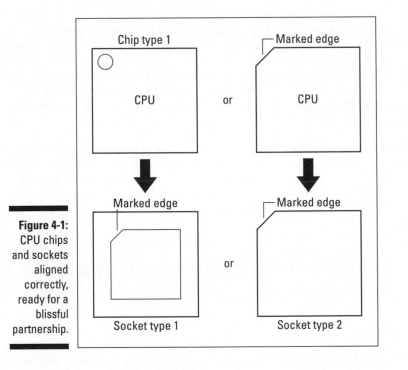

Figure 4-1: CPU chips and sockets aligned correctly, ready for a blissful partnership.

4. **If your motherboard has a ZIF socket for the CPU, raise the lever on the side of the socket.**

   Your motherboard manual should show you how to lift the lever; this step unlocks the ZIF socket so that you can insert the chip.

5. **Carefully place the CPU chip on top of the socket.**

   The edges of the chip should match the edges of the socket, and the stubby corner should match the socket marker. Look at the chip from the top and the side to make sure that the pins that you can see are on top of their matching holes.

6. **Okay, take a deep breath and relax — then use your fingers to gently push down on the edges of the chip.**

   Apply even pressure to the top of the CPU. After some initial resistance, the chip should settle into the socket. Press evenly on the CPU until the pins aren't visible from the side.

7. **If your motherboard has a ZIF socket for the CPU, lower the lever on the side of the socket.**

   Push the lever down to lock the ZIF socket so that the CPU chip is held in place.

Never, never, *never* try to force a CPU into a motherboard. If it doesn't feel like it's correctly seated and all the pins fit, back off and check your motherboard manual to make sure that the chip is aligned correctly. If the CPU is not correctly aligned and you try to force it into the socket, you'll bend some of the pins (which can be fixed, but only by an experienced technician). In the worst case, you'll break a pin. If this happens, you may as well bury the chip in your backyard and get another CPU.

All processors made these days need fans on top or on the side to keep the chip cool; the fan is clamped to the top of the chip (usually with an intervening layer of conductive glue to help transfer heat). This fan will have a separate power cable that you need to connect, so refer to your CPU and motherboard documentation to find the fan connector.

Add RAM Until the Mixture Thickens

If you bought RAM with your motherboard, it should come preinstalled. If you bought your RAM chips separately or you scavenged them, here are the rules of the game:

- ✔ **DDR and DDR2:** The most common memory modules used with Pentium and Athlon PCs are double data rate (DDR) modules, which are effectively twice the speed of older synchronous DRAM (SDRAM) memory. The latest version of this type of memory is the DDR2 module, which doubles again the data transfer between RAM and your PC — however, the new DDR2 design is still relatively new, so it's less common (and more expensive) than the older DDR standard at the time of this writing. DDR and DDR2 memory modules have one notch on the connector and two notches on each side of the module. Figure 4-2 illustrates a typical DDR module, just waiting for someone to reach out and install it.

- ✔ **RDRAM:** Yet another high-performance variety of RAM — but this older species is on the decline. In fact, Rambus dynamic random access Memory (RDRAM) modules are now disappearing from the market as DDR2 memory grows more popular. (I know, the doggone acronyms are as bad as the full names.)

Figure 4-2:
Is it a potato
chip? A
chocolate
chip?
No, it's a
DDR chip.

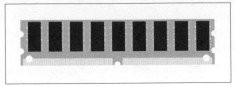

Athlon and Pentium PCs use DIMM memory — short for *dual inline memory module* — and older Pentium-class computers use SIMM memory, short for *single inline memory module*. First-generation Pentium motherboards used extended data output (EDO), 72-pin SIMMs. Because they're no longer manufactured, these antiques are now actually gaining in value! (Forget gold coins; invest in old silicon.)

While you're out shopping for RAM, remember that DDR and DDR2 memory is assigned a speed rating as part of the name, so it's commonly listed as DDR266/PC2100 or DDR2 400. As you might guess, the faster the memory speed, the better the performance, so the bigger numbers tell you that 333 (or 2700) is faster than 226 (or 2100). The speed rating that you choose should be determined by the memory speeds that your motherboard supports.

In the days of the 486 and the original Pentium, SIMMs were typically grouped in pairs, although most of today's motherboards can accept two to four DIMMs.

- ✔ **Compatibility:** To avoid mix-ups and stragglers, it's better to order all your RAM at one time from the same dealer. In general, RAM modules made by different manufacturers are *supposed* to work together as long as they're all rated at the same speed, although I've heard horror stories on the Internet about compatibility problems. Whenever you can, order the same brand.

- ✔ **Amount:** Check the design that you created in Chapter 2 for the recommended amount of RAM that you should use, but don't forget this Mark's Maxim:

The more RAM, the merrier! This is especially true with Windows XP and Windows 2003 Server Edition. The more RAM you can add, the better and faster your system runs.

Ready to install your memory modules? Good — follow these steps:

1. **Touch something metal to banish the static monster.**

2. **Cover your work surface with a piece or two of newspaper and lay your chassis down on top of the newspaper.**

   Again, don't plug the chassis in yet — wait until the end of the chapter.

3. **Locate the memory slots, which you can generally find at one corner of the motherboard, close to the CPU itself.**

   If Picasso designed your motherboard, check the manual, which should include a schematic drawing to help you find the memory slots. You should also find instructions on which bank of slots to fill first — make sure that you add the memory in the order specified by the manual. (The banks are usually marked on the motherboard itself, just to avoid confusion.) In general, most people fill bank 0 first, and then bank 1, and so on.

4. **Position the motherboard so that the DIMM memory slots are facing you. The slots should look like those shown in Figure 4-3. (*Remember:* DDR modules have different notches, but they're installed the same.)**

   The clever little locking mechanism uses friction to lock the DIMM firmly in place. Notice that the notches cut into the connectors at the bottom of the module match the spacers in the memory sockets; you can't install DIMM or DDR chips the wrong way. The notch is an example of good thinking on someone's part.

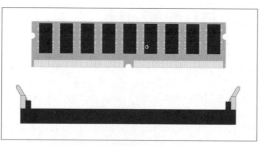

Figure 4-3:
A DIMM socket, ready for action.

5. **Align the metal teeth at the bottom of the module with the socket, and then push down lightly to seat the chip, as shown in Figure 4-4.**

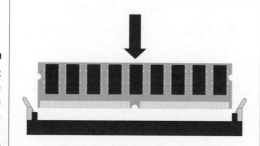

Figure 4-4:
Inserting the DIMM chip safely into its socket.

6. **As the module moves into place, make sure that the two levers at each side of the socket move toward the center, as shown in Figure 4-5, until that clever little locking mechanism clicks into place.**

Figure 4-5:
The locking
levers on
a DIMM
socket.

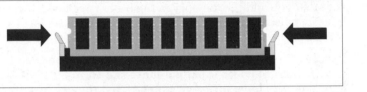

That's it! When correctly installed, the module should sit vertically on the motherboard, and the two levers should be flush against the sides of the module.

Time to Meet Your Bus Slots

While you have your case open and you can see everything clearly, take a moment to determine what type of bus slots you have. (And note that the type of slots has nothing to do with the processor, memory, and motherboard's bus speed.) If you add internal adapter cards to your computer, they fit into these bus slots (becoming, in effect, an extension of the motherboard itself). If you're confused about which types of slots you have, check your motherboard manual.

Most motherboards that you buy today have a mixture of the following slots:

✔ An accelerated graphics port (AGP) slot or a PCI-Express x16 slot reserved for a video card

✔ Four or five peripheral component interconnect (PCI) slots

✔ A number of PCI-Express x1 slots for PCI-Express adapter cards (other than a video card)

This information becomes really important really quickly because you'll need to buy the proper type of adapter card for many other parts in your computer. If the card doesn't match your available slots, you can't use it! These slots are a series of long, parallel connectors on your motherboard, and most motherboards come with anywhere from five to seven slots. Figures 4-6 and 4-7 illustrate the two most common types of slots on Pentium and Athlon motherboards: the super-fast AGP video card slot and the high-speed 32-bit PCI bus slot. (You'll also find more about the AGP and PCI-Express video card slots in Chapter 6.)

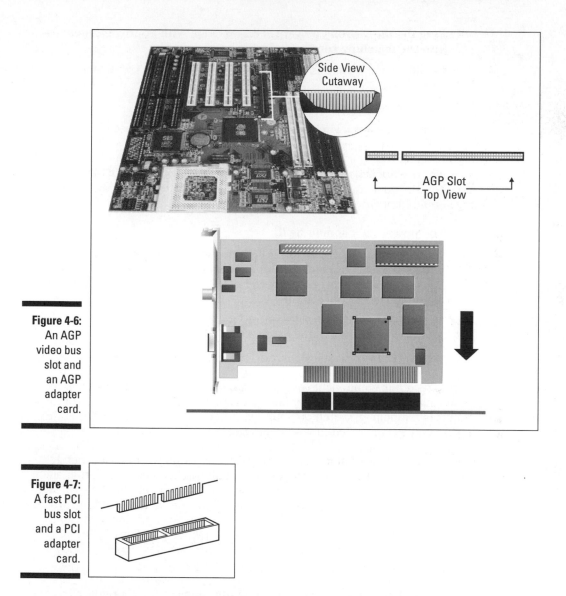

Figure 4-6:
An AGP
video bus
slot and
an AGP
adapter
card.

Figure 4-7:
A fast PCI
bus slot
and a PCI
adapter
card.

If you're rapidly becoming tired of the word *slot,* here's good news: We're fin-ished with it, at least for this chapter!

Fire That Puppy Up!

Time to test your work and see how well you did. Although your computer doesn't even have a monitor or keyboard connected yet, you can still check out your assembly so far. Follow these steps:

1. **Plug the three-prong power cord that came with your computer case into the matching connector on the power supply.**

   Go ahead and push this one in pretty firmly. You don't want it to wiggle free.

2. **Plug the power cable into your friendly wall socket.**

3. **Push the power switch on the front or back of your case.**

If you connected your cables to the motherboard correctly, and *if* your switches are hooked up correctly (both of which are covered in detail in Chapter 3), and *if* your CPU and RAM chips are installed correctly, the following should happen:

✔ **The power light should be lit.**

   Troubleshooting: If the power light doesn't go on and the fan on your power supply is turning, reverse the connector attached to the power light pins on the motherboard. For all the information on motherboard connections, refer to Chapter 3.

✔ **The fan on the CPU should be spinning.**

   Troubleshooting: If the fan isn't spinning, check to make sure that you've plugged in the cable from the fan to your power supply.

If the preceding components are in working order, your motherboard is receiving power, and the power light is correctly connected. (If none of these things is happening, switch off your computer and reverse the order of the power cables connected to your computer.)

Your computer might blurt out a series of beeps. Don't worry — it's merely trying to tell you that it can't find a video adapter, a keyboard, and other such components. (You install and attach those elements in later chapters.) In fact, the beeps are your friends, and you can use them later in the assembly process to help you diagnose problems. For example, if the machine emits one long beep followed by three short beeps, you have a video problem. If your PC sounds eight or more long, continuous beeps, it's telling you that it's encountering a memory problem.

That's about all the testing you can do at this stage. After your chassis passes all these tests, you're ready to add more components to your computer.

Chapter 5

The Three PC Senses: Ports, Mouse, and Keyboard

*1*n today's world of graphical user interfaces (read that as Windows XP, Windows 2000, Linux, and Mac OS X), a keyboard is no longer enough. To get the most from modern computer programs, you need to drag and drop and double-click. In other words, your computer needs a mouse (or another pointing device). In fact, pointing devices have been around for more than a decade or two, and they were standard equipment on other computers (such as the Atari ST and Commodore Amiga) long before the arrival of Windows 3.0 on the PC. Most computer techno-wizards prefer the speed of keyboard commands, but for better or worse, the mouse is here to stay. Both your mouse and keyboard connect to your computer through special connectors plugged into *ports* on the front or back of the case. Your computer also needs a port for sending information to your printer as well as a port for sending and receiving data through an external modem. Although some of these ports have changed over the years, others are virtually unchanged since the arrival of the first PC.

In this chapter, you find out how to add ports to your computer (if required), how to connect your keyboard and mouse, and the many different types of pointing devices available today.

If you bought a new motherboard, it should have several of these ports built in already. For example, all motherboards have a built-in keyboard connector. However, older "antique" motherboards might require you to buy an adapter card that adds a FireWire port to your computer. If you installed an ATX motherboard into an ATX case, your ports are already set! (For all the details on cases, see Chapter 3.) If your motherboard came with built-in ports but without connectors, you still need to attach the port connectors to the motherboard and then add the ports to your case. So don't skip this entire chapter; instead, jump to the "Connecting Built-in Ports" section.

Pursuing Your Port Preferences

Prepare to be amazed by the variety of ports that you can add to your computer! Your computer definitely needs the first three or four ports mentioned in the following list (and illustrated in Figure 5-1), although the rest are optional ports that handle the special hardware that power users just love.

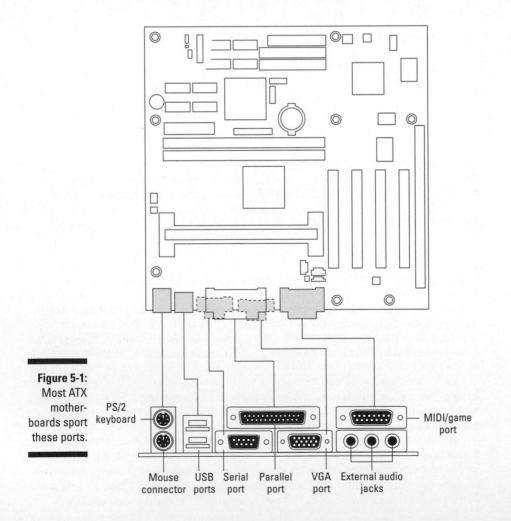

Figure 5-1:
Most ATX motherboards sport these ports.

PS/2 keyboard

MIDI/game port

Mouse connector

USB ports

Serial port

Parallel port

VGA port

External audio jacks

✔ **Keyboard port:** Keyboard ports come in two varieties: One type fits the IBM PS/2 connector shown in Figure 5-2. An older type of keyboard port is larger than the PS/2 connector. All motherboards made in the last five or six years have a keyboard port that accepts the smaller PS/2 plug. If you want to use a keyboard that has a good feel to it but uses the older-style, round connector (usually called an *AT connector*), you can pick up a converter that enables you to plug the older keyboard into a PS/2-style port.

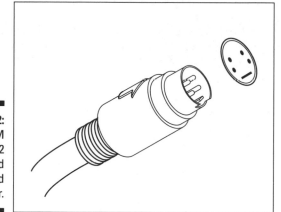

Figure 5-2:
The IBM
PS/2
standard
keyboard
connector.

✔ **Serial port:** These ports have been around since the early days of the PC (and were once the standard port for connecting an external modem). In current computers, serial ports are primarily reserved for some exotic types of joysticks and game controllers. A serial port is commonly called a *COM port* (short for *com*munications *port*). Most motherboards offer two serial ports (but can have more than two), and each of these ports is typically assigned one of four standard COM port designations — COM1, COM2, and so on — which identifies that particular port to the computer.

In the past, computers used serial ports to handle your modem, your digital camera, and your mouse. If you're a real technological old-timer, you might have even used this type of port to plug in a strange type of printer called a serial printer. And if you remember that, you may also recall that these ports used to come in two varieties (a male 9-pin version and a male 25-pin version), but the 9-pin serial port is the only one in use today. (By the way, a *male* connector has pins, and a *female* connector has holes for those pins. Go figure.) With as many as four COM ports on the same computer, you can run multiple modems on the same computer. Some companies still use modem servers on their networks, and others use one incoming line for a fax/modem while using another line for an Internet connection.

✓ **Parallel printer port:** Although it's hard to believe, one type of port hasn't changed much since the early days of PC XT and AT class computers. Parallel printer ports look and operate pretty much as they did in the early 1980s. Their primary purpose is to provide a connection for your printer. (For several years past, parallel ports also performed double duty as connections for external devices, such as scanners and Zip drives. Today's hardware, however, is almost exclusively connected through a USB or FireWire port.) Unlike serial ports, parallel ports transfer data on several wires rather than on just two. Unfortunately, scavengers often mistake parallel ports for the older 25-pin serial port on older PCs (sounds like a case for more computer case labels, as I suggest at the end of this section). Unless you're using a scavenged serial card from an older computer, you probably won't run into a 25-pin serial port, so if you see a rectangular port with two rows of pins (or holes) on the back of your PC, it's practically guaranteed to be a parallel port.

✓ **PS/2 mouse port:** This port is a dedicated mouse port, which frees up your serial ports for other things. You'll find the PS/2 port on computers built after 1995 or so. (As I mentioned earlier in this chapter, older computers enabled you to connect the mouse using one of the serial ports.)

✓ **USB port:** This high-speed port is the universal method for attaching all sorts of peripherals (such as digital cameras and external modems) to your computer. The first version of the USB port (usually called USB 1.1) could accommodate as many as 127 daisy-chained (that is, connected) devices — probably even enough for Bill Gates, and it provided transfer rates of as much as 12 megabits per second (Mbps). USB 2.0 ports go even further, moving data at speeds as fast as a blistering 480 Mbps (and it's backward compatible with version 1.1 USB hardware). Plus, any peripheral that you plug into a USB port is automatically recognized by Windows 2000 and Windows XP (as it should be), and you can remove that same device without rebooting your computer. Figure 5-3 illustrates the USB ports and connectors on both the PC and peripheral ends.

USB now reigns as king for connecting scanners, joysticks, controllers, digital cameras, printers, and even some mice and keyboards. If you're shopping for a new motherboard, make *sure* that it comes with USB 2.0 ports, and you can kiss port confusion goodbye!

✓ **FireWire port:** Otherwise known as your friendly neighborhood IEEE-1394 high-performance serial bus, a FireWire port transfers data as fast as 400 Mbps, which has made it a popular choice for connecting expensive toys that generate lots of data, such as digital camcorders, video-conferencing cameras, super-fast scanners, and color laser printers. Like USB, FireWire is automatically recognized by Windows 2000 and Windows XP; it supports as many as 63 devices connected together on a single FireWire port. (Although the USB 2.0 port could surpass FireWire in a speed race, FireWire allows your computer to control digital devices as well, so it's likely to hang around. A new FireWire 800 standard has appeared on a few high-end PCs and can pump an unbelievable 800 Mbps to external devices, but these super-fast connectors aren't likely to be as popular in the PC world as USB 2.0 for some time to come.)

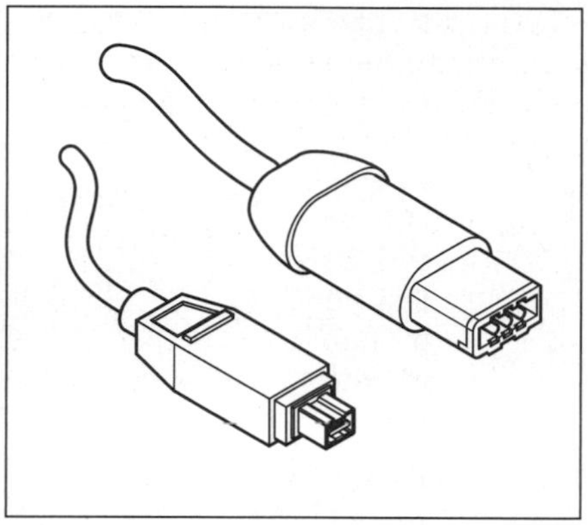

Figure 5-3:
The USB connec-
tors that conquered the world.

If you're planning on editing digital video or participating in videoconfer-encing, consider adding a FireWire port to your PC. Figure 5-4 illustrates a FireWire and USB port panel that takes the place of a drive bay cover on the front of your PC — as you might imagine, having these ports on the front of your computer (instead of hiding out in back) is a great con-venience when connecting digital cameras, digital video (DV) cam-corders, and external hard drives.

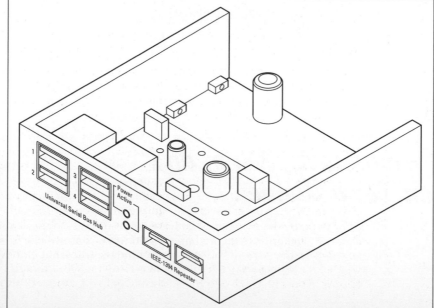

Figure 5-4:
A front-
panel port expander that fits in the front of your PC case.

✔ **Game port:** If you plan to add a sound card to your computer, the card might also have a game port for your joystick or gamepad. If not, most multiple in/out (I/O) port adapter cards also provide a game port onboard along with the standard serial and parallel ports. Game ports have 15 pins, and one port can connect two standard, two-button IBM joysticks. (Or, you can decide to opt for a USB game controller, although many gamers get very attached to their expensive flight joysticks, steering wheels, and throttles.)

✔ **MIDI port:** You use this type of specialized port for connecting MIDI-capable musical instruments to your computer. MIDI (musical instrument digital interface) ports are usually added along with your sound card. (You find out more about sound cards and MIDI in Chapter 9.) Again, you can also get a USB-to-MIDI port adapter.

✔ **Infrared port:** If you have a laptop computer or handheld device with an *infrared port,* you might want to consider adding one to your new computer. An infrared port lets you transfer data and files between two computers without the need to string cables between the two machines. An infrared port comes in handy if you travel often and like to keep your data synchronized between your laptop and desktop systems. Infrared ports are typically installed on an adapter card, with some sort of external infrared sensor (which looks something like the infamous "red eye" from your TV's remote control).

✔ **SCSI port:** If you install a small computer system interface (SCSI) adapter card in your computer (which I cover in Chapter 11), the card also offers an external SCSI port to connect scanners, CD recorders, and other SCSI devices.

Label your ports, and you will rejoice later.

Put that label maker that you got for Christmas to good use. Even though you might remember *now* which port is which, I heartily recommend that you create labels for your ports after you install them. If you label your ports (or at least copy the port layout on the back of your PC on paper), you eliminate any identification problems in the future.

Of Keyboards, Mice, and Men (and Women)

"Grandpa, in your day, did they really have only one kind of mouse and one kind of keyboard?" Things have *really* changed — now you can choose from a dizzying array of pointing devices and keyboards (and even combinations of both).

The mouse has mutated

If you're at a loss about which pointing device is best for you, here are some guidelines to steer you in the right direction:

✔ **Standard mouse:** The basic mouse is still around; it comes in two-button and three-button varieties. Some mice even carry smaller buttons on the sides! If you choose a mouse that has sprouted more than two buttons, you might be able to program the additional buttons. (For example, the software that came with my trackball enables me to program the middle button to double-click.) A mouse is still a good choice for a traditional pointing device, although it's harder to use for delicate work and requires lots of desk space. And these pointing devices get dirty often. You should clean your mouse at the first sign of skipping or sloppy response. (To avoid this onerous chore, buy an optical mouse, which doesn't use a ball and doesn't require any cleaning.)

Most fashionable mice now sport a wheel between the buttons, which enables you to scroll Web pages and documents up and down (and even left and right) by turning the wheel with your finger — nice!

✔ **Wireless mouse:** This type of mouse doesn't trail cords, a desirable feature for many computer owners. Going wireless also enables you to control a presentation with much more freedom than a standard mouse. Be prepared to feed this monster new batteries often, though (or buy a rechargeable model), and check the box to see just how far you can stray without losing the signal.

✔ **Trackball:** As shown in Figure 5-5, this pointing device resembles an upside-down mouse: Rather than move the housing around, you move the ball with your finger or thumb. Trackballs are a little harder to use at first; they stay in one place, however, so they require much less desktop space.

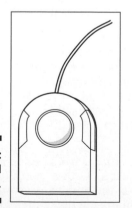

Figure 5-5:
A typical
trackball.

TIP

If you decide on a trackball for your computer systems, consider buying my favorite pointing device: an *optical trackball*. They never require adjustment or cleaning, and they have fewer moving parts than standard trackballs or mice. These trackballs use balls covered with a pattern of dots, and optical sensors in the body of the trackball "read" these dots to determine movement.

✔ **Touchpad:** This pointing device has been popular on laptops, but it's also available for desktop computers. To use a touchpad (as shown in Figure 5-6), you move your finger across its surface, and the cursor follows your movements onscreen. To click, you can either press a button on the touchpad or tap the pad surface twice in quick succession. No pen or other stylus is required. Like trackballs, touchpads take up little space. They don't require cleaning, although they do need to be adjusted every few months by running a special program. Some people feel that a touchpad is better for fine detail work on a computer.

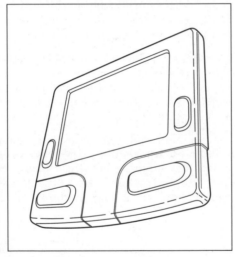

Figure 5-6:
Okay, so a touchpad looks a little strange, but it works!

✔ **Drawing tablet:** This pointing device is a larger version of the touchpad. A *drawing pad* is designed specifically for computer art and drafting. It allows freehand drawing on the tablet, which then appears on the screen. Depending on the size of the tablet, you can even use a ruler or stencil, but don't use a regular pen or pencil, please! (Use only the stylus that comes with the tablet.) The drawing tablet can also double as a regular touchpad when you're not drawing.

✔ **Fingertip mouse:** Another pointing device that started out on laptops is the fingertip mouse. There's really not much to it other than a tiny button about the size of a pencil eraser that sits in the middle of a smooth case. (Many laptops feature a fingertip mouse in the middle of their keyboards, or you can buy a desktop keyboard with a built-in fingertip mouse.) To use a fingertip mouse, you nudge the button in the direction that you want the cursor to travel onscreen. The longer you push, the farther the cursor travels; the harder you push, the faster it moves. To click, you press a button on the case. As with a touchpad, you need to adjust a fingertip mouse from time to time by running a program.

The key to keyboards

One keyboard is *not* just like another! For example, if you've been given an older 84-key keyboard, I suggest hanging it up in the barn as a good luck charm along with the horseshoes. You can easily recognize these keyboards because they don't have a separate set of cursor control keys or a separate numeric keypad. If you're using any version of Windows, you need at least a standard 101-key keyboard.

More expensive keyboards have additional features that can make your life at the computer considerably easier. For example:

✔ **Extra keys:** Windows 2000 and XP both support extra keys. In fact, one key even looks like the Windows logo. Pressing these keys make drop-down menus appear within programs, display the task list, print special characters, and much more. (That crazy Gates fellow . . . it wouldn't surprise me if he ends up adding new symbols to the alphabet!)

✔ **Ergo, ergonomics:** Recognizing the evils of carpal tunnel syndrome, many keyboards today are ergonomically designed. This design usually includes a wrist rest and a more human-friendly shape. The ergonomic keyboard shown in Figure 5-7 is a good example.

Figure 5-7: Catch the wave! An ergonomic keyboard helps reduce wrist strain.

✔ **Mouse/keyboard combos:** Need every inch of desk space? Consider a keyboard with a built-in trackball or touchpad. These integrated keyboards reduce hand movements and make you a more efficient, meaner typing machine.

✔ **Detached connectivity:** For the couch potato who has everything. Look Ma, no wires! A *wireless* keyboard enables you to lounge on your futon while composing that Great American Novel — but don't forget the batteries, and remember that these keyboards are significantly more expensive than their wired brethren. (My tech editor recommends a pair of binoculars, if your futon is more than three or four feet away!)

If you decide to use a wireless keyboard or mouse, rechargeable batteries are the smart power user's investment. Although you pay more up front for the special reusable batteries and charger unit, you more than make up for that in savings over the years. Oh, and here's my two-cent recommendation on rechargeable batteries: Go with lithium ion (LiIon) batteries, which last longer and don't require charging as often as nickel cadmium (NiCad) batteries.

✔ **Multifunction buttons:** Many computer *multifunction* keyboards look more like your car's dashboard these days. Buttons have been added to allow you to check your e-mail, visit certain Web sites, display help for your operating system and applications, connect to the Internet, and control your optical drive. (One of my computers even has a rotary volume control on the keyboard, which I find much handier than the volume control on the Windows taskbar. Besides, it reminds me of my old stereo receiver.)

Although these keyboards are convenient, remember that a multifunction keyboard requires its own proprietary software; if you've scavenged one of these keyboards and didn't get the software, all those extra buttons become window dressing. Also, you have to program many of those keys on a multifunction keyboard. Sounds a little strange, doesn't it? What you're doing is identifying what function each of these specialized keys is supposed to perform. (You should have to do this only once.)

If you're using a desktop case or a huge 21-inch monitor, I recommend a *keyboard shelf,* which looks like a drawer that fits under your computer. The shelf slides out to give you access to the keyboard. After you're finished typing, you can simply push the shelf back inside the unit. This device saves desk space, and it puts your keyboard at the proper typing position.

If you're buying a new keyboard, always try it out before you pull out your credit card. Because keyboards are all made differently, they have a different typing and comfort "feel" to them. People can be finicky about their keyboards, and typing a long document on a bad keyboard is roughly equivalent to poking a soggy sponge or a hard rock repeatedly with your fingers.

Installing a Port Adapter Card

If your motherboard doesn't have built-in USB 2.0 or FireWire ports, it's time to add your port adapter card. These cards typically have one USB 2.0 and one FireWire port on the side of the card itself, and some allow you to add cables that take up another slot on the back of your case to add even more ports. Check the manual that came with your port adapter card to determine what connectors are actually on your card and which must be added separately.

Your adapter card manual should also fill you in on any *dual inline packaging* (DIP) switch or jumper settings that have to be configured — I discuss both DIP switches and jumpers in Chapter 3. Now is a good time to move any required jumpers, before your card is mashed between several other cards and you have to be a contortionist like the Great Zambini to reach it. I do have good news about most port adapter cards: The factory default settings are usually just what you need, although it never hurts to check first.

To install your port adapter card, follow these instructions:

1. **Don't handle anything until you touch a metal surface.**

   Have you been shuffling your feet through that deep, plush carpeting all day? Dissipate yourself of excess electrostatic energy. I'm talking Static City!

2. **Haul your open case on top of your work surface.**

   Do not plug it in yet.

3. **Locate an adapter card slot of the proper length at the back of your case.**

   I cover the different types of adapter slots in Chapter 4, but here's a refresher just in case: peripheral component interconnect (PCI) cards use the short slots, and 16-bit industry standard architecture (ISA) cards are twice as long. Because USB 2.0 and FireWire port adapter cards are PCI, you'll need a PCI slot. Also, make sure that any notches cut into the connectors on your card match any spacers within the slot. These spacers help ensure that you don't try to stick a 16-bit card into a PCI slot. Found an empty slot of the right length? Good! Move along to the next step.

4. **Take your trusty screwdriver and remove the screw and the metal slot cover at the back of the case, as shown in Figure 5-8.**

   Stick both these parts in your parts box.

   You might need this slot cover later to close your case if you decide to remove an adapter card.

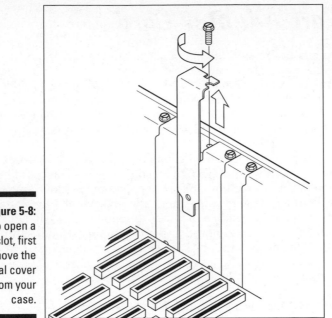

Figure 5-8:
To open a
slot, first
remove the
metal cover
from your
case.

5. **Pick up the adapter card by the top corners and then line up the connector on the bottom of the card with the slot on the motherboard, as shown in Figure 5-9.**

The card's metal bracket should align with the open space created when you removed the slot cover. If the adapter card has extra connectors that aren't positioned above the slot, you're trying to fit the wrong type of card into the wrong slot. Look for a slot that has matching connectors and notches.

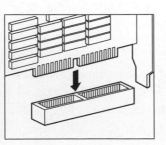

Figure 5-9:
Make sure
that the
connectors
on the
bottom
of the card
line up with
the slot.

6. **Houston, are we go for launch? If so, apply even pressure to the top of the card and push it down into the slot on the motherboard.**

   Although you won't hear a click, you should be able to tell when the card is firmly seated. The bracket should be resting tightly against the case.

7. **Add the screw that you removed in Step 4 and tighten down the bracket — but don't overtighten it.**

Your computer is now equipped with at least one external USB port or FireWire port.

Connecting External Ports

If your computer uses a standard ATX motherboard and case (which I discuss in Chapter 3), your ports are already connected. (If you recall, they stick out the back of the PC through that funky cutout.) Therefore, you can skip this section with a smile (unless you've installed a sound card that offers separate ports for MIDI or optical connections).

However, if you need to attach *external* ports to the front or back of your case and connect them to your motherboard, you're in the right place. External ports for the back of your case should look something like metal slot covers, sporting one or two ports on the outside and separate ribbon cables for each port. External ports for the front of your case are usually built into the case already, complete with cables for connecting to your motherboard.

External ports are not the same as the ATX-standard ports that are permanently attached to your motherboard — they need to be connected manually.

To install external ports, follow these instructions:

1. **Don't handle anything until you touch a metal surface.**

   Put down that slick, plastic, handheld video game; you might be carrying static now.

2. **If you're connecting an external port on the front of your case, skip to Step 5. If you're installing an external port on the back of your case, remove the screw and the metal slot cover at the back of the case and save both in your parts box.**

3. **Insert the slot cover with the ports into the vacant slot.**

4. **Add the screw that you removed in Step 2 and tighten the bracket.**

5. **Check your motherboard manual and find the connectors for the external ports.**

   These connectors are similar to the motherboard connectors for your reset button.

6. **Attach the cables to the connectors on your motherboard as instructed by your motherboard's manual.**

   Pin 1 on the motherboard connector should align with the marked wire on the cable; this marking is usually a red stripe or red lettering.

Connecting Your Keyboard and Pointing Thing

It's time to add those all-important parts that let you argue directly with your computer: your mouse and keyboard. As I mention earlier in this chapter, computers use one of two types of keyboard connectors, and a mouse can be connected to a serial port or a separate mouse port. The steps that you follow are determined by your motherboard and what it provides.

Installing a keyboard

Connecting the keyboard is as easy as plugging in the cable through the case and into the keyboard port. To install your keyboard, follow these instructions:

1. **Locate the keyboard port on the back of your case.**

   If you have an older keyboard, the port should be as thick as a permanent marker. If you have a PS/2 keyboard port, it should be about the thickness of a pencil eraser. If your keyboard connector is the same size as the keyboard port, rejoice and continue. If the connector is the wrong size, grumble, visit a local computer shop, and ask for an adapter to make an older keyboard fit a PS/2 keyboard port (or the other way around).

2. **Place the tip of the keyboard connector into the port and rotate it slowly while applying light pressure.**

   The connector should fit into the port only one way, so you should be able to feel when the pins line up. If your connector has a little arrow or a flat area on the outside, that indicator usually points up (although not every motherboard has the decency to define "up" the same way).

3. **When the keyboard connector is correctly aligned, push it in firmly.**

Installing a non-USB mouse (or other pointing thing)

If you've invested in a USB mouse, you already know the drill: just plug it in. However, if you've grown attached to an older non-USB mouse — my goodness, that sounds somewhat racy — you'll be happy to know that all of today's motherboards still offer a PS/2 mouse port.

Follow these steps to install the mouse:

1. **Locate the port on the back of your case.**

2. **Place the tip of the connector into the port and rotate it slowly while applying light pressure.**

    The connector should fit into the port only one way, so you should be able to feel when the pins line up. If your connector has a little arrow or a flat area on the outside, that marker usually points up (although the direction that "up" takes seems to vary in the eyes of some engineers).

3. **After the connector is correctly aligned, push it in firmly.**

Check It Once, and Check It Twice!

Even though your PC is now sporting all of its ports, you really have no way to test them — but all is not lost. You can test your keyboard right now. Just push the power switch on your computer case.

If you've connected your keyboard to the port on your motherboard correctly, all three keyboard lights should flash — the Num Lock, Caps Lock, and Scroll Lock indicators. If these indicators light up, your keyboard is correctly installed. If these lights don't illuminate, remove the keyboard connector from the keyboard port and try plugging it in again. If you still have no luck, try another keyboard to make sure that the port is working, and then check your motherboard manual to make sure that you're connecting the keyboard to the keyboard port. (Remember that the port is the same size and shape as your mouse port; look for a keyboard icon next to the correct port.)

Chapter 6

Images "R" Us: Adding Video and a Monitor

*W*hile you're building your computer, you'll be dazzled by more features, functions, acronyms, and assorted hoo-hah surrounding your video display than just about any other component of your computer system. Computer components such as your floppy drive and your keyboard remain largely unchanged since the 486-class computers of old, but today's multimedia applications and operating systems demand monitors and video cards that deliver photographic-quality color and sharp detail. Game players and multimedia techno-jocks will also spend their dollars freely for advanced 3-D graphics and good-quality digital video.

In this chapter, I help you understand the buzzwords and acronyms that surround the technology behind all those video features so that you can make an intelligent decision on what to buy. I give you the inside information about your video subsystem, which has two parts: the video adapter card that fits inside your computer and the monitor that displays the images. You find out how to select the features that you need and how to install your video components.

I'm Okay, You're a Video Card

Your video card plays an important role in your computer: It sends the visual output produced by a program to your monitor, which displays the output on its screen. That visual output could be alphanumeric characters that form words, high-resolution graphics such as a photograph taken with your digital camera, or even the realistic 3-D shape of a monster in your favorite PC action game.

Get set because, in this section, I take you on a whirlwind tour designed to help you find the video card that's exactly right for your applications.

Full speed ahead with accelerated graphics

Unless you've been living under a rock in the Mojave Desert for more than a decade, you've most likely encountered a Windows program running on a computer. Graphical operating systems such as Mac OS X and Windows XP were designed to make computers easier to use by making the displays more visual.

You probably agree that the graphical point-and-click interface is a good development, but when this type of interface was introduced, computers were nowhere near ready to handle the graphics. The first Windows programs ran abysmally slow, and the splashy graphics took too long to display — hence, the popular nickname for Windows 3.0 became *WinDoze*.

By the way, I have a rare copy of Windows 2.1, which is the precursor of Windows 3.0. It runs on antique 80286 PCs. Windows 2.1 takes up a whopping seven floppy disks, and they're the old 720K disks to boot! (And no, it doesn't run Half-Life 2.)

As time went by and Windows slowly developed into the operating environment of choice, computer hardware designers decided to tackle the problem of slow graphics by beefing up the standard PC video adapter. These enhancements enabled the computer's CPU to concentrate on running programs and performing calculations. With the arrival of the accelerated graphics card, techno-nerds around the globe breathed a collective sigh of relief. Finally, graphics were moving full speed ahead!

Accelerated cards have a separate processor onboard (often called a GPU, for *graphics processing unit*) to handle complex graphics functions, such as drawing 3-D objects and displaying menus (which means that your CPU doesn't need to worry about these tasks). In the past, accelerated cards cost dramatically more than standard video cards, but now they're standard equipment with any PC that you buy. When you're shopping for a fast video card, keep these guidelines in mind:

✔ **Look for AGP or PCI-Express:** You get the best performance from an accelerated graphics port (AGP) or PCI-Express video card. Sticking a fast video card in a standard peripheral component interconnect (PCI) slot is a little like forcing a thoroughbred horse to pull a plow: It will do the job, but you're holding it back. Only the AGP and PCI-Express bus types provide the super-fast throughput that your new video card needs to work its magic. (Chapter 3 includes more information on selecting a motherboard with support for AGP and PCI-Express adapter cards.)

✔ **Compare speed:** Most video card manufacturers provide benchmark figures advertising the speed of their accelerated cards; you can use these figures for speed comparisons. As an example, the manufacturer of my video card measures its card's speed using the *3DMark05* utility from FutureMark (www.futuremark.com), which is a well-known benchmark program for graphics hardware under Windows.

✔ **Get driver support:** Make sure that your new card is fully supported with drivers for Windows XP and Windows 2003 Server, OpenGL, and Direct3D. (The last two in that list are the high-performance graphics subsystems that gamers use when playing today's most demanding 3-D games under Windows.) With the right software drivers, just about any operating system can benefit from the same accelerated video adapter.

If you're looking for a specific software driver, I heartily recommend Driverzone.com, at www.driverzone.com, which is a comprehensive Web site that provides links for just about every manufacturer and every type of computer component that I've ever seen.

Video cards are one computer component that simply don't "scavenge well" — that's because Windows video standards are constantly evolving, and a video card that's only a couple of years old is already an antique. Therefore, I strongly recommend that you install a new video card if performance is your goal! Stick with an AGP or PCI-Express video card designed for today's Athlon and Pentium computers.

If you're building an inexpensive, low-end PC, you can save money by choosing a motherboard with *integrated* (built-in) video hardware. An integrated video card offers mediocre performance at best when compared with a separate AGP or PCI-Express video card, but you may find the integrated solution a money-saver if games are not high on your list.

Will 3-D video transform my entire existence?

You might have seen 3-D computer graphics on television or in the movies, but what good is a 3-D video card if you're not running an expensive graphics program? Computer gamers will tell you that there's no better piece of hardware to

TECHNICAL STUFF

Catching a ride on the magic bus

If you're familiar with the history of motherboards and the various bus architectures that have been used in computers, you're probably lots of fun to talk to at parties. With all this technical knowledge at your disposal, you might also know that 486 computers used a nifty bus called the VESA Local Bus (VLB), which was faster than the original 16-bit ISA standard bus.

Back in the days of the 486, VLB offered the fastest access to your system's CPU and RAM, and it had the same purpose as the PCI slot in the first Pentium machines: connecting your video adapter card and hard drive controller card to provide the fastest possible flow of data. Unfortunately, VLB wasn't fast enough and has faded into the history of yesterday's technology; VLB isn't suitable for use on any Pentium-class motherboard (including the original first-generation Pentiums). Even the PCI bus, which is roughly 30 percent faster than VLB, has been declared yesterday's technology — these days, a card using an AGP or PCI-Express bus delivers the fastest video performance. (In fact, PCI video cards have all but disappeared.)

---

improve 3-D games such as Unreal Tournament, Halo 2, Half-Life 2, and Doom 3. With a 3-D video card, objects in these games look so realistic that you can practically reach out and touch them, and these games will run much faster, too.

If you're a nut for computer graphics, you might have already entered the world of 3-D; if not, here's a quick introduction. Today's 3-D video cards take care of *rendering* — that's the computer term for drawing objects in three dimensions and overlaying a pattern on the surface of the object. For example, a square wooden block is originally rendered as a simple cube object, but when a wood grain pattern is added, it suddenly looks just like a wooden block. Of course, that wooden block can just as easily become a complex object, such as a tentacled mercenary with a phased plasma rifle from the planet Quark. Modern 3-D computer games work with your 3-D video card to realistically render your enemies, who then proceed to try to render *you* (limb from limb, if you get my drift). These advanced games even provide realistic lighting, shadow effects, and weather effects such as rain and snow.

A 3-D video card handles the complex math necessary to produce 3-D images (just like an accelerated video card does for Windows), thus enabling your CPU to focus on handling the program. Figure 6-1 illustrates my favorite rendering program, trueSpace (www.caligari.com), with a representative cool 3-D graphic (in this case, a giant walking robot).

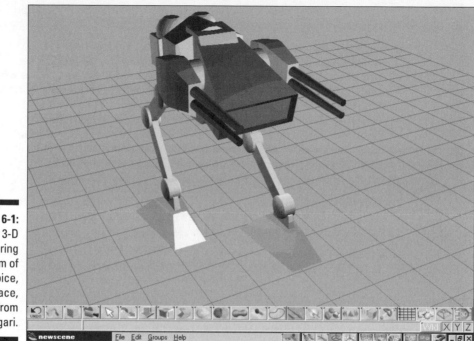

Figure 6-1:
My 3-D
rendering
program of
choice,
trueSpace,
from
Caligari.

A 3-D video card speeds up just about every operation in today's hottest
computer games (as well as "serious" programs such as trueSpace,
Photoshop CS2, Premiere Pro, and other multimedia bigwig applications).
The most popular 3-D video cards use chipsets from the following two top
manufacturers:

✔ **NVIDIA:** Home to the older RIVA TNT and TNT2 (both of which have been
   big favorites of computer gamers for years), NVIDIA (www.nvidia.com)
   is known in the 3-D world for its GeForce chipset. At the time of this writing, the GeForce 7800 GTX chipset is found on the most powerful 3-D
   video cards available.

✔ **ATI:** The ATI Rage series of 3-D video cards was a mainstay for years in
   the retail PC world because they were cheap and reasonably powerful.
   The company (www.ati.com) continues to update its Radeon GPU
   chipset (currently the Radeon X850 series) to compete head-to-head
   with GeForce, so it's also a 3-D video card to compare.

Speaking of comparisons, what should you look for in a 3-D video card?
Here's a quick shopper's checklist:

✔ **Go for memory:** Look for the most onboard RAM that you can afford. Most cards feature anywhere from 32MB to 512MB.

✔ **Compare speed:** Check common benchmarks between cards to determine which is actually faster. As an example, the 3DMark05 benchmark utility that I mention earlier in this chapter can help determine which card is truly the fastest at performing a standard rendering test. You typically find these benchmark figures in the card's specifications on the box or on the company's Web site. (Some video card manufacturers also list the frame rate that a card can achieve while running a popular game such as Unreal Tournament, Doom 3, or Half-Life 2; the higher the frame rate, the better the performance, which makes it a good figure to use while comparing video cards.)

✔ **Get driver support:** Your card should offer full OpenGL and Direct3D support. These two drivers are the most popular for today's computer games and rendering programs.

✔ **Go for color and resolution:** The deeper the color depth and the higher the resolution, the better. Find out more about these features in the next section.

For reviews and benchmarks of the latest video cards (along with comparisons between the newest NVIDIA and ATI chipsets), visit Tom's Hardware at www.tomshardware.com.

Thanks for the memory

Your computer's motherboard isn't the only part of your computer that has its own RAM. Your video card needs memory as well. In essence, your video adapter uses RAM to store colors and pixel values; the more RAM on your video card, the more colors you can display and the higher the video resolution you can use. I recommend a minimum of 32MB of video memory for a PC running an office suite and Internet applications or a minimum of 128MB if you're running graphics-intensive games and applications on a 3-D video card.

Because colors and resolution are important in selecting a video card, I attack them separately.

More about colors

In the early days of computers, you were lucky if you could display 4 or 16 colors on the screen at one time. These old standards were color graphics adapter (CGA) and enhanced graphics adapter (EGA). People were satisfied with CGA and EGA colors for a surprisingly long time, mostly because computer hardware in those days cost a fortune, and why would anyone need more colors to run (chortle) *DOS* programs? Even game players were happy with 16 colors. (And some still say that the games had more depth and imagination back then because games didn't rely on flashy graphics. Go figure.)

How deep is your color?

You hear techno-nerds talk about color depth all the time, especially when they argue about the Web. *Color depth* refers to the number of colors in an image; popular color depths are 256 colors, 64 thousand colors, and 16 million colors. Most graphics on the Web use a color depth of 256 colors because the lower the color depth, the less time it takes to download the image to a Web browser using a standard dial-up analog connection. Still, some people who create Web pages like to use 16 million color graphics because those graphics look better. Eventually, the popularity of broadband Internet access will allow Webmasters to strut their stuff with more confidence, but for now the battle rages on.

With the arrival of the video graphics array (VGA) standard of 256 colors and the debut of Windows 3.0, everything changed. Suddenly, the rush was on for flashier and more realistic color. Most computers now use the super video graphics array (SVGA) standard, and even the most rudimentary video card on the market these days can provide more than 16 million colors on the screen at one time. That's true photographic-quality color.

Have you scavenged a video card with 16MB or less RAM? I'd use it as a boot scraper. At the time of this writing, you can pick up a 64MB video card for less than 30 bucks — and that card is far more likely to work with today's games, video-editing, and graphics applications.

More about resolution

Extra video RAM lets your monitor display images at a higher resolution. To explain resolution, I need to introduce you to a single dot on your monitor: a *pixel*. The display on your monitor is built from thousands of pixels arranged in lines, each pixel displaying a certain color. Your video system's resolution is expressed in the number of pixels displayed horizontally and the number of lines displayed vertically. For example, a resolution of 1024 x 768 means that the monitor displays 1024 pixels horizontally across the screen and 768 pixels vertically.

At lower resolutions, graphics look big and chunky, with ragged edges and blocky shapes. Any resolution lower than 800 x 600 is pretty much unusable these days.

At higher resolutions, such as 1024 x 768, 1152 x 864 (my favorite), 1280 x 1024 or even 1600 x 1200, you can fit more images, data, icons, and information on your screen at one time. With such a higher resolution, you can work on an entire brochure in your desktop-publishing program without zooming out. Or you can fit more of your favorite Web page on the screen without scrolling. Details look better, too, and you can work more efficiently.

But wait — it couldn't be that easy, could it? Nope, you're right: There's a trade-off between resolution and the readability of the fonts and graphics on your screen. For example, I simply can't work for long with a resolution of 1600 x 1200: my older (read that *wiser* and *more mature*) eyes end up producing a whopper of a headache trying to read text while I'm writing.

Note that LCD (or *flat-panel*) monitors typically favor one resolution, which the manufacturer usually specifies as the *native* resolution. If you switch an LCD monitor to a resolution other than the native resolution, the screen is likely to look fuzzy or out of focus.

What's your favorite display resolution? Only you can tell — the decision is completely personal, like choosing that keyboard that feels "just right." After installing your video card, try a wide range of resolutions to see what suits you best. But remember, every monitor has a maximum resolution it can display, so keep your experimentation within the limits of your hardware!

Digital video 101

"What exactly is digital video, and why do I need a video card that displays it?" Well, like the digital audio stored on audio CDs, you can also store video in digital format. In fact, this technology has been around as long as the laser disc.

On the computer, however, digital video has come of age only within the past decade. The first big breakthrough occurred when Windows 95 arrived and became the PC operating system of choice because it contained support for digital video in the Microsoft AVI format. (DOS had no built-in support for displaying video.) Computer games and the Web have also helped to popularize digital video on the computer screen.

The big drawback with digital video has been the sheer amount of space that it takes up. A few minutes of uncompressed digital video (recorded at full-screen resolution with stereo sound) can easily take up 500MB of storage space on your hard drive. This massive storage space required for digital video is one of the reasons for the popularity of the DVD recorder, which can store 4.7GB of digital video on one disc (or 8.5GB on a dual-layer DVD disc).

Notice that I said *uncompressed.* That's where MPEG comes in: It's one of two or three compression formats that greatly reduce the size of a digital video file. The video is compressed (encoded) while it's recorded, and then an MPEG software program decompresses (decodes) it on your computer. In the days of the Pentium II, that decoding took time and quite a bit of the CPU's resources, resulting in the slow, stuttering video playback that you might remember seeing on older computers — or video playback in a window the size of a postage stamp. Today's video cards are far more powerful, and many have built-in MPEG encoding and decoding in hardware for full-screen video that's smooth as butter.

Look out! Digital video from the planet MPEG!

Yep, video cards are just chock-full of acronyms, and this one is a real winner: MPEG stands for *Moving Pictures Expert Group.* Now that's a trivial fact that you can toss around to your friends, right? At least the name suggests something of value — MPEG is the buzzword for digital video on your computer.

If you plan to use your computer extensively to edit digital video, make sure that your video card has *hardware MPEG support,* which can encode (and decode) MPEG digital video all by itself without bogging down your CPU.

What else do I need from a video adapter?

By this time, you might be shrugging your shoulders in disgust, thinking that you'll probably have to pay $1000 for a good-quality video adapter with a top 3-D chipset, at least 128MB of RAM, and hardware MPEG decoding. Perhaps you'll have to take a second mortgage on the house?

Fear not, good citizen! A good-quality, 3-D gaming card with the NVIDIA GeForce FX 5200 chipset and 128MB of memory, for example, has all these features and even a few more — and you can pick it up at a local computer store for well under $60. (Other comparable cards are around the same price.) Not a bad price for a power user part, eh?

Knowing about a few other features can help you determine which video card to buy. Along with the 3-D features that I mention earlier in this chapter, here's a short checklist of features that add value to any video card:

- **Higher refresh rate:** If you spend hours at the PC, your eyes will feel much better at the end of the day if your video card offers a refresh rate of 75 to 85 Hz. (I discuss refresh rate in more detail later in this chapter, in the "Feeling refreshed?" section.)

- **Support:** Before buying a video card, check the company's Web site. Here are some questions to ask: How often does the manufacturer update its drivers for the card that you're considering? Does it offer tech support over the Web, or will you end up getting put on hold, waiting for the next available customer service rep?

- **DVI output:** Oh joy, yet another strange abbreviation created by engineers to confuse normal humankind. In this case, the seemingly random collection of letters stands for *digital visual interface* (often called *digital* *video interface* as well), which refers to a relatively new port that connects your video card to many new flat-panel liquid crystal display (LCD) and digital cathode ray tube (CRT) monitors. A DVI port looks nothing like a standard VGA port, but it provides the fastest transfer of video data (hence the best performance) and the highest-quality digital video signal (compared with the tired analog signal offered by a standard VGA port). As long as your current monitor uses a standard VGA connection, you don't need a DVI port . . . but there's always the future, right?

✔ **Bundled software and Windows utilities:** Most video adapters available today include bundled software on CD-ROM. The software usually highlights the top features of the video card. (For example, a 3-D video card typically includes one or two games that take advantage of the card's 3-D hardware.) Other favorites are multimedia encyclopedias and educational multimedia software for kids, as well as a software DVD player program. The best cards have utilities that add functionality to Windows, such as enabling you to quickly change the resolution of your desktop. Look for the software bundle that best fits your needs.

✔ **TV output:** If you create business presentations or broadcast-quality animation on your computer, how can you display your work on your television (or transfer it to videotape)? The easiest method is to buy a video adapter that can display output from your computer on a TV, VCR, or camcorder as well as on a monitor.

A video card with *TV output* is not the same thing as a *TV card*. Don't expect to be able to watch TV just because your video card has TV output. For that, you need a TV card, which is an adapter with a built-in TV tuner that enables you to watch TV in a little window on your monitor. It's just the thing for sports fanatics and those who refuse to miss their soaps.

✔ **Video panning:** If you have the necessary RAM, some cards enable you to pan (move) your screen around a huge image or document, rather like how a movie camera pans to keep an actor in view while he or she moves from one part of the set to the other. This feature lets you view the whole image or document even if it's so big that it doesn't fit all on one screen. If you're going to edit large graphics in Photoshop or perhaps edit large documents or brochures in a desktop-publishing package, video panning might be a valuable feature for you.

✔ **Dual display:** A card with this feature can support two monitors at once, placed side-by-side — Windows XP allows you to use the two monitors as one super-large desktop, or you can display two different desktops at the same time. *Sweet!* (Of course, you'll have to spring for a second monitor — such is the techno-wizard's lifestyle.)

✔ **DPMS support:** A video card with display power management signaling (DPMS) support can shut down your monitor to save energy in case you leave your computer unattended for a preset amount of time. (This feature requires a DPMS monitor, which I cover later in this chapter.)

DVD details

I'm willing to bet that you're already familiar with *DVD,* which is abbreviation-speak for *digital video disc* (or *digital versatile disc,* depending on the abbreviation that you encounter first). This type of disc, called "the new generation of CD-ROM," is rapidly replacing the VHS tape for home movie distribution.

Single-layer, single-sided DVDs hold about seven times the data of a standard CD-ROM — a tasty 4.7GB — so they have the storage capacity required to hold even the longest movies. (Dual-layer DVDs will hold a whopping 8.8GB!) Plus, DVDs carry Dolby Digital Surround sound, and there's even plenty of room for niceties such as subtitling in multiple languages. Finally, DVDs use a form of MPEG encoding called MPEG-2, which provides a picture as good as commercial satellite TV (much better than your average VHS tape). For complete coverage of DVD drives meant for PC use, see Chapter 8.

Staking Out Your Visual Territory

Luckily, there's less to remember about your computer's monitor than there is about your video adapter, although it's still just as important in providing you with the best possible display. In this section, I discuss the selling points of a good monitor.

Like a keyboard, a monitor is something that you really need to try in person. You need to *see* the monitor and its display with your own eyes before you buy it. Often, the only difference between two monitors with similar prices is that one simply looks better to you.

If you live in a large town with at least one or two computer stores, visit each store and take a look at the monitors they offer. Before you decide to buy, write down the brand name and model number of the monitor and see whether you can buy it online or through mail order for less. (With the brand name and model number, you can easily use Price Watch at www.pricewatch.com to locate the best prices across the entire Internet.)

Whichever monitor you choose, it *must* be capable of displaying SVGA graphics. Without an SVGA monitor, even the best video card and the most powerful Pentium or Athlon computer will look like those old Pong games from the early 1980s. (Luckily, it's getting harder to find a VGA monitor these days, for exactly that reason.)

Deciphering monitor sizes (and choosing the one for you)

You can buy a monitor in several different sizes (all measured diagonally, like a TV): 15-inch, 17-inch, 19-inch, 21-inch — even larger, which is especially useful for those doing desktop-publishing or computer-aided drafting. Which is the right size for you?

You can compare the size of your monitor with the size of your car. A 15-inch monitor is like a '71 Volkswagen Beetle, and a 21-inch monitor is like a Cadillac sports sedan. They both do the same job — driving you where you want to go — but one is faster, bigger, and more fun to drive (as well as much more expensive). You can stretch out in the Caddy, and it has all the latest controls and a gaggle of automatic functions that keep everything in sync — it's the same with the 21-inch monitor.

In general, the larger the monitor, the easier it is on your eyes, especially if you'll be chained in front of your computer for hours at a time. At the same resolution, the 17-inch monitor displays the same images as the 15-inch, but the image is physically bigger and the details stand out more clearly. When you increase the resolution of your desktop (to 1024 x 768 or so), the monitor size becomes more important because the smaller monitor needs to shrink everything to fit the entire desktop on its screen.

Ever heard the adage "How big is a 19-inch TV?" Computer monitors suffer from the same inaccuracy. Although two monitors might both be advertised as 17 inches, one of them might have an actual viewing area of 15.9 inches, and the other might have a viewing area of 16.1 inches. (Remember, we're measuring the diagonal size of the screen.) As you might expect, the second monitor displays more than the first. The first monitor probably looks the same size, but you'll probably be paying for more plastic case. When you're shopping for a monitor, it's worth paying a few dollars more for the monitor with a larger actual viewing area.

For general home use, a 15-inch monitor is fine. But if you prefer larger text and graphics, plan to do graphics-intensive work for several hours at a time, or are a hard-core gamer, I would point you toward at least a 17-inch or 19-inch monitor.

Comparing dot pitch among monitors

Although *dot pitch* sounds like a cartoon character, it's actually another important figure that you can use to compare monitors while you're out shopping. Rather than go into an exhaustive techno-nerd discussion of electron guns, cathode ray tubes, and magnetic fields, just keep this in mind: The lower a monitor's dot pitch, the more detailed and precise the display. (In fact, *dot pitch* refers to the distance between pixels; the smaller the dot pitch, the closer the pixels and the more detailed the image.)

Although more expensive CRT monitors boast a .22 or .24 dot pitch, typical LCD monitors have a .26 dot pitch, which is fine for most computer users. Any dot pitch higher than .26 loses a noticeable amount of detail, thus resulting in a grainy appearance at higher resolutions. The higher the dot pitch, the worse the image becomes.

Feeling refreshed?

Another feature to look for while shopping for a CRT (or tube) monitor is a high *refresh rate,* which refers to the number of times per second that your video adapter card redraws the image onscreen. The higher the refresh rate, the better. Although the human eye can't see it, most monitors redraw each pixel on the screen 60 times a second (for a refresh rate of 60 Hz). The screen is drawn line by line, starting at the top-left corner; Figure 6-2 shows you this process.

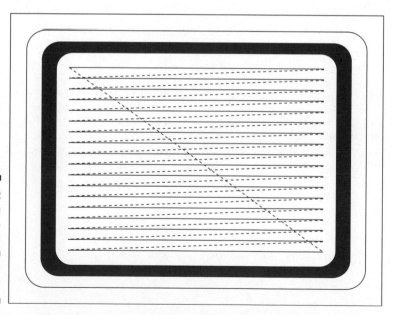

Figure 6-2:
Can you imagine repeating this path 60 times a second?

Although you can't see the screen being redrawn, the human eye *can* discern the difference between 60 Hz and 70 Hz. The more times that the screen is redrawn every second, the sharper, clearer, and more stable the image appears. (You might be able to notice the flicker of your screen refreshing at lower refresh rates by looking slightly above or to the side of the screen because your peripheral vision can pick it up more easily.) The best monitors now have average refresh rates of between 75 Hz and 85 Hz. If you plan to

Attack of the dot-pitch piranha

There you are, shopping for a monitor at your local computer chain store. The salesperson swoops down like a vulture and leads you to a remarkably cheap 19-inch monitor. "Isn't this a great deal?" he crows. "You get a 19-inch monitor for about the same price as a 17-inch!"

Here's your response: Stare him straight in his beady little eyes and ask him, "Okay, slugger, what's the dot pitch on this great deal?" If his answer is something outrageous, like "a .39 dot pitch," you can bet that the monitor probably won't reach a higher resolution than 1024 x 768 — and the display won't be very readable, either! At best, you might find a monitor like this

one suitable for playing computer games at 800 x 600 resolution, although using it under Windows will eventually drive you insane from the grainy, smudgy-looking fonts.

These cheap monitors are usually an off-brand because no major monitor manufacturer (such as NEC, Sony, or Hitachi) would want to produce such a monster.

Oh, and don't forget to smile condescendingly at the oh-so-helpful salesperson . . . who probably just missed out on a fat bonus for selling you a super-cheap monitor.

spend long hours in front of your monitor, you'll probably feel less fatigued and your eyes will be in better shape with a monitor that offers a higher refresh rate. (Personally, I can't use a system running at anything less than 75Hz.) Your video card needs to support a higher refresh rate, too.

Common refresh rates for today's PCs are 72 Hz, 75 Hz, 80 Hz, and 95 Hz. (As I said, I recommend anything above 75 Hz.) However, some very expensive high-performance monitors (commonly used for computer-aided drafting) can handle refresh rates over 100 Hz. Under Windows XP or Windows 2000, your computer can automatically set the optimal refresh rate for your particular hardware combination.

Remember that the best judge of a monitor's display is your own eye, so *use* it!

Therefore, I recommend that you select a monitor by shopping at your local computer stores; then buy it online to save money.

What else makes a great monitor?

When you're familiar with the major features of a good monitor, you're almost ready to go shopping. In this section, I list a number of extra features that you should look for while selecting the monitor that works best for you. Keep in mind that these features can appear on a good 17-inch monitor as well as on an expensive 21-inch model:

✔ **Flat screen:** If you can imagine writing a document, playing a game, or answering your e-mail on the surface of a basketball, you get some idea of why computer owners crave CRT monitors with screens as flat as possible. Old monitors with curved tubes tend to distort the display, especially if you're doing fine detail work, such as drafting or desktop-publishing layout.

✔ **Flat panel:** Although they're still significantly more expensive than standard tube monitors of the same size, these color displays are a dream come true. LCD flat-panel monitors use the same liquid-crystal technology as laptop computer screens, so they require only 15 to 20 percent of the depth of a regular monitor. With a flat-panel monitor, you get a truly flat, edge-to-edge display with no distortion and gorgeous color. Flat-panel screens also give off very little heat and use much less electricity. And, unlike a monitor with a tube, a flat-panel display emits virtually no radiation, so it's easier on your eyes, and you can spend longer periods of time in front of your computer without discomfort. Once available only in 15- and 17-inch models, larger 19-inch and 21-inch flat-panel displays are becoming affordable now that the price of the technology has dropped.

If you decide on an LCD flat-panel monitor, make sure you note the *response time* (given in milliseconds, such as 8 ms, 16 ms, or 20ms) — the lower the response time, the better a flat-panel monitor will be for gaming and digital video. If you're a gamer or you're into digital video, I strongly recommend an LCD monitor with a 16ms response time or lower.

✔ **Antiglare coating:** As a general rule, whatever you create or do on your computer should shine — *not* the monitor itself! An antiglare screen can be a big help in an office that is brightly lit or has many windows. If you decide on a monitor that doesn't have an antiglare coating, you can still buy an antiglare panel and attach it to your monitor later.

✔ **Energy Star/DPMS compliant:** All Pentium and Athlon-class motherboards sold these days have the Energy Star power management system built in. (Before Energy Star became a standard, these motherboards used to be called *green* or *power-saver* boards.) You can configure an Energy Star motherboard to power down the computer while you're off getting doughnuts. If your monitor is Energy Star-compliant, your computer can shut the monitor down too. When you return, press a key or move your mouse to wake up your computer, and then congratulate yourself on saving both your money and your environment.

Some video cards can also perform this power-down function for your monitor; see whether your card's manual mentions that it's Energy Star/VESA DPMS compatible. If so, follow its instructions for enabling the power-saving features.

✔ **Low radiation:** All computer monitors emit some electromagnetic radiation. As I mentioned earlier in this section, flat-panel LCD monitors emit the least (virtually none at all). Depending on what you read, you might feel that computers also attract Bigfoot or UFOs — but the radiation is real. Your monitor is responsible for virtually all the electromagnetic emissions from your computer, which makes sense when you think about it: You're sitting in front of a big glass tube, on the other side of which are three big electron guns shooting a bazillion electrons at hyperwarp speed right at your head. Before you decide to go back to using an abacus, let me reassure you that computer monitors are safe to use! However, many monitors are designed to further reduce electromagnetic emissions to the MPR II standard, set by the Swedish Board for Technical Accreditation, or the more stringent European TCO standard. If you plan to spend hours every day in front of your monitor, it's reassuring to know that you won't get a sunburn.

✔ **Digital controls:** Older monitors have thumbwheel controls, which you use to adjust everything from contrast and brightness to vertical and horizontal positioning. This method is fine until your 4-year-old starts messing with them. Techno-nerds like me favor more precise digital controls with an on-screen display (OSD) of easy-to-follow menus that make fine-tuning your monitor's picture more like setting your DVD player.

Most monitors with digital controls also offer separate programmable configurations that you can store in memory. If a particular program changes the characteristics of your screen, you can load a special configuration to take care of it rather than manually adjust your monitor each time.

✔ **Color configuration:** Does that pink really look like pink to you? If your monitor supports *color configuration,* you can change the hue of the colors displayed by your monitor. This feature is a real killer for users who do desktop publishing and image editing — they can adjust their colors to match the Pantone color chart used by printers.

✔ **Built-in speakers:** Built-in speakers aren't for everyone because they usually add a considerable amount to the price of your monitor, and the stereo separation from speakers that are only a few inches apart is pretty dismal. (Remember that the sound card has jacks that enable you to add your own external speakers, which typically sell for less than $30 a pair. For more information, see Chapter 9.) However, if you're looking for convenience and you want to save desktop space, you can investigate a monitor with built-in speakers.

✔ **Tilt/swivel pedestal:** Older CGA and EGA monitors usually came with little pop-up legs, but any good-quality monitor that you buy today should have a base that tilts and swivels. Your neck will thank you! If you've scavenged an older VGA monitor without a base, you can also pick up a tilting monitor stand at most computer stores.

Take it from someone who spends hours a day writing at the keyboard: Elevating your monitor correctly is important. You should be able to sit down at your keyboard and type naturally, with your monitor at eye level and at least two feet distant from your eyes. With a properly positioned monitor, you should be able to work without undue strain on your neck or your eyes.

✔ **Warranty:** Because you can use an SVGA monitor with just about any IBM-compatible computer that you might build in the foreseeable future, it's worth paying extra for a longer warranty. Most top monitors these days have a three- to five-year warranty; economy models typically offer only a one-year warranty.

Installing a Video Adapter Card

In this section, I show you how to add your video adapter card to your chassis. Your video adapter card will have one VGA port on the side of the card itself.

Today's video cards are *jumperless,* or *plug and play,* which means they configure themselves automatically for your computer. For example, Windows XP and Windows 2003 Server can usually set up a plug-and-play video card automatically. If you have one of these video cards, congratulate yourself for your good choice, although it's still a good idea to check your manual for any last-minute instructions that might apply to your operating system.

To install your video adapter card, follow these instructions:

1. **Touch a metal surface before you handle your video card (or anything else on your computer).**

   Let me guess: You've been making balloon animals to amuse your kids? If so, your skin is now one big conductor for static electricity, and that static could damage your video card.

2. **If your computer chassis is plugged in, unplug it.**

3. **Locate an adapter card slot of the proper length at the back of your computer case.**

   If you have an AGP or a PCI-Express video card and an Athlon or Pentium 4 motherboard, you should be able to easily locate the single AGP or PCI-Express slot. (It's usually in the middle of the motherboard.) If you have a 32-bit PCI video card, use one of the shorter PCI adapter card slots. (Need help identifying what type of card slots you have? Chapter 4 illustrates these slots.)

   Most video adapter cards meant for Pentium-class computers these days fit only in an AGP slot or a PCI-Express slot.

4. **When you locate the slot, take your favorite screwdriver and remove the screw and the metal slot cover at the back of the case.**

   Stick both parts in your spare-parts box.

5. **Pick up your video adapter card by the top corners. Line up the connector on the bottom of the card with the slot on the motherboard.**

   All the connectors and any notches on the video card should line up with the slot; the card's metal bracket should align with the open space created when you removed the slot cover.

   Does the adapter card have extra connectors that aren't positioned above the slot? If so, you're trying to fit a "square peg into a round hole"! Look for a slot that has matching connectors and notches.

6. **If everything lines up as it should, apply even pressure to the top of the card and push it down into the slot on the motherboard.**

   Although you won't hear a click, you should be able to tell when the card is firmly seated, and the bracket should be resting tightly against the case. Remember: Never apply undue force — the card should pop in easily!

7. **Add the screw to the corresponding hole in the bracket and tighten down the bracket, but don't overtighten it.**

Connecting Your Monitor

Connecting your monitor to your computer is a simple task. Luckily, the VGA video port and cable connect only if they're correctly aligned. (The same is true for a DVI connector, although most PC owners still use the VGA port.)

To connect your monitor to a VGA port, follow these instructions:

1. **Locate the VGA video port on the back of your case.**

   Although the port is about the size of a serial port, notice that the VGA port has 15 pins. (You can see this illustrated in Chapter 5.)

2. **Align the connector on the end of the monitor cable with the video port.**

   The angled edges on the connector are designed to make sure that it goes in only the right way.

3. **When the connector is aligned correctly with the video port, push the connector in firmly.**

4. **If you want, you can tighten the connector by turning the knobs on the connector clockwise.**

   Some connectors use screws instead, and you'll need a very small screwdriver to tighten these connectors. If you feel that the connector is in firmly, you can leave it as is.

5. **Plug the three-prong power cord that came with your monitor into the matching connector on the back of your monitor's case.**

   Push the plug in firmly to make sure that it doesn't pop out.

6. **Plug the monitor's power cable into your friendly local wall socket.**

   If your wall socket accepts only two prongs — indicating that it isn't grounded — I would heartily recommend that you relocate your computer to a socket that *is* grounded instead of sticking an adapter plug on the cable.

In case you noticed, the connector on the monitor end of your monitor's power cable and the connector on the computer end of your computer's power cable are probably similar — in fact, they're likely to be interchangeable unless you're using a new flat-panel LCD display. Interchangeable cables were one of the first things that someone designed correctly for the IBM line of personal computers. Interchangeable cables let you grab whatever standard power cable is around and use it on either your computer or your monitor. Most techno-types have at least one or two spare power cables in their parts box.

Hey, I Can Finally (Kind of) Boot!

That's right, you're finally going to see something on the screen after completing this chapter's tests. You can also visually check to make sure that your CPU and RAM modules are correctly recognized by your motherboard at this point.

Is a screensaver really necessary?

Do you need to protect your monitor by using a screensaver? This question is asked so often by new computer owners that I'd like to answer it for you here: No. Modern SVGA color monitors don't suffer from burn-in, as did the old monochrome monitors that were originally paired with IBM PCs, XTs, and ATs. Burn-in was a particularly horrible fate for a monochrome monitor; if left on for hours on end with the same display, the image would be literally burned into the monitor tube. That shadowy image would be visible even while you worked on other programs. Even today, you can still see one of these relics from time to time; check out the screen on your bank's ATM machine!

However, if you run Windows XP or Windows 2000, you get one or two screensavers for free anyway — those screensavers do come in handy for the following:

✔ **Password protection:** If you need a simple measure of security at your home or office, you can password-protect a screensaver, which prevents anyone else from using your computer. Be careful, though, because it is still possible to bypass the screensaver by *rebooting* the computer (turning it off and then on again).

✔ **Messages:** You can configure some screensavers to display a scrolling message, which is perfect for letting fellow workers know where you are and when you'll be back.

✔ **Anger management:** Some screensavers are humorous enough to keep you from losing your cool on a particularly bad day.

If you've unplugged your PC, plug it back in now. Push the power switch on your monitor and then push the power switch on the front or back of your case.

To make sure that your computer recognizes all your stuff correctly, you should turn on your monitor and any external parts, such as your modem or printer, before turning on your computer (or at the same time). The easiest and most convenient way to do this is to connect all the power cables from your various computer devices into the same surge protector or uninterruptible power supply (UPS). This way, you can turn the entire system on or off with a single flip of one switch, and your entire system is also protected against indirect power surges from lightning strikes or alien encounters.

If you've correctly installed your video adapter and connected your monitor cable, the following should happen:

1. You should see a message on your screen, which identifies either the video adapter or the motherboard.

   It doesn't matter which you see. The important thing is that your monitor is *displaying* the message.

   Troubleshooting: If your monitor doesn't display any text, check the installation of your video card and then make sure that the monitor cable is firmly connected and that you plugged in your monitor. Also, make sure that you've set both the contrast and brightness on your monitor to medium.

2. After a few seconds, you should see your computer counting the amount of RAM on your motherboard.

   Actually, your computer is testing your computer's RAM, so watch to make sure that you have all the memory that you should have and that no error messages are displayed.

   Troubleshooting: If your computer returns an error message about your system memory or RAM, go to Chapter 4 and check your RAM to make sure that you installed it correctly. You might also need to consult your motherboard's manual to make certain you chose the right bank in which to add RAM.

3. If the RAM test goes okay, your computer will probably show a screen detailing all the parts it can find (such as what CPU you have), how much RAM you have, and how many ports it can locate.

   Troubleshooting: If your computer locks up, return to Chapter 4 and double-check your CPU installation.

4. At this point in the boot process, your computer tries to find a hard drive or floppy drive and promptly gets upset when it doesn't find them.

   Poor thing — your computer will probably beep once or twice and then sulk in frustration.

   Troubleshooting: No beep? Check your PC's internal speaker to make sure that it's properly connected.

5. Turn off your computer, pet the case affectionately, and reassure your half-assembled chassis that you will be adding a hard drive and floppy drive in Chapter 7.

   If your machine completed this test, you've successfully added your video adapter and monitor to your system — good going!

Chapter 7

Make Room! Your Hard Drive and Other Storage Devices

Ah, the quest for storage. Whose domicile ever has enough closets and room for all your stuff? (Even Bill Gates probably needs another closet.) Likewise, your new computer needs a warehouse to permanently store all those programs and all that data that you'll be using. And for that, you need a hard drive. Of course, you could simply run your trusty Web browser, jump to your favorite online hardware mega-super-colossal-mall and buy the first hard drive that you see. If you're looking for the best value, however, you should take your time and consider your options. To make an informed choice while you're shopping (and to make the installation easier), you need to know which hard drive features and specifications are most important.

Although you can consider a hard drive to be the main memory "closet" of your computer, it isn't the only magnetic storage device that your computer can use. In this chapter, I also introduce you to alternative data storage options such as

- ✔ Floppy disk drives
- ✔ Tape backups to protect against the loss of your valuable data
- ✔ 2GB universal serial bus (USB) drives no bigger than a key chain

You can also store data by writing it to CD or DVD using laser light — hence the moniker optical drive — but I cover that in Chapter 8.

"Be Vewy Quiet . . . I'm Hunting for Hawd Dwives!"

If you've started looking in ads or online for hard drives, you're probably drowning in techno-babble and funny numbers and odd acronyms. Is it EIDE or E-I-E-I-O? Who would want to buy something that's SCSI (skuzzy)? Little Miss Muffet SATA on a tuffet? (Okay, that last one was a stretch, but I couldn't help it.)

To help you select a hard drive that's suitable for your system, get ready because the acronyms and jargon are going to flow fast and free through this section. You'll find out more about what types of hard drives will fit in your computer, and the advantages and disadvantages of each breed of hard drive. Then you use this information to determine which type of hard drive is appropriate for your needs.

Luckily, today's PCs use only three major types of internal hard drive technology.

Enhanced IDE hard drives

An *enhanced IDE* (commonly known as *EIDE*) hard drive is the successor to the IDE (or integrated drive electronics) throne, which in turn was based upon the ATA interface standard introduced back in the hoary days of 1986. The *enhanced* part of the name simply means that these drives are smaller, run faster, and have more storage capacity. As you can guess from its name, an IDE drive carries onboard most of the electronics that were located on a hard drive controller card. Enhanced IDE is the single most popular hard drive technology, and this type of drive is used in just about every PC manufactured today. Most EIDE adapter cards can control a maximum of four EIDE devices (including hard drives, tape backup drives, and CD/DVD recorders).

By the way, EIDE drives are also called PATA (that's short for *Parallel ATA*) devices. This gets important in the next section, as you'll see.

Figure 7-1 illustrates the business end of a modern EIDE drive. Note the appearance and position of the power connector, the ribbon cable connector, and the master/slave jumper set. (*Note:* You need to be familiar with all three components when you install your hard drive.) These components might be in different spots on your particular hard drive, but they're there somewhere — check your hard drive documentation for their exact location. The master/slave jumper is particularly important: The setting that you choose for this jumper determines whether the drive is the *primary* (master) drive or the *secondary* (slave) drive in a PC with two hard drives. If you have only one drive, you should select master drive. Your hard drive jumper diagram (which usually appears printed on top of the drive) provides the settings for the master/slave jumper, and you'll find more about jumpers in Chapter 3.

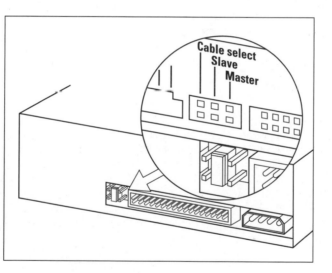

Figure 7-1:
The EIDE hard drive is the workhorse of today's PCs.

Serial ATA hard drives

For most PC owners, an EIDE (PATA) drive is probably the best choice — but if you're willing to spend a few dollars more, you can join the ranks of the SATA faithful (short for *serial ATA*, as opposed to *parallel ATA* for EIDE drives). The SATA interface delivers data back and forth between your PC and your hard drive significantly faster than EIDE/PATA — about 20 MBps faster — and the cable itself is smaller (which allows for better airflow inside your PC's chassis), about half an inch wide.

SATA devices also require a different power connector, which uses 15 pins — therefore, you'll never mix up a SATA power cable with a standard EIDE/PATA power cable, which has only 4 pins. In fact, many SATA hard drives include one of each type of power plug (like you see in Figure 7-2), just in case you're using an older power supply that doesn't have a SATA plug. If your SATA device doesn't have a legacy 4-pin power plug, you'll have to pick up a converter at your local computer store; one end of the converter connects to the 4-pin plug from your power supply, and the other fits your SATA drive.

Besides the simplified cable connections and the performance boost, SATA drives have one huge advantage: no master/slave jumper! A SATA drive is designated as primary or secondary according to the cable connection you make on the motherboard, so there are no jumpers to set. (Remember, today's motherboards are typically equipped with two SATA connectors and two EIDE/PATA connectors. For each type of interface, one connector will be called the primary and one will be called the secondary.)

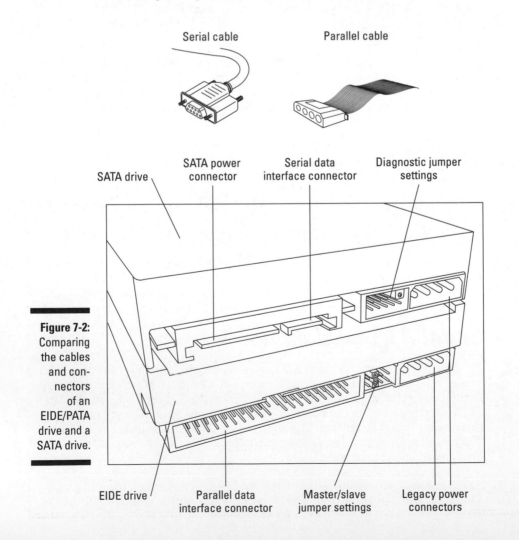

Figure 7-2: Comparing the cables and connectors of an EIDE/PATA drive and a SATA drive.

Okay, I almost forgot another plus for SATA drives: They can be unplugged and swapped without turning off your PC (a procedure called *hot swapping*). This is more of an issue for server PCs that normally never get turned off, but recently I've seen consumer desktop and tower cases that offer slide-in/slide-out device bays that allow techies to easily swap SATA drives.

SCSI hard drives

SCSI is short for *small computer system interface,* which is a power user's dream. (Unfortunately, you really do pronounce it *scuz*-zee.) Many SCSI adapters can move data far faster than even a SATA drive. SCSI hard drives are often found on network server computers, dedicated high-power gaming machines, and 3-D graphics workstations. (The SCSI hard drive was once the standard for all Macintosh computers — something to remember for your next techno-trivia game.)

SCSI speed isn't limited to hard drives, however: A typical SCSI adapter can connect as many as seven SCSI devices to your computer (including scanners and CD recorders). Some variants of SCSI can support as many as fifteen devices. (For complete details on SCSI and what it can do for your PC, jump to Chapter 11.)

Ah, but there's a caveat: SCSI adapter cards, drives, and devices can be the most aggravating beasts on the face of this planet to install and configure.

A hard drive genealogy

Hard drives have developed quickly over the years, and the hallowed family of older abbreviations and acronyms is proof. In fact, the following acronyms are so old that I don't even bother spelling them out.

In the beginning, computers used MFM and RLL drives, which were big, heavy clunkers that actually used voice coil magnets (the kind of magnets used in stereo speakers). These hard drives took up half the computer's case. Most of us old-timers fondly remember an MFM drive thrashing around on our desktops — and because these drives used speaker magnets, they would literally shake from time to time. You can't buy one of these drives these days unless you jump into a time machine.

The next arrival was the ESDI interface, which was a hot, new item that took hard drives to faster speeds and larger capacities. ESDIs needed new controllers, and every power user jumped on the bandwagon. Again, you can promptly forget about them.

IDE drives were next on the horizon, and some are still around. These drives were much smaller, lasted longer, and ran faster than earlier models. You can still find IDE drives on some 386 and most 486 computers, happily chugging away with aplomb. (They have no idea they're antiques.)

Unlike EIDE, which requires you to set only a single jumper (or SATA, which needs no jumpers), a SCSI device chain requires correct termination and a unique SCSI ID number for each device. Many a computer guru has snapped from the frustration of trying to force a cantankerous SCSI card to work properly. (Usually these cards get thrown off a local bridge and settle to the bottom, where they irritate even the fish.)

Comparing EIDE, SATA, and SCSI hard drives

"Okay," you say, "SCSI or SATA wins, right?" Wrong, believe it or not. EIDE/PATA is still the hard drive of choice for three important reasons:

✔ **Less expensive:** EIDE drives and adapter cards are typically less expensive than SCSI and SATA hardware, which makes EIDE more popular with computer manufacturers.

✔ **No significant performance difference:** Not every computer application sees a dramatic performance increase from faster SATA and SCSI hardware. For example, your word processor doesn't perform any better with a SATA drive than with an EIDE drive because hard disk access isn't important while you're typing.

✔ **More popular with hardware manufacturers:** At the time of this writing, most CD/DVD recorders, internal tape drives, and internal cartridge drives still use EIDE connections — and as long as the common denominator is still EIDE/PATA instead of SATA, EIDE will remain King of the Hill!

I agree that SATA is indeed superior to EIDE hardware, and it is slowly but surely replacing EIDE as a standard. In a couple of years, it will be harder and harder to buy a new EIDE drive, and many techs are predicting the upcoming demise of SCSI as well.

Don't give up entirely on SCSI, though. I describe it in detail in Chapter 11 and even show you how to install it. In fact, you can mix SCSI, SATA, and EIDE hardware in the same computer; if you find that you need a SCSI device chain after your computer is up and running with an EIDE or a SATA drive, you can add it. (This is a great idea for those that want a speedy high-resolution scanner or multiple DVD recording system added to their existing PC.)

More stuff about hard drives

What specifications does a smart shopper look for in an EIDE drive? Here are a few:

✔ **Storage capacity:** No big mystery here. The more storage capacity, the more data you can store on a drive. Although an obsolete MFM drive of 50MB was considered overkill in its day, modern EIDE drives hold anywhere from 60GB to more than 300GB. Hard drive capacities are always increasing over time.

On average, most home computers running Windows XP need at least 20GB of hard drive space. For an office computer, the size of your hard drive is more dependent on what type of programs you run; some office software suites take up an entire gigabyte of space all by themselves. My personal recommendation? It's always a good idea to buy a drive so large that you can't imagine ever running out of space — believe me, my friend, you'll fill it up! I would suggest a drive of *at least* 60GB, which will set you back less than $75. Remember, that's a bare minimum; gamers, digital photographers, and digital video connoisseurs will want far more room.

✔ **Access time:** A drive's *access time* (sometimes called seek time) is a measurement of how fast the drive can read and write data. The lower the number, the faster the drive. This time is measured in milliseconds (ms), and it's usually listed next to the drive in advertisements. Naturally, the faster the drive, the more expensive it is. (Just once, I'd like the best of something to be the cheapest.)

Today's fastest EIDE drives have access times of around 7 ms, although any speed under 10 ms should be fast enough for your Pentium computer. If you're a power user with a Pentium 4 or Athlon XP processor, stick with a drive below 10 ms. Super-fast SATA drives often deliver access times around 5 ms.

✔ **rpm:** At last, an abbreviation that most of us understand! Yes indeed, this is your old friend, *revolutions per minute,* and it measures the speed at which the platters within your hard drive are moving. (The *platters* are the spinning discs in your hard drive that store data magnetically.) In general, the faster the rpm, the faster the drive can retrieve data. Before you strap a tachometer onto your drive, however, you should know that rpm is not as accurate as *access time* in predicting a drive's performance. I recommend a drive with a minimum of 7200 rpm (my Western Digital Raptor SATA drive spins at 10,000 rpm, and Windows XP feels like a Ferrari).

✔ **Size:** Most drives are 3½ inches, which means that they fit in a standard 3½-inch bay. (Most PC cases have one of these bays left open: It's reserved for your floppy disk drive. However, these bays can be covered as well, without an outside opening — perfect for a hard drive's nest.) If you have an available standard half-height 5¼-inch bay in your case, you need a drive cage kit to enable the 3½-inch drive to fit. A *drive cage* is simply a metal square that holds the smaller 3½-inch drive inside; in turn, the cage is fastened to the computer chassis as if it were a 5¼-inch device.

✔ **Cache:** A hard drive's *cache* (sometimes called a *buffer*) holds data that's used frequently (or will soon be needed) by your central processing unit (CPU). With a disk cache, the hard drive itself doesn't have to re-read that data. As you might guess, the larger the cache, the better (and usually the more expensive) the drive. I recommend a drive with at least an 8MB cache.

✔ **Warranty:** A hard drive is one of the few parts in your computer that is both complex and has moving parts of its own. A typical hard drive has a reliable lifetime of about six years or so under normal use. The standard industry warranty for hard drives is three years, although you can find drives with warranties as long as five years.

If you're contemplating using a scavenged drive, consider the condition of the drive carefully before using it. For example, if the drive is more than three or four years old (or if it's been used for several hours every day for two or three years), it's already well past middle age, and it's certainly not fast enough for a new Pentium 4 system. In essence, you'll be slowing down your entire computer if you use it. Also, older drives usually hold well under 20GB and perhaps as little as 5GB. With the size of today's Windows operating systems, a lower-capacity hard drive under 20GB doesn't give you much room for additional programs or data files. I urge you to consider a new hard drive that uses the latest technology.

The Ancient Floppy Still Lives

Once upon a time, long before modems and networks, only one way existed to transfer information from one computer to another, back up your computer files, or store data offsite: the floppy disk. The floppy disk was an icon, a universally recognized symbol that everyone revered, and if you didn't have a drawer full of floppies — well, Bucko, you just weren't *with it!*

Why aren't floppies trendy anymore?

A number of things have led to the gradual decline in importance of the floppy disk:

✔ **Too fragile:** Floppy disks are the most fragile of magnetic media. Even the plastic case of a 3½-inch floppy disk isn't much protection, and floppy disks are infamous for simply losing data through exposure to magnetic fields, heat, and simple old age. (*Ahem:* Never, *never* put floppy disks on top of your stereo speakers. The next time that you play Jimi Hendrix, they're goners!)

✔ **Too small:** The development of really big programs — that is, programs that would require forty floppy disks — produced the perfect environment for the arrival of the CD-ROM. (For the full story on CD-ROMs and DVDs, hop over to Chapter 8.)

✔ **Too slow:** A program that takes 20 seconds to load from a floppy is loaded in less than 1 second from a hard drive. It's not practical to run a program from a floppy drive or access files regularly from a floppy.

Despite all these drawbacks, floppy drives are still standard equipment on computers partly because of the universal nature of 3½-inch floppy disks. They've been around for so long, and everyone's so accustomed to them, that no computer manufacturer wants to take the plunge and produce a computer without a floppy drive. (Unless, of course, you're interested in a new Macintosh computer such as the G4 desktop or the iMac — but if you are, why are you reading this book?)

Another reason for the continued survival of the 3½-inch floppy is that all computer users still need some form of removable storage, and floppy drives are cheap. Better forms of removable media have been developed — for example, the Zip drive, which I mention later in this chapter. However, these other removable media drives are more expensive to produce and aren't universal.

IBM once attempted to make 2.88MB disks a standard, but that concept was met with hoots of derision by most of the computing world. By that time, digital video and audio had arrived on the Web and on CD-ROM, and even a small digital video or digital audio file probably wouldn't fit on a single floppy disk, even if that floppy could hold 2.88MB. (Hence the hoots.)

Also, important data still resides on 3½-inch floppies around the world. (On unreliable, potentially unstable floppies. Makes you shudder thinking about it, eh?)

Selecting a floppy drive

There isn't much in the way of features to look for when you're buying a floppy disk drive. Color is one, however — you can easily buy a black floppy drive to match that smashing ebony case you bought for your new system.

Don't Forget Your Controller Card

Many motherboards sold these days feature more than just integrated serial ports and parallel ports. All modern motherboards already have at least a built-in EIDE hard drive and floppy drive controller. A *controller* directs the flow of data to and from your hard drives, floppy drives, and any additional devices.

Here are three other features that you should consider for your motherboard's built-in controller:

- ✔ **SATA support:** Motherboard manufacturers are rapidly adopting the SATA standard, but it's still easy to buy a motherboard that doesn't include SATA support. If you're itching to push the performance of your PC to the limit, make sure your new motherboard has the SATA connectors you need.

- ✔ **RAID support:** Great, another acronym. This one stands for *redundant array of independent disks*. In plain speech, a RAID is a combination of two or more hard drives linked together by your motherboard's onboard controller. A RAID can be configured to boost the transfer speed for the files on the array's hard drives or to provide redundant (backup) copies of those files in case one of the hard drives fails. Either way, most home PC owners should probably steer clear of a RAID — just make sure you back up your data. (Heck, even a RAID needs to be backed up regularly.)

- ✔ **Cache:** A controller memory cache stores data that's used often or that your CPU will probably require very soon. It improves performance because the CPU can retrieve the data from the memory cache, which is much faster than re-reading it from the drive. Don't spend any extra on a caching controller, however, unless you're a power user intent on cutting-edge gaming or professional-quality video editing (or you plan to use your computer as a network server or something equally taxing). A "Cunningham Edition" home PC or a simple office PC really doesn't need such high-speed disk access.

Backing Up Your Data

One thing that floppy disks were once good for was backing up your hard drive. Of course in those days, a hard drive held 50MB or 75MB, so you needed only a box or two of 3½-inch high-density floppies to do the job. However, no one would even consider backing up one of today's 180GB hard drives on 1.44MB floppy disks. No one deserves punishment like that. (Well, maybe spammers and hackers.) To be honest, many computer owners don't back up their data.

Now, consider that statement carefully because, unfortunately, it's true. The vast majority of computer owners in the world have absolutely no recourse if their hard drive fails or if they happen to delete the wrong file or directory. If your data is important to you — and I'm certainly assuming that it is — can you really afford to lose it all in a few seconds? If you answered, "No," keep reading. If you answered, "Yes," I'm wondering why you need a computer in the first place.

Three popular solutions exist for backing up your data easily: a tape backup unit, a Zip drive, and a CD or DVD recorder. I discuss tape backups and the Zip drive in the following sections, and I attack CD and DVD recorders in Chapter 8.

I should also mention that some companies now sell external hard drives that are especially made for backing up your internal hard drives. A USB 2.0 or FireWire external drive is well-suited for backing up data, as long as you keep that external drive safely stored away while you're not using it.

Whichever method you choose to back up your data, I *strongly* urge you to make it a habit to back up once a week or once a month, depending on how often the important data on your drive changes.

I back up my entire system to DVD+RW once a week. However, to back up individual files conveniently, you can still use floppy disks. Although they can only hold 1.44MB, floppy disks work well to back up smaller files that you're working on — Word document files or address book data, for example. These files are small enough to fit easily on a single floppy, and no fancy backup software is required. For example, I simply copy the latest versions of the files that I'm working on to a floppy, and copy the files back to my hard drive in case I do something really dumb. Remember, however, that you can't rely on floppy disks as permanent backup — instead, consider a 512MB or 1GB USB flash drive, which is much more reliable and scads faster than a floppy!

Selecting a Tape Drive

Before I leap into the discussion of tape backups, I should note why they're still around. After all, backups made to CD and DVD are more reliable in the long run than any tape backup because optical storage is superior to magnetic storage! However, the huge capacities of today's hard drives keep tape backup systems in vogue because a tape can hold much more than even a DVD disc. This is especially attractive when backing up a network server or if you schedule automated backups. With a tape drive, you can back up your 120GB drive with three tapes; that same backup to DVD+RW would take twenty-eight discs!

Tape drives vary widely in speed and capacity. Older QIC-80 models, which used to be the standard, maxed out at about 250MB per tape (with compression — the tape actually held only 120MB, but the backup software compressed the data as it was written to tape, so you could squeeze as much as 50 percent more data onto one tape). Typical speeds were about 10MB per minute, although some drive manufacturers offered proprietary tape drive adapter cards that could boost speeds to as much as 19MB per minute.

However, even backing up 250MB at a time has become anachronistic, so the QIC-80 standard was updated to a technology named *Travan,* which can hold anywhere from 10GB to 40GB of compressed data per tape. These drives can typically save data at anywhere from 100 to 240MB per minute. Figure 7-3 shows a typical Travan drive.

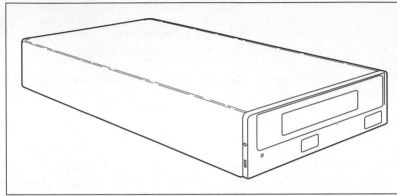

Figure 7-3:
A standard Travan internal tape drive, which holds as much as 40GB of data per tape.

Most Travan drives are internal drives and take up a single half-height bay. Although some Travan drives require a separate controller card (which should be provided along with the drive), most either connect to your floppy drive cable or act as another EIDE or SCSI device. You can also find external tape backup units that connect to your USB. These external tape drives are good for office use or if you have both a laptop and a desktop computer and want to back up the data on both of them, although they're typically somewhat slower than the EIDE or SCSI model. You can pick up a Travan drive for less than $300.

The Cadillac of tape backup units is the digital audio tape (DAT) drive, which is several times faster than a Travan drive in both backing up and restoring files. Digital audio tapes can hold anywhere from 4GB to 80GB of data on a single tape, so if you're looking for a backup solution with the least amount of tape swapping, DAT is your choice. As you might expect, these drives are more expensive, averaging about $600. Digital audio tapes are far more reliable than older magnetic backup tapes, and they're faster than Travan drives.

Hey, You Just Removed Your Media!

In this section, I tell you about an old friend that enables you to take 750MB of data and run with it — or mail it, or toss it to a co-worker, or even lock it in a safety deposit box. I'm talking about the popular Zip removable-media drive from Iomega (www.iomega.com). A removable media drive enables you to insert and remove cartridges (or, in some cases, actual hard drive platters) so that you can take your data with you.

Do you really need removable storage, or are you just fascinated by toys?

To be honest, you don't absolutely need a removable storage drive unless your primary application fits one of these criteria:

✔ **File size:** If you plan to send or receive files that can't be efficiently sent over the Internet or by floppy disk (perhaps because the files are just too big), you'd benefit from a removable media solution. For example, publishers and printers love to use Zip drives to send desktop-publishing files.

✔ **Security/portability:** If security is an issue and you want to protect your data, the best way to do so is to take your data with you or

lock it up so that others have no access to it. Zip drives make taking your important data with you easy.

✔ **Archiving:** If you want to store information without filling up your hard drive, a Zip drive can act as a warehouse for archiving data.

Sounds good, doesn't it? Ah, but don't forget that a DVD-RW or DVD+RW disc can hold far more at 4.7GB! If you're planning on adding a DVD recorder to your PC, a Zip drive is less important. Instead, consider Iomega's new REV removable-cartridge hard drive, which can store 35GB on a single cartridge.

The Zip drive: The floppy with muscle

Iomega caused a minor revolution by introducing the *Zip drive,* which uses a cartridge similar in size and shape to a standard 1.44MB 3½-inch floppy. The original Zip drive held 100MB; the newest model holds 750MB of data and accesses that data much faster than your old friend, the floppy drive. The Zip drive features an average seek time of 29 ms. (See "More stuff about hard drives," earlier in this chapter, if you're not sure what seek time, also called access time, is.)

Although each Zip disk sells for anywhere from $10 to $25, the ability to store 750MB means that you can carry those digital video and audio files, or perhaps the contents of an entire Web site — all on a disk that you can carry in your pocket. Techno-nerds around the globe can breathe a sigh of relief.

With the set of Zip utility programs that come with the drive, you can pass-word-protect a disk or catalog the contents of all your disks so that you can locate a single file easily. Iomega also includes a simple-to-use backup and restore program with both versions of the Zip drive.

The Zip drive is available in external USB and internal EIDE versions. At the time this chapter was written, both versions were about $150.

Of course, Zip drives have disadvantages as well:

- ✔ Zip drives are far slower than recordable CDs and DVDs
- ✔ Every PC that needs to read your disk needs a Zip drive as well
- ✔ CD-RW and DVD-RW drives and media are cheaper than Zip drives and media

For these reasons, both my technical editor and I prefer rewriteable CD-RW discs to Zip disks — a CD-RW can be read on just about any PC, and much faster to boot.

The REV has landed

If you want a removable media drive with 35GB of capacity and a wealth of connection options, you're asking for the Iomega REV drive. REV cartridge drives are available with USB, FireWire (or IEEE 1394), and SCSI external connections and with internal EIDE, SATA, and SCSI drives. At a street price of around $350 for the internal versions (and around $60 per cartridge), the REV is an economical choice, too. The REV cartridge is essentially a hard drive subsystem, with the platters enclosed and protected. When you load the cartridge into the REV drive, you end up with a complete hard drive, ready to use. These cartridges are sturdy enough to mail or ship across town or around the world — but remember, the person on the receiving end will need their own REV drive to read that cartridge!

The average access time for the REV drive is close to that of a traditional hard drive — much faster than a CD or DVD disc — so it's a good choice for retrieving digital video and sound files for your multimedia projects. You can also use the REV drive as a fast backup unit for selected directories on your hard drive; a simple backup application is included with the drive.

If you're running multiple operating systems — for instance, Windows XP and Linux on the same PC — removable cartridge drives such as the REV make it easy to store files that you use with "that other operating system" when you're not using it. For example, a friend of mine stores his Linux source code and compiler files on his REV drive so that they don't take up valuable space on his hard drive — and he can carry them with him when he travels out of town!

Connecting Your Drive Controller

A hard drive is an expensive doorstop unless you connect it to your motherboard — and in this section, I'll show you how to connect that all-important EIDE or SATA cable. Remember that your EIDE or SATA controller is built into your motherboard — congratulate yourself. After you've completed this section, continue to the installation of your hard drive and floppy drive, which I cover in the following sections. These same steps apply also to built-in SATA connectors.

Ready? Then follow these steps to connect your cables:

1. **Oh, my goodness — you've been struck by lightning! Now is *not* the time to install a computer component. In case you can't wait, however, touch a metal surface before you handle anything.**

   This action discharges any static electricity that your body might be carrying.

2. **If your computer chassis is plugged in, unplug it.**

3. **Check your motherboard manual for the location of two connectors:**

   • One connector attaches one end of the hard drive cable to the motherboard (either EIDE or SATA).

   • The other connector attaches one end of the cable from your floppy drive to the motherboard.

4. **Attach the cables that came with your controller or motherboard to these connectors, as shown in your manual.**

   No manual for your scavenged motherboard? Check the manufacturer's Web site, or visit your local computer repair shop and ask a tech to identify them for you.

   Make sure that you connect the correct cable to each connector. The floppy drive cable usually has a twist in it toward the end that connects to the drive.

For any flat ribbon cable connector that you attach to an EIDE drive or your motherboard, pin 1 on the male connector must always match the hole for pin 1 on the female connector. In almost every case, pin 1 on the male connector is the pin in the upper-left corner of the connector. "Okay," you say, "but how can I tell which side of the ribbon cable is wire 1?" No problem — every ribbon cable has one wire that's painted red or somehow marked with a design (or lettering, perhaps). That wire is wire 1, which should always connect to pin 1. Figure 7-4 illustrates this phenomenon.

Installing Your EIDE Hard Drive

Installing an EIDE hard drive is a simple procedure. Follow these steps:

1. **Just finished combing your hair? Now that you look marvelous, touch a metal surface before you handle your drive.**

   This action discharges any static electricity that you might have picked up.

2. **If your computer chassis is plugged in, unplug it.**

3. **If you're installing only one drive, check the jumper settings on your hard drive to make sure that they're set for *single drive, master unit.***

   This setting is the default factory setting for most drives, although it never hurts to be sure. If the jumpers aren't set correctly, move them to the correct positions for *single drive, master unit.* If you're installing two devices (or a second device on a PC that already has one EIDE hard drive), your EIDE hard drive must be set as *multiple drives, master unit,* and the other device should be set as *multiple drives, slave unit.*

4. **Select an open drive bay for your hard drive.**

   Depending on the size of your drive, it might fit in a 3½-inch bay, or you might have to use a 5¼-inch half-height bay. If you want to fit a 3½-inch drive into a 5¼-inch half-height bay, you need a *drive cage kit,* which contains rails that fit on the side of the hard drive, bringing its total width to 5¼ inches.

5. **If your drive needs a cage kit, attach it by using the screws that came with your drive to attach the cage rails onto both sides of your drive.**

   If the drive is the same size as the open bay, you don't need a cage kit and you can simply skip to Step 6.

6. **Slide the drive into the selected bay from the front of the case.**

   The end with the connectors should go in first, and the electronic stuff should be on the bottom, as in Figure 7-5.

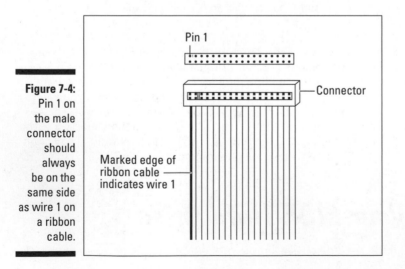

Figure 7-4:
Pin 1 on the male connector should always be on the same side as wire 1 on a ribbon cable.

Pin 1

Connector

Marked edge of ribbon cable indicates wire 1

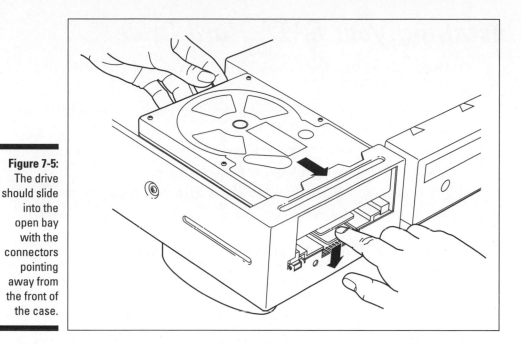

Figure 7-5:
The drive should slide into the open bay with the connectors pointing away from the front of the case.

7. **Carefully slide the hard drive back and forth in the drive bay until the screw holes in the side of the bay line up with the screw holes on the side of the drive. Unsheath your mighty screwdriver and use the screws that came with the drive (or your cage kit) to attach the drive to the side of the bay.**

   You generally use four screws to secure the hard drive to the bay.

8. **Connect one of the power cables from your power supply to the power connector on the hard drive.**

   This connector fits only one way. Press it in firmly to make certain that it doesn't pull out.

9. **Connect the ribbon cable coming from the controller card (or your motherboard if it has a built-in controller) to the back of the hard drive.**

   Remember: The wire with the markings is wire 1. If you're unsure which pin on the drive's connector is pin 1, check your drive's manual. The connector should fit snugly, so after it's correctly aligned, press it all the way on. Many drive and cable manufacturers now block one hole and one pin on the two connectors (a trick called *keying*) so that the cable fits only one way!

Good job! You don't have to be an electrician to install a hard drive.

Installing Your SATA Hard Drive

Okay, so installing a SATA drive is even easier than adding an EIDE drive! Follow these steps:

1. **Finished wiping your windows? Make sure that you touch the metal chassis before you get started!**

2. **If your computer chassis is plugged in, unplug it.**

3. **Select an open drive bay for your hard drive.**

4. **Slide the drive into the selected bay from the front of the case.**

   Again, slide the end with the connectors in first, with any exposed circuitry facing down.

5. **Slide the hard drive back and forth in the drive bay until the screw holes in the side of the bay line up with the screw holes on the side of the drive. Use the screws that came with the drive to attach the drive to the side of the bay.**

   You generally use four screws to secure the hard drive to the bay.

6. **Connect one of the SATA power cables from your power supply to the power connector on the hard drive.**

   Remember, your SATA hard drive may have a legacy 4-pin power connector — if not (and your power supply doesn't have SATA connectors available), run to your local computer store and pick up a 4-to-15 pin (EIDE-to-SATA) power converter.

7. **Connect the SATA cable coming from the controller card (or your motherboard if it has a built-in SATA controller) to the back of the hard drive.**

Don't forget to dance the jumperless SATA Superiority Dance!

Installing Your 3½-Inch Floppy Disk Drive

Follow these steps to install your 1.44MB 3½-inch floppy disk drive:

1. **Now that you're done dusting the furniture and building up static, touch a metal surface before you install your floppy drive.**

   This action discharges any nasty static electricity that you might be carrying.

2. **If your computer chassis is plugged in, unplug it.**

3. **Select an open drive bay for your floppy drive.**

   All cases come with at least one 3½-inch bay especially for your floppy drive, so use that one.

   If you have a computer case from the planet Quark that doesn't have a 3½-inch drive bay, you can even use a 5¼-inch half-height bay if you get a drive cage kit.

   Is your 3½-inch drive bay sitting vertically so that it's sideways in the case? Never fear — you weren't sold a mutant case; floppy drives work both horizontally *and* vertically. Smile knowingly to yourself and continue the installation.

4. **Slide the drive into the selected bay from the front of the case. (The end with the connectors should go in first.)**

   If you're installing the drive horizontally, the button that ejects the disk should be on the bottom; if you're installing the drive vertically, it doesn't matter which way it faces.

5. **Slide the floppy drive back and forth in the drive bay until the screw holes in the side of the bay line up with those on the side of the floppy drive. Use the screws that came with the floppy drive to attach the drive to the side of the bay.**

   You generally use two screws to secure the floppy drive to the bay.

6. **Connect one of the power cables from your power supply to the power connector on the floppy drive.**

   To avoid mistakes, this connector fits only one way. Push it in as far as possible.

7. **Connect the ribbon cable coming from the controller card (or your motherboard if it has a built-in controller) to the back of the drive.**

   If you're installing this floppy drive as your drive A: (the standard configuration for PCs), use the last connector on the cable (the one after the twist in the cable). This connector goes on only one way and should fit snugly. When the connector is aligned correctly, press it all the way on.

Installing Your Internal Tape Backup Drive

If you've chosen to install a Travan or DAT drive for backups, you'll be happy that you did after you've filled up several gigabytes of hard drive space. Follow these steps to install an internal EIDE tape backup drive:

1. **Silk sheets on the bed? Say no more — touch a metal surface before you touch the inside of your computer.**

   This action discharges any static electricity that might be hiding on your person.

2. **If your computer chassis is plugged in, unplug it.**

3. **Select an open drive bay for your tape drive.**

   If your tape drive fits in a 3½-inch drive bay, use that drive bay. Otherwise, you can use a 5¼-inch half-height bay and a drive cage kit.

   Unlike a 3½-inch floppy drive, your tape drive *must* sit horizontally in your computer case, so you can't use it in a vertical drive bay.

4. **Slide the tape drive into the selected bay from the front of the case.**

   The end with the connectors should go in first. Check your drive manual for the correct orientation. (Most units have some sort of label on the front that tells which end is up.)

5. **Slide the tape drive back and forth until the screw holes in the side of the bay line up with those on the side of the drive. Use the screws that came with the tape drive (or your cage kit) to attach the drive to the side of the bay.**

   You generally use four screws to secure the tape drive to the bay.

6. **Connect one of the power cables from your power supply to the power connector on the drive.**

   This connector fits only one way, which makes life easier for everyone. Make sure that you push it in tightly.

7. **Connect the EIDE cable from your motherboard to the back of your tape drive.**

   Check your tape drive manual to see which jumpers need to be set, and follow the instructions for connecting the cable.

Setting Up Your PC and Configuring Your Hard Drive

In this section, you configure your new hard drive and format it. To get started with your hard drive setup, make sure that the monitor and keyboard are connected and that your computer is plugged in. Then follow these steps:

1. **Check your motherboard manual and see what key or key combination displays your computer's CMOS setup screen.**

   CMOS stands for *complementary metal-oxide semiconductor,* which is a type of RAM that stores data even after your PC is turned off. Usually, the key you press to display this screen is the Delete key (or perhaps F1). If you can't find the key, don't panic — all motherboards display the setup key when you turn on the computer — just watch closely and be prepared to press the key.

2. **Push the power switch on the front or back of your case.**

3. **When you see the screen prompt to enter your setup screen, press the indicated key.**

   Although the screen that appears varies with every motherboard, you should see a menu with at least one entry for EIDE HDD Auto Detect, SATA HDD Auto Detect, Hard Drive Auto Detection, or something similar. Use your cursor keys to select that function and follow the onscreen instructions. Your motherboard should identify your hard drive's characteristics automatically.

4. **After you enter the hard drive settings, select the standard settings screen and set your drive A: as a 3¹/₂-inch 1.44MB floppy drive.**

   On this same screen, set the computer's internal clock with the current date and time.

5. **Make sure to save the values you entered, and then exit the setup screen.**

   Usually, you see a separate menu item to Save values and exit. Your computer should now reboot.

Your PC can now recognize its hard drive and floppy drive. For your floppy drive, that's all that's necessary. Your hard drive, however, must now be formatted before your computer can access it.

Formatting Your Hard Drive

At this point, your new computer knows that it has a hard drive and a floppy drive and the specifications of those drives. However, the hard drive isn't partitioned or formatted, so when you reboot your PC, it can't access the hard drive — and thus, you can't load that fancy operating system you've been hankering to use. In nontechnoid terms, *partitioning* means to divide your hard drive into one or more drive letters. You must create at least one partition to store data on your drive. After you've created one or more partitions, it's time to *format* those partitions — this process prepares them to hold data by creating areas to store information on the magnetic surface of the platters (as well as creating a directory that stores the location of all the files that you save to your hard drive).

After you exit the setup screen in the last step of the preceding section, your PC will automatically reboot. Then, after what will seem like an agonizing wait, your computer beeps and informs you that there's been a hard drive failure. Smile quietly to yourself, insert the formatting utility disk provided by the hard drive manufacturer, and continue the boot process by pressing the indicated key. The floppy drive should spring to life, and eventually the drive manufacturer's partitioning and formatting program appears.

If you have a scavenged drive that already has existing data, it should boot correctly if it was drive C: (the primary hard drive) on the original PC. I would still recommend that you partition and format it, however, to ensure that the formatting will be completely compatible with your hard drive controller.

"But Mark, I bought this hard drive used, and I didn't get a formatting utility disk!" Don't panic! Instead, boot your system by using a Windows XP installation CD-ROM and then follow the instructions that appear. The Windows XP Setup program can automatically prepare your hard drive before it installs XP! (Pretty snazzy, yes? Hoo-ah, Redmond!)

Part III
Adding the Fun Stuff

The 5th Wave   By Rich Tennant

"Now, when someone rings my doorbell, the current goes to
a scanner that digitizes the audio impulses and sends the
image to my PC where it's converted to a Pict file. The image
is then automated, compressed, and sent via high—speed
modem to an automated phone service that sends me an
e—mail message back to tell me someone was at my door
40 minutes ago."

In this part . . .

You add all the fancy bells and whistles that any multimedia computer needs these days, such as a DVD recorder, a 3-D sound card that plays MP3 music, and a dial-up modem (or DSL/cable connection) for the Internet. Get ready to blast the toughest game invaders, surf the Web, or listen to audio CDs while you work on a spreadsheet!

Chapter 8

Putting the Spin on CD-ROM and DVD

*I*t's becoming hard to remember the days of old. I'm speaking of prehistoric times, before computers had CD and DVD-ROM drives. (As frightening as it sounds, most young folks don't remember a computer *without* one!) You already know that a modern multimedia computer requires at least a CD-ROM drive for installing software and games, digital video, interactive encyclopedias, and silliness such as talking bears . . . but you can actually do much more than that in the world of optical media. Today's technology enables you to record your own data DVDs, data CDs, and audio CDs, or watch DVD movies with Dolby Digital Surround sound that you've recorded yourself!

In this chapter, I explore all the CD and DVD hardware that's available, and I discuss the features that help you determine which drive is right for your new computer. After you install your drive and the software that it requires, you're ready to access the world of multimedia — and don't forget to take a few minutes to explain to the younger generation the historical relevance of floppy disks.

By the way, if you'd like a complete guide to CD and DVD recording — in fact, an entire *For Dummies* book devoted just to the subject — I can highly recommend *CD & DVD Recording For Dummies,* 2nd Edition, written by yours truly (what a coincidence!), by Wiley Publishing, Inc. It gets into the technical stuff, provides you with all the tips and tricks that I've learned in a decade of burning CDs and DVDs, and shows you how to create all the different types of discs that I mention in this chapter.

Discovering the Details about CD and DVD

Ready for a long, highly technical discussion of bits and bytes, reflected laser light, and variable speed motors?

If so, you're reading the wrong book! The good thing about CD and DVD technology is that you don't *have* to know anything about the man behind the magic curtain. Most drives are built in the same manner, are used in the same way, and perform equally well. However, a number of extra features often help determine the price of your CD-ROM or DVD drive, and this section helps you "decode" all the options while you're shopping (or scavenging).

Name your CD-ROM/DVD interface

CD and DVD drives can be *internal* (installed inside your PC's case) or external. I prefer internal drives over external drives because internal hardware costs less and takes up less space on your desk. (See the upcoming section "The battle of the drives: Internal versus external" for a comparison of external and internal optical drives.)

Internal drives

An internal read-only CD-ROM or DVD-ROM drive should set you back about $30. Just like with hard drives, you can choose from three standard connection interfaces for your new internal CD-ROM or DVD drive:

- **Enhanced integrated drive electronics (EIDE):** Most optical drives today use the same EIDE technology as the most popular type of hard drive, so you can connect your CD or DVD drive to the same controller as your hard drive. (I talk about EIDE technology in Chapter 7.) Enjoy this kind of convenience because it doesn't happen very often in the PC world.

- **Serial advanced technology attachment (SATA):** If you're building a PC using serial ATA devices, you can add a SATA CD or DVD drive as well. These drives are significantly faster and typically easier to install, but you may pay an extra ten bucks for your new drive over a similar drive that uses an EIDE connection. (Serial ATA is covered like a blanket in Chapter 7.)

✔ **Small computer system interface (SCSI):** You might want to choose a SCSI optical drive for its pure, raw, unadulterated speed — just like the SCSI hard drives that I discuss in Chapter 7. SCSI CD-ROM and DVD drives transfer data significantly faster than their EIDE counterparts, and some even surpass SATA speeds. (For more details on the SCSI interface, jump to Chapter 11.)

External drives

Because external drives have their own case (and sometimes their own power supply as well), they cost significantly more than an internal drive. For example, an internal DVD recorder runs about $50, and an external DVD recorder drive starts at around $100. You have three interface choices for connecting an external optical drive:

✔ **SCSI:** If your PC has a SCSI card installed, you can choose either an internal or an external SCSI CD or DVD drive. (The ultimate in convenience!) For more details on SCSI technology, see Chapter 11.

✔ **USB:** Is it any wonder that the USB (universal serial bus) port is so popular these days? Here's yet another peripheral that you can connect. And, as with the other USB hardware that I discuss throughout this book, you don't have to reboot your PC when you add or remove your external USB CD or DVD — make sure, though, that you buy only USB 2.0 hardware, and *make sure* that your new PC has USB 2.0 ports available. (USB 1.1 is barely able to keep up with 4x CD recording, and forget about burning DVDs with a USB 1.1 connection.)

✔ **FireWire:** Because an external FireWire CD or DVD drive is super-fast, you can compare it favorably with an internal CD or DVD drive. A FireWire port transfers data much faster than the older USB 1.1 standard, so these drives can usually read faster as well. (USB 2.0 drives are actually faster than first-generation FireWire drives.) Again, if you're looking for an external CD or DVD recorder with the best performance, FireWire or USB 2.0 are your best connection bets. If your computer doesn't have either a FireWire or a USB 2.0 port, you have to add a port adapter card. (You'll find more about FireWire and both flavors of USB in Chapter 5.)

The great CD-ROM and DVD speed myth

If you're shopping for a CD or DVD drive, you're going to be pelted with numbers: 16X, 24X, and 48X, for example. Those numbers aren't size figures for NBA basketball shoes — the number in front of the *X* indicates how fast the CD or

---

What really goes on in my optical drive?

Okay, if you absolutely *must* know, your CD (or DVD) drive uses a laser to read a long series of tiny pits in the surface of a disc. These pits represent *digital data* — a string of zeros and ones — which your computer can recognize as program data or music. In fact, your computer's CD or DVD drive is internally similar to a regular audio CD player. Ready for a totally useless fact? If you unraveled all the pits in a typical CD-ROM, they would stretch over three miles!

This is how the laser reads these microscopic pits: The laser light is directly reflected from the smooth areas of the disc *(lands),* and the pits scatter the light and do not reflect it. A lens in your CD or DVD drive picks up the reflected light and therefore can tell the difference between pits and lands. The reflective surface on a disc is a thin layer of metal, which gives the disc a shiny appearance.

DVD can transfer data (its *transfer rate*). By transferring, I'm talking about either reading data from a disc or writing data to the disc from your hard drive.

Original single-speed CD-ROM drives could read data from the disc at about 150 kilobytes per second (KBps); the *X* figure indicates a multiple of that original speed. For example, an *8X* drive (usually read as *eight speed* by CD-ROM racing enthusiasts) can read data eight times faster than the original single-speed drives. So, an 8X CD-ROM drive can transfer about 1200 KBps from the disc to your computer.

Okay, so where does the "myth" come in? Well, most of today's games and applications don't need the whopping-fast transfer rate of a 48X or 52X CD-ROM drive. Because the typical CD-ROM game or application is still likely to recommend a 16X drive, the biggest benefit of these is that they give techno-weenies a chance to brag about their speedy drives. (Coincidentally, this is the reason why most retail computers still come with 32X or 42X drives. Those manufacturers know the fact behind the myth as well as you do!) DVD read-only drives, on the other hand, fall between 4X and 16X speeds when reading a DVD; in a similar vein, this "X-factor" relates to a multiple of the first DVD-ROM drive speed.

Because most programs and games don't need the blazing speed of a 48X or 52X CD-ROM drive, most computer owners are still quite satisfied with a 32X drive. If you want to save some money by buying or scavenging a used CD-ROM 32X drive for your new Pentium 4 computer, I say that you can go for it with a clear conscience.

Don't get me wrong. High-speed drives are nice in certain situations. For example, a 52X CD-ROM drive installs one of those huge 3GB productivity applications or 3-D games to your hard drive much faster than a 16X drive, so a fast drive can save you time. If your primary application revolves around digital video or you have the spending money and simply hate waiting, a fast CD or DVD drive is probably a better choice.

The battle of the drives: Internal versus external

As I mentioned earlier in this chapter, CD or DVD drives that use the EIDE, SATA or SCSI interface are internal drives. They fit in an internal half-height drive bay in your computer case (just like a floppy or hard drive).

External CD and DVD drives can be convenient if you have a laptop computer that has a SCSI, USB, or FireWire port but no internal CD or DVD drive. You can connect the external drive to your laptop, carry the drive with you when you travel, and then simply reconnect the drive to your desktop computer when you return to your home or office.

External drives also eliminate much of the heat inside your case because the laser in the drive generates more heat than just about any other part in your computer. Naturally, external drives are more expensive because you're also paying for a separate case, power supply, and external cable.

If you need to share an external CD or DVD drive among more than one PC and they all have USB 2.0 ports, you're in luck! A portable USB CD or DVD drive will be a perfect fit for your needs.

Turning your computer into a jukebox

If you want your PC to do double duty as a stereo, you'll be happy to know that multiple CD and DVD changers for your computer are alive and well,

---

A tale of CDs and CD-ROMs

What's the difference between an audio CD and a computer CD-ROM? Like everything else in the computer world, of course, the answer is hidden by abbreviations and acronyms! An audio CD *(compact disc)* holds digital audio in the standard international format called Red Book. A computer CD-ROM (short for c*ompact disc-read only memory*) is written with the Yellow Book standard, and contains files that your PC can read or programs that you can run. (You absolutely do not need to remember this type of trivia, and you won't be tested on it.) An audio CD player can't read a data CD-ROM that has files on it (or a DVD-ROM data disc that contains files), but a computer CD or DVD drive *can* read both audio CDs and computer CD-ROMs.

except that it's usually called a *jukebox* (in honor of those vinyl-playing Wurlitzer dinosaurs that everyone wants for the den). Jukeboxes are available in several different sizes, including half-height internal drives that can switch between four discs. Drives with a higher capacity don't fit internally, so they sit outside the computer in an external case. Although a jukebox holds multiple discs, it can read from only one disc at a time.

External jukeboxes are usually SCSI devices, so make sure that you get everything you need when buying a jukebox, including a SCSI adapter (if you don't have one), an external SCSI cable, and all the software drivers for your operating system. A jukebox can set you back anywhere from $200 to $500, depending on the number of discs that it holds as well as the speed (and type) of the drive.

Reading multiple CDs at once

If you need to access multiple CDs or DVDs at once, check out a tower drive array. Nothing exotic here: A *tower system* is simply a large external case that holds from four to eight half-height, internal USB 2.0/FireWire/SCSI optical drives, including a separate power supply and fan. Sounds a little clunky, right? Well, don't laugh too hard; unlike jukeboxes, tower drive arrays can read from each of those discs *simultaneously!* Tower arrays are typically used on office networks and Web servers that need immediate access to a wide range of discs. For a small office, a tower system enables one person to retrieve an image file from one disc at the same time that another person is searching a database on another disc.

Will that be caddy or tray?

The earliest computer CD-ROM drives all used a flat plastic cartridge called a CD-ROM *caddy.* (Sorry, Tiger — it won't help you choose the right club for that difficult par 3 on the 17th.) This type of caddy holds the disc inside the drive and helps keep the disc away from dust and fingerprints. (You could store a disc in the caddy, if necessary.) Figure 8-1 shows a caddy CD-ROM drive.

As CD-ROM technology advanced, however, more and more drives turned to a motorized tray system for holding the disc. As you can see in Figure 8-2, a tray-loading optical drive looks more like a standard audio CD player. You press a button to extend the tray, and then you press the button again to retract the tray and load the disc into the innards of the drive. Of course, this procedure is much more convenient than opening a plastic caddy each time that you want to load a disc, so tray drives are preferred by the hip multimedia crowd.

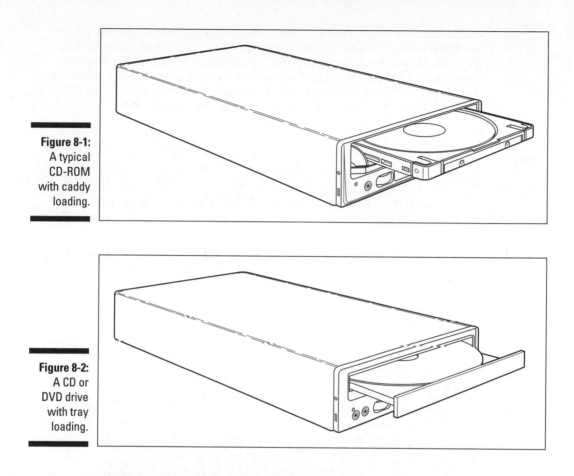

Figure 8-1:
A typical
CD-ROM
with caddy
loading.

Figure 8-2:
A CD or
DVD drive
with tray
loading.

Other read-only CD-ROM and DVD features to covet

In actual operation, you can find few differences between an expensive, name-brand CD or DVD read-only drive and a cheaper drive of the same speed from a smaller manufacturer. Both drives read and transfer at about the same speed, and both can be controlled from within your applications. (For example, you can eject a disc from your audio CD program with either drive.)

So which features really make a difference? Here's a checklist that helps you separate the wheat from the chaff when you're shopping for a CD or DVD drive:

✔ **Access time:** If you're not careful, you can easily confuse a drive's *access time* with its *transfer rate* (measured as 48X or 52X, as I discuss in the section "The great CD-ROM and DVD speed myth," earlier in this chapter). Access time is the actual time required for your CD or DVD drive to locate a specific file on the disc. Older drives have access times of about 150 milliseconds (ms), and today's faster CD and DVD drives average an access time of around 100 ms for reading CDs and 150 ms for reading DVDs.

In Chapter 7, I discuss how access time is important when choosing a hard drive. Most hard drives have access times of around 7 to 11 ms (much faster than the typical 80 ms for an optical drive), which is another reason why hard drives are still the champions of the multimedia world. Besides, reading and writing everyday data, such as a letter to Aunt Mildred or that Great American Novel, is much easier with a hard drive.

✔ **Audio controls:** When the first CD-ROM drives appeared on the market, many of them didn't even have a stereo headphone jack or a volume control — after all, who knew that playing audio CDs through a multimedia computer system would become so popular? Manufacturers have learned their lesson, though, and most drives now include a headphone jack and volume control. Some external drives come with everything necessary for dual use as an audio CD player and a computer CD or DVD drive: separate channel connectors for your stereo and even a full collection of control buttons, such as skip track, pause, and play.

✔ **Cache:** Just like a hard drive, a CD or DVD drive uses a special set of onboard random access memory (RAM) modules to hold data that your computer needs often . . . or will probably need soon. The larger this cache (also called a data buffer), the fewer interruptions you experience in the transfer of data. If you plan to use a DVD drive for watching digital video, consider a drive with at least 2MB of cache RAM.

✔ **Support:** Does your drive's manufacturer offer tech support through the Web, or will you end up spending your two bits calling long-distance for support over the telephone? (Remember, scavengers, that you won't be getting free tech support.)

What You Need to Know about DVD

Unless you don't own a TV, you've probably already heard about *DVD,* which is short for *digital video disc.* (Some folks are starting to say that the abbreviation stands for *digital versatile disc.* Although it's probably an urban legend, I've heard that a computer novice recently asked a computer salesman for a PC with a *digital voodoo disc.*) DVDs look similar to standard audio CDs or computer CD-ROMs, but they can store much more data. They also feature a higher transfer rate than standard CDs. The current generation of DVDs holds anywhere from a hefty 4.7GB (that's the equivalent of seven standard CD-ROMs) to 9.4GB. In fact, the DVD specification allows for discs holding as much as a whopping 17GB each!

Before you get really upset at the computer hardware industry for replacing your traditional CD-ROMs with this new voodoo, here's the good news: A DVD drive can also read your standard audio CDs and computer data CDs, so you don't need two drives. However, some older DVD drives can't read discs created by a CD recorder.

Although DVD drives work the same as CD drives, they use a different type of laser, and the pits carrying the encoded data on the surface of the disc are smaller and packed more tightly. The denser the data, the more data a single disc can hold, as shown in Figure 8-3.

"Why on earth do I need that kind of space?" you might ask. Think (and thank) Hollywood. DVD technology has practically replaced VHS tape in the video rental market. Today's digital video takes up gigabytes of space. Quality, storage capability, and durability are much better with digital video than with VHS. A typical Hollywood movie fits nicely on a single DVD, with room to spare. A CD simply doesn't have the capacity for all that digital video.

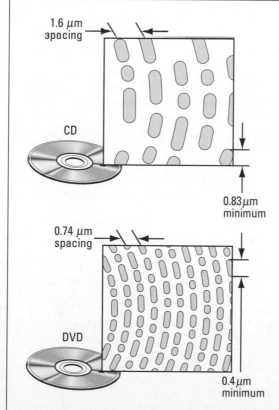

Figure 8-3:
DVD
technology
packs more
of your data
into the
same space
than a
CD-ROM
does.

The extra room on a DVD even enables manufacturers to include such luxuries as running commentary from the director, multiple language versions of the same film, or parts of the film that were edited out in the big-screen version.

Most DVD movies you buy today feature Dolby Digital Surround sound, which is typically supported by today's video cards or your PC's DVD player software. Some even feature Dolby DTS, which sounds even closer to the audio you hear in your local GooglePlex 32-screen theater.

Do I need DVD for my computer?

If you've played one of the latest computer games, it's probably obvious why DVD is becoming more attractive: A single CD-ROM simply doesn't have the storage space required by today's hottest games. For example, it's not uncommon for a sophisticated 3-D video game to ship on two or three CDs. DVD ends the irritation of disc swapping for millions of game players (at least for a few years, anyway).

Although DVD was once considered revolutionary for the home video market, it's pretty much MOTS for computer owners. (Sorry about that — acronyms have begun to take over my brain. MOTS is short for *more of the same.*) Computer DVD drives can read much more data and do it faster, although discs are used for the same purposes: multimedia games, educational titles, digital video, and audio. So far, I've heard no announcement that DVD will replace those irritating free demo CD-ROMs that you get in the mail from Internet service providers and software developers. I use those free discs as coasters for parties, or you can make a really interesting DMFYBC (short, of course, for *digital mobile for your baby's crib.*)

So how long will it take before you really *need* a DVD drive in your computer? That depends on how quickly software manufacturers switch completely from CD-ROM to DVD technology, and whether or not you're set on watching DVD movies on your PC. For the foreseeable computing future (meaning another two or three years), you're certainly safe in selecting a standard CD read-only drive or CD recorder for your system.

If you decide to add a DVD drive to your computer, make sure that your PC has the horsepower to handle it. I recommend a bare minimum of a Pentium Celeron or an AMD Sempron CPU. The faster your CPU, the better. (In Chapter 4, I explain the Intel and AMD CPU models in detail.) Your video card should be capable of displaying 16 million colors at a resolution of at least 800 x 600, and you need a super video graphics array (SVGA) monitor with at least a .28 dot pitch. (See Chapter 6 for more information on video cards and monitors.)

The whole decoder thing explained

The digital video on DVDs is compressed by using the MPEG-2 standard to save space. The *MPEG-2 decoder* built into your video card (or performed in software by your DVD player) decompresses the video and handles the Dolby Digital audio. Without the decoder card, you can't watch the same discs that you can use in a home DVD movie player.

The Dolby Digital sound standard is also referred to by audiophiles as *AC-3* technology, so you might see AC-3 listed in the description of a DVD drive that includes a decoder card.

One more stumbling block stands in the way of your Dolby Digital listening pleasure: You need a PC sound card, stereo amplifier or a stereo receiver that supports Dolby Digital sound, as well as the proper speaker system. And don't forget that you have to run wires from your computer to your stereo.

What You Need to Know about CD and DVD Recorders

CD recording is just plain neat. With CD-R (short for c*ompact disc-recordable*) technology, you can record (or, in techno-wizard parlance, *burn*) your own commercial-quality audio CDs with as much as 74 minutes of music or save as much as 700MB of computer data. Plus, you can play these discs on any standard CD drive (although older DVD drives can't read them). Need more space? A DVD recorder can pack that golden 4.7GB that I mentioned earlier onto a single disc, and most DVD recorders can create movie discs that you can use in your TV's DVD player!

A decade ago, CD recorders were so expensive and hard to use that most computer owners simply thought that they were out of reach. The good news is that this technology (CD recorders, blank discs, and related software) has dropped in price. A spindle of one hundred blank CD-R discs are now available through the mail for less than $20, and recorders that were sold for more than $1000 have dropped to $50 — for a complete kit that includes the drive and the recording software.

A DVD recorder for well under $100 is easy to find, and a spindle of one hundred recordable DVDs will set you back less than $50. Two types of record-once DVDs are available: DVD-R and DVD+R. As you can guess, these two formats are not compatible, and you must buy the right type of disc for the recorder that you choose. (If you've invested in a multiformat DVD recorder, you can write 'em both — but note that DVD+R recording speeds are generally faster than DVD-R recording speeds on the same drive.)

CD and DVD recording software has also become easier to use. Programs such as Drag-to-Disc from Roxio (www.roxio.com) enable you to write data directly to a CD or DVD recorder under Windows XP, just as though the recorder were a huge floppy drive.

In case you're wondering, when you aren't using a CD recorder to create CDs, it doubles as a standard CD-ROM read-only drive, so you need to buy only one drive. (The same is true of a DVD recorder, which can read CDs and DVDs as well as burn them.)

Remember that copyright restrictions determine what you can legally record! Unless you're sure that you can copy the material, I strongly advise you to contact the copyright owner for permission.

Make sure that you check the system requirements for a drive before you buy it. I recommend that you dedicate at least 1GB of hard drive space to recording with a CD recorder, and at least 6GB for a DVD recorder. (You need that space to hold all the data that you intend to record.) If you select a SCSI or SATA recorder, you need the corresponding connectors (either built-in to the motherboard or located on an adapter card you've installed). Windows 2003 Server and XP are currently the best operating systems for CD and DVD recording on the PC.

Why record my own CDs and DVDs?

A number of computer applications can benefit from a CD recorder — in fact, they'd sit up and beg for one if only they could speak. If your primary application appears on this list or you're interested in any of the following applications, you should consider a CD recorder (or, in some cases, a DVD recorder) rather than a simple read-only CD-ROM drive:

✔ **Creating audio CDs:** If you're an audiophile with a ton of hard-to-find vinyl albums (or a stack of irreplaceable cassettes or tape reels gathering dust in a corner of your home), you can transfer those musical treasures to compact disc. Today's higher-end recording programs enable you to rearrange tracks in any order, print a cover for the CD jewel box with a list of the track names, and even remove some of the crackle, pop, and hiss associated with older media.

If you have found a used CD recorder and will be using it primarily for recording audio, make sure that it supports a recording format called *disc-at-once;* this format enables you to create discs without irritating clicks between each of the tracks.

✔ **Archival storage:** How would you like to remove those three-year-old tax records, spreadsheets, and word processing documents from your hard drive and free up all that space — without losing a single byte of that data in case you need it in the future? Although you could back up that data to tape, you'd have to restore it to your hard drive to use it, and magnetic tape has a limited shelf life. If you use CD-Rs to archive your data, however, you can be assured that those old files will be available for years to come and can be read on any CD-ROM drive. Plus, you can run programs and read data files directly from the disc, so you don't have to restore anything. The 4.7GB capacity of a recordable DVD makes a DVD recorder an even better storage solution.

How long does a recorded CD or DVD last? Although companies cite many different figures, the average shelf life of a recorded disc is usually stated as somewhere around ten years. (I'm betting it's much longer, but only if you take proper care of your discs and store them in a cool environment.)

✔ **Moving data:** Do you have a presentation or slide show to perform on a business trip? A recorded disc is a perfect way to carry gigabytes of data with you wherever you go without worrying about magnetism or X-rays in airports (two dreaded enemies of exposed film in cameras and magnetic media, such as floppies and backup tapes). With the universal acceptance of CD and DVD, it's now a safe bet that the computer at your destination will be able to read your disc.

✔ **Digital photo albums:** If you have a recorder and a digital camera (or a scanner that can digitize regular photographs), you have everything you need to create your own custom photo albums on a disc. You can display these photo albums on any computer with a corresponding optical drive and an SVGA color monitor.

You can even include on your CD-R a trial version of a graphics program, such as Adobe's Photoshop Elements (www.adobe.com), so that family members who don't have a graphics viewer can install one right from your disc. (*Shareware* programs offer you a free trial period, but you need to pay the author if you continue to use the program.) Paint Shop Pro has an excellent slide show feature that can display your pictures automatically.

✔ **Small business:** A CD or DVD recorder is practically a requirement these days for distributing beta copies of most software or even distributing the finished product if you don't want the expense of duplicating a large number of CDs at a commercial replicating plant. A good example is a CD-ROM that contains all the templates, clip art, and documents that a new employee might need. Having everything on one recorded disc beats scurrying around and looking for the company logo clip art.

✔ **Movies, movies, movies:** If you love your DV camcorder, you can burn that digital video onto a DVD and create your own DVD movies. Depending on the DVD creation software that you use — such as MyDVD Studio from Sonic, at www.mydvd.com — you might even be able to add your own menus, animated backgrounds, and slide shows of digital photographs to your DVD movie. (Wait 'til Grandma sees the kids on her DVD player, complete with menus she can operate with her DVD remote control . . . she'll be so busy watching your movies, she'll burn her apple pie!)

If you have a large number of people who will be accessing the same archival data on a network or Web site, consider recording a disc with the data instead of storing it on a hard drive. You can save time because you don't have to back up the data if it's stored on a disc, and after your network administrator has configured the drive properly, everyone can access the data from a single disc on the server.

What's the deal with rewriteable discs?

All CD recorders today are CD-RW drives, which stands for *compact disc-rewriteable*. Unlike an older, blank CD-R, which can be recorded only once, you can reuse and re-record a CD-RW. (DVD rewriteable discs come in three flavors: DVD-RW, DVD+RW, and DVD-RAM. The first two formats are the most popular for those burning DVD movie discs, and the older DVD-RAM format is usually used for backing up your hard drive. Like a CD-RW, you can record, read, and erase these rewriteable discs hundreds of times.)

A rewriteable CD or DVD sounds like the ideal choice, until I mention the downside: CD-RWs can be read only on drives that support CD-RW, which means that virtually no CD-ROM drives or audio CD players older than four or five years can read CD-RWs. Although all new CD-ROM drives can read both, check the specifications of a drive (or call the manufacturer's technical support) to make sure that a specific drive can read CD-RWs. When it comes to compatibility, CD-R is clearly the winner: A standard CD-R can be read on standard computer CD-ROM drives and audio CD players that have been around for almost two decades.

Doin' the LightScribe thing

Are you old enough to remember laser-etched vinyl record albums? (My favorite was Styx's *Paradise Theater*.) These albums played normally on your turntable, but carried cool-looking labels and borders around the edge of the album that were etched into the vinyl using a laser. About right now, you should be saying, "Hey, my DVD recorder uses a laser too! I wonder . . ."

Before you try and patent the idea, let me tell you about *LightScribe* drives and media. If your CD or DVD recorder supports this new technology and you record a CD or DVD using the proper media, you can flip over that new disc you've burned and use your drive's laser to burn a silkscreen-quality label onto the top of the media! No printer or paper labels needed. The laser-etched label looks awesome and will make you the envy of all of your techno-friends at your next party.

One downside (you knew there'd be at least one): A spindle of fifty LightScribe blank DVD+R discs is more than $90 at the time of this writing, so they're three times as expensive as their less flashy brethren.

Likewise, not every computer's DVD drive or TV DVD player will recognize all rewriteable disc formats. However, virtually all PC DVD-ROM read-only drives and TV DVD players can read a DVD-R because the format has been around for several years. Why is this? The DVD rewriteable disc formats that I mentioned earlier aren't as well established as CD-RW — none of the three formats are compatible. (Sigh. Can't we all just get along?) For example, you can't use a DVD+RW in a DVD-RW drive. At the time of this writing, the format battle rages on. For the best compatibility, I recommend a dual-format DVD recorder, which can burn both DVD-RW and DVD+RW discs.

Prices for CD-RW hardware, software, and blank discs are only slightly higher than standard CD-R prices, so the decision is a simple one: If you need to record discs that everyone can read, stick with CD-R. If you're recording discs for use on your own computer and the convenience and savings of using rewriteable discs appeal to you, go with CD-RW. This is true also with DVD-recordable and DVD-rewriteable discs.

Table 8-1 should help you sort things out between the different CD and DVD recording formats.

Table 8-1	CD and DVD Recording Formats		
Format	*Capacity*	*Rewriteable?*	*Compatible With*
CD-R	700MB	No	All PC CD-ROM drives and PC DVD drives
CD-RW	700MB	Yes	Most PC CD-ROM drives and PC DVD drives
DVD+R	4.7GB	No	DVD+R drives; many DVD players
DVD+R DL	8.5GB	No	DVD+R drives; many DVD players
DVD+RW	4.7GB	Yes	DVD+R drives; few DVD players
DVD-R	4.7GB	No	All DVD drives and DVD players
DVD-RW	4.7GB	Yes	DVD-R drives; few DVD players
DVD-RAM	9.4GB	Yes	All PC DVD-RAM drives

Remember, all but the last type of drive in Table 8-1 can create both data CD-ROMs and audio CDs — the exception, DVD-RAM, can't write to CD-R or CD-RW discs.

Caring for your CDs and DVDs

Contrary to popular opinion, optical discs are not indestructible. Here's a quick checklist of the most common archenemies of any compact disc — avoid them all, and you'll never lose a byte of data (or a single musical note)!

✔ **Heat:** Keep those discs cool! The same hot car seat that claimed your favorite cassettes (or those videos from the rental store) could melt your discs or render them unreadable.

✔ **Dust:** Like any audio CD player, a few specks of dust can cause a CD or DVD drive to skip to skip to skip. (You get the idea.)

✔ **Liquids:** Anything from water to grape juice to prussic acid can mess up a disc. If you're lucky, you might be able to remove a liquid stain with a little isopropyl alcohol.

✔ **Fingers:** Oily fingerprints can lead to dirty discs, and your drive will occasionally refuse to read them. Handle your discs by the edges or use your finger as a spindle by sticking it through the hole in the center of the disc.

✔ **Sharp objects:** A surface scratch on the reflective side of a CD or DVD can deflect the laser light, which leads to lost data. If you're handling a recordable disc, make certain that you don't scratch the gold or silver layer on the top side of the disc. And stay away from ballpoint pens when labeling your discs — use a permanent (nonsmudging) felt-tip marker.

That said, you are human and might get gunk on your discs anyway. If you already have an expensive, hi-tech compact disc cleaning apparatus, you can use it on your computer CDs and DVDs as well. However, I really don't think that these James Bond contrivances are necessary. Compact discs were designed to be easy to clean. I recommend a lint-free *photographer's lens cloth* for dusting the bottom of your CDs (and, if necessary, a bit of isopropyl alcohol disc-cleaning solution).

To clean the bottom surface of a CD or DVD, wipe from the center spindle hole straight toward the outside of the disc. Never wipe a compact disc or DVD in a circular motion because that can scratch the surface and result in lost data.

Installing Your EIDE CD or DVD Drive

Have you already installed an EIDE hard drive in your system, as I demonstrate in Chapter 7? If so, you might need to unplug some connections. Why? Your EIDE CD or DVD drive might use the same controller and cable as your EIDE hard drive. If you like, take a permanent marker and mark the cables in their current position (with a "To Hard Drive 1" on the cable, for example) so that you can restore the existing connections quickly after you have your optical drive in place.

If your CD or DVD drive ever swallows your disc and won't eject it, it's time to straighten a paper clip. Locate the emergency manual eject hole — it's an unmarked hole under the tray (about the diameter of a piece of wire). Stick the end of the paper clip into the manual eject hole and push firmly; the tray should pop out of the drive.

If your computer uses a single EIDE hard drive configured as *single drive, master unit* (which is the default hard drive installation that I describe in Chapter 7), you need to change the jumper settings on your hard drive so that it's set for *multiple drive, master unit.* Until you complete this task, your computer can't correctly recognize the CD/DVD drive. Just follow these steps:

1. **Now that you've taken off that heavy wool sweater, touch a metal surface before you handle your drive.**

   This step discharges any static electricity that your body might be carrying.

2. **If your computer chassis is plugged in, unplug it and remove the cover.**

3. **Check the jumper settings on your CD/DVD drive to make sure that it's set for *multiple drive, slave unit.***

   Multiple drive, slave unit is the default factory setting for most CD/DVD drives, although it never hurts to be sure. If the jumpers aren't set correctly, move them to the correct position. (Your CD-ROM/DVD manual shows where the jumpers are located on your drive and how to set them.)

4. **Select an open drive bay for your CD/DVD drive.**

   A CD-ROM/DVD drive requires a 5¼-inch half-height bay. External USB, FireWire, and SCSI drives have their own case and don't need an internal drive bay. (In fact, you shouldn't be following this procedure at all if you're installing an external drive.)

5. **From the front of the computer case, slide the drive into the drive bay.**

   The end of the drive with the connectors should go in first. Usually, a label or some kind of writing on the front of your drive indicates which end is up.

6. **Attach the drive to the side of the bay.**

   Slide the drive back and forth until the screw holes in the side of the bay line up with those on the side of the drive. Secure the drive with the screws (usually four) that came with the drive.

7. **Connect one of the power cables from your power supply to the power connector on the drive.**

   Note that the power connector fits only one way.

8. **Connect the ribbon cable coming from the controller card (or your motherboard, if it has a built-in controller) to the back of the drive.**

   A second connector should be on the ribbon cable, connecting your hard drive to your controller. That's the connector for your second EIDE device, which in this instance is your CD/DVD drive. The wire with the markings is on the side with pin 1. If you're unsure which pin on the drive's connector is pin 1, check your drive's manual. The connector should fit snugly, so press it all the way on after you correctly align it.

Loading Drivers and Testing Everything

Because Windows 2003 Server and Windows XP recognize standard optical drives without requiring you to load additional drivers, you can jump right to testing your installation.

After you install your drive and reboot Windows, load a computer game or application CD-ROM into your drive and double-click the My Computer icon on your desktop. Double-click the icon for your new CD or DVD drive to display the directory of the disc in Windows Explorer. (If the disc that you loaded runs automatically, you won't even have to lift a finger . . . the program's installation menu will appear all by itself!)

Your new optical drive has a separate drive letter, just like your hard drive. If you've installed a single hard drive, for example, your computer will probably assign drive D: to your new DVD recorder.

If your drive doesn't seem to be working, make sure that it's receiving power: Is the drive's power indicator lit? If not, check the power connection to the drive.

If the drive is receiving power but doesn't seem to be able to read a disc, you might have the cable upside down. Reverse the EIDE cable connected to the back of the drive by flipping it over and reconnecting it.

This procedure completes your CD/DVD drive installation! In Chapter 9, I show you how to add a sound card to your PC to enjoy digital audio and music.

Chapter 9

Let Your PC Rock!

In This Chapter

▶ Buying the right type of sound card

▶ Figuring out wavetable technology

▶ Taking a look at MIDI

▶ Playing MP3 music

▶ Understanding 3-D spatial sound

▶ Figuring out surround sound

▶ Selecting and installing a microphone for your system

▶ Choosing and installing speakers for your system

▶ Shopping for and installing a subwoofer

▶ Installing your sound card

▶ Testing your work

*F*ace it — the days of the computer as a big, silent monolith have passed. A perfect example is how computers are portrayed by Hollywood: These days, multimedia computers in movies sound more like video games. More than anything else, this change in perception on the part of the public — computers evolving from room-filling silent machine to R2-D2 — is because of the audio revolution that started with the Macintosh many years ago, which has culminated in home and office PCs that speak, sing, scream, and even sob! (What, you've never heard a computer sob? Try running Quicken on my computer; it must be hard to balance my financial mess.)

In this chapter, I walk you through the process of adding real, honest-to-goodness, high-quality stereo surround sound to your PC — you can make your games (and even your serious word processor) come alive. I discuss the speakers and subwoofer that will satisfy even the most demanding computer audiophile. No more silly beeps from that archaic internal PC speaker. You're going to add a multimedia sound system, and your new PC will suddenly sing like a bird.

Sorting Out Sound Card Basics

Remember the last time that you went shopping for a new CD player, satellite radio, or receiver for your stereo system or your car? Despite all the fancy jargon and the pretty brushed chrome, some of the equipment just didn't *sound* good enough. And, if you're like me, you might have found that the most expensive models often didn't sound much better than the less expensive ones.

As you probably already know, the best way to select audio equipment is to listen with your own ears. Understandably, that presents a bit of a conundrum when choosing a sound card from a mail order catalog. The secret is to know which of the computer audio buzzwords actually improves the sound that you hear. Luckily, teaching yourself the lingo of computer audio is pretty easy. If you're an audiophile, you want to make a good choice when shopping for your sound card because it's the most important component in your computer when it comes to sound quality.

Recognizing common breeds of sound cards

You'll find two common types of sound cards available today: the integrated sound card (which is built-in to your motherboard) and the PCI bus sound card. Both types of sound hardware can produce spectacular sound, and each has particular advantages over the other.

PCI bus audio

The PCI card is today's state-of-the-art sound card. (More about the PCI slot appears in Chapter 4.) Good 32-bit PCI sound hardware can deliver spectacular stereo sound effects for your games (including 3-D spatial sound, which I get into in a moment) and can record in stereo with CD quality at 44 KHz. In other words, the audio that you hear from one of these cards, which usually start around $50, can reach (or even surpass) the clarity and low noise level that you enjoy with audio CDs. The sound card that you select for your PC might also include a game port for your joystick or even a built-in FireWire port. Many top-of-the-line PCI cards come with a panel designed to fit in an empty slot in your PC's case, providing plugs and separate volume controls.

Don't get confused if your new sound card is listed as providing the highest-quality *24-bit sound* — it's still a 32-bit PCI card. Before you pull out your hair in frustration, let me explain. When sound card manufacturers talk about 24-bit audio, they're talking about the sound quality (or *bit rate*) that the card can produce — and not the type of card slot. 24-bit sound quality is top-of-the-line these days and is offered by companies such as Creative Labs (www.creativelabs.com) and their Audigy 4 Pro series of cards. But never fear; it's still pumped out by a 32-bit PCI card.

Figure 9-1 shows the 32-bit Sound Blaster Live! sound card.

Integrated audio

The majority of today's motherboards include onboard integrated audio hardware, complete with attached ports. Typically, this integrated sound hardware is a good choice for a PC dedicated to casual gaming, office applications, and Internet fun. Depending on the features of the onboard sound, you may even get bells and whistles like 3-D spatial sound or MP3 hardware compression (buzzwords that I explain later in this chapter).

8-bit or 16-bit audio

If someone gives you an original 8-bit or 16-bit Sound Blaster-compatible card, promptly run over it with your car — repeatedly. These older cards may not support true stereo recording or stereo effects, and they are usually the cheapest sound cards that you can find. Unless you found one of these in an Egyptian tomb and you're not interested at all in the quality of the audio produced by your PC, steer clear of these cards. They make great boot scrapers.

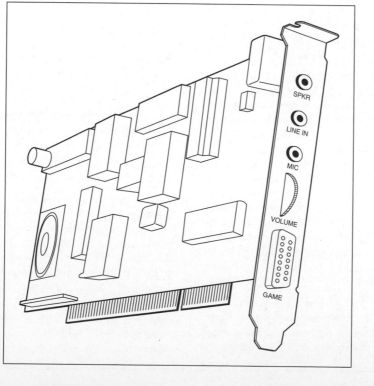

Figure 9-1:
The basic standard for today's PCI audio cards is the Sound Blaster Live! card.

Surfing the sounds of the Web

You'll probably encounter many types of sound and music files in the multimedia world, especially if you spend lots of time on the Internet and the Web. If you have the right software or browser plug-in, your sound card should be able to play these other files, too:

✔ **WAV:** The WAV format is the Microsoft standard for recording, storing, and playing digital sound (and it's a popular format on the Web). Both Netscape Navigator and Internet Explorer can recognize and play WAV files automatically. The sound quality of WAV files can range from compact disc quality to mono sound files of telephone quality. (The lower the sound quality, the smaller the file size — and the less time that it takes to transfer over the Web.) Windows 2000 and XP include simple sound-editing tools, and any sound-editing program worth installing can save and play WAV files. You'll find a hard drive's worth of WAV files at my favorite audio site, The Daily .WAV (www.dailywav.com).

✔ **AU:** You often encounter AU sound files on the Web. This sound format was developed by Sun Microsystems, and AU files are popular in the Unix and Linux worlds. Because AU files are compressed, they require less time to download. Although most sound-editing programs can play AU files, it's more important that your Web browser support them so that you can hear them directly while surfing. For example, if you connect to a Web site featuring sound files and click one of the recordings, you can hear voices speak within your browser. If you're using Mozilla Firefox or Internet Explorer, AU support is built in.

✔ **AIFF:** The AIFF format is a popular sound standard for Macintosh computers. Most sound-editing programs can import AIFF files, so you can play them if you download them to your hard drive. Like the Windows WAV format, AIFF files are CD quality, but they're usually not compressed like WAV files. Therefore, they're not all that popular on the Web because of their size.

✔ **MP3:** MP3 format music files have taken the Internet by storm. Depending on their file size, MP3 files can be even better than CD quality (and yet still be very small compared with the same music in WAV format). An entire underground of Web sites has developed to distribute dance, pop, and alternative singles in MP3 format — illegally, I might add, because many of these songs are (of course) copyrighted. You can create MP3 files on your PC, and pocket MP3 players that resemble everything from portable cassette players to ballpoint pens are all the rage these days.

✔ **WMA:** Microsoft's answer to MP3, WMA files are slightly better in quality than MP3 files and are considerably smaller. However, Bill and his gang have saddled the WMA format with extensive copy protection that severely restricts how you listen to your music (and even how often you can burn it to an audio CD). Therefore, many audiophiles steer clear of WMA. WMA is the preferred format within Windows Media Player and is supported by most portable music players (except the iPod).

✔ **AAC:** A relatively new format, AAC was developed by Apple for use on the iTunes Music Store, so all the songs you purchase and download from the Music Store are in AAC format. AAC files are similar in quality to MP3, but they're actually slightly smaller because of better compression. As you might expect, the Apple iPod music player supports AAC songs — unfortunately, most other MP3 players don't.

Don't forget the software part!

Make sure that the sound card you choose is well supported with software and drivers written for the operating system you're using. (Appendix A is an introduction to all the truly chic PC operating systems.)

If you scavenge a used sound card and don't get any software along with it, check the company's Web site (if possible) to find out whether you can download the latest drivers. One online resource for drivers that I use is The Driver Zone at www.driverzone.com. If you can't connect to the Internet, call the manufacturer's technical support line to get the software.

If you're buying a new sound card, it should include the drivers that you need and also a number of nifty software toys. These programs often include an onscreen "stereo deck" that lets you play audio CDs, digital sound files in Windows WAV format, MP3 files, or MIDI music. (See the upcoming section, "Do I need MIDI ports?" for more.) Figure 9-2 shows an audio mixer that came with my sound card. You might even get a voice-recognition program or a text-to-speech program that lets your computer talk to you and "read" text files aloud.

Figure 9-2:
Hey, that looks like my stereo, man. Can your new computer play my Maroon 5 CD?

Riding the wavetable

Virtually all of today's sound cards offer wavetable technology. Exactly what is this advanced hoo-hah all about?

Rather than get bogged down with a discussion of waveforms and analog/digital processing, here are the real facts on wavetable: It is indeed worth its reputation. 8-bit sound cards (and most older 16-bit sound cards) used a technique called *frequency modulation* (FM), in which the sound card creates the closest possible imitation of a sound. For example, if your PC should sound like a grand piano, an FM sound card produces the closest possible sound to that of a grand piano. It would probably be a fairly close imitation, but you can still tell that the sound is computer generated.

A wavetable card, on the other hand, stores the real sound of a grand piano in digitized form (within a certain chip on the card itself) and plays that instead — a big improvement! Whether you're playing a game with background music or listening to MIDI music, a sound card with wavetable support definitely sounds better (which is why musicians and audiophiles who own computers usually invest in a wavetable card with a huge selection of sound samples). Most wavetable sound cards can also be upgraded with additional onboard RAM, which enables them to offer more than one sound for the same instrument.

However, wavetable technology means nothing when it comes to digitally recorded music or digital sound effects in WAV format (which are actual sounds recorded as data on your hard drive or an audio CD). Wavetable support only improves computer-generated music, and it doesn't make an audio CD played on your computer's CD-ROM drive sound any better.

Why do I need 3-D for my ears?

Another feature offered by many advanced sound cards is — get ready for a real mouthful here — 3-D spatial imaging. This type of sound has several applications:

✔ Playing audio CDs

✔ Playing digital audio files

✔ Playing sound effects within games

Sound cards with 3-D spatial imaging provide an auditorium or concert hall effect — the music sounds as though the speakers are separated farther apart than they actually are.

Computer game players are the ones who can really take advantage of 3-D imaging. If you're playing a game that supports one of these 3-D cards, a laser bolt streaking past the right side of your ship actually comes from the right speaker. If you hear the deep, guttural growl of a dragon to your left, it would behoove you to turn your character to the left quickly (and with sword drawn)!

If you're a game player, I definitely recommend that you spend a few extra dollars for a card that supports 3-D spatial imaging. If you're not an audiophile or you're not into computer games, this feature might not be important to you.

The software in many game programs provides a less effective form of 3-D spatial imaging that plays on standard sound cards. However, you always get better sound effects when you have a sound card with hardware that supports 3-D imaging.

"Send help — I'm surrounded by sound!"

Take 3-D spatial imaging one step further — including both sound effects *and* music — and you have surround sound, just like the super-realistic audio that you've experienced in movie theaters and with the best home stereo systems. Home DVD players usually offer Dolby Digital Surround sound built in, and more are arriving on the market that offer Dolby DTS (which delivers even higher quality surround sound). You can join in the fun with your PC, however, if you add both a DVD drive and a sound card with Dolby Digital Surround support to your computer. You can play games, watch commercial movies, and even enjoy audio discs recorded in surround sound. (For more information on DVD drives and MPEG decoding, read Chapter 8.)

You need five, six, or even seven speakers and a game, movie, or audio CD that's encoded for surround sound. As the line between your PC and your traditional stereo system continues to blur, however, you'll be seeing more of surround sound, and it'll be less expensive to add to your existing PC.

MP3 fanatics, pay attention!

Do you have a collection of thousands of songs in MP3 format taking up gigabytes of space on recorded CD or DVD discs or an old hard drive? You can enjoy these CD-quality sound files through your computer's sound system, or you can even record them directly to an audio CD if you have a CD or DVD recorder. (For more information on CD recording, make a note to visit Chapter 8 when you're finished here.) MP3 files are all the rage on the Internet, and hundreds of different models of personal MP3 players (similar to personal cassette players) are on the market. I've even seen a number of MP3 car audio decks that have appeared recently!

If you're already an MP3 fanatic and you're shopping for a sound card, I can't stress this advice enough: *Buy a card that supports high-quality MP3 encoding and digital effects!* This type of card is especially valuable when you create your own MP3 files or listen to your collection. For example, my Sound Blaster Audigy 2 card allows me to add environmental effects to a recording to simulate a concert hall or stadium, and I can record the highest-quality MP3 files from a number of different audio sources (including analog and digital CD audio, of course).

Do I need MIDI ports?

All right, it's time to come face-to-face with MIDI (a rather cute acronym for musical instrument digital interface), which is an international standard shared by computers, synthesizers, and many types of specialized musical instruments (such as drums and keyboards). MIDI music is shared in the form of data files, which enable most computers to play the same music. MIDI files make it possible for musicians to record and play music using computers. MIDI files are often found on the Web; in fact, the EMBED HyperText Markup Language (HTML) command enables your Web page to play a MIDI song as background music. Most sound cards can play MIDI music files without extra hardware or software, and a wavetable card can sound great while playing MIDI. (See the earlier section, "Riding the wavetable.")

However, most sound cards do *not* provide the MIDI interface connectors (ports) that enable you to hook up a synthesizer or other musical instrument that supports MIDI directly to your computer. These connectors are usually offered as an upgrade that you can buy and install later, or they come with the card for a higher price — you might even find that a motherboard with integrated audio includes a MIDI port. Naturally, musicians get a big kick out of connecting a musical instrument to their computer. If you're running music-editing software with MIDI support, you can play notes on the instrument and create MIDI music directly, or you can instruct your computer to "play" the instrument automatically.

But do you really need MIDI interface connectors (sometimes referred to as MIDI daughterboards) or a USB-to-MIDI converter? If you're not a musician, I recommend against spending extra money on a sound card with MIDI connectors. However, if you are a musician and you want to experiment with computers in your music, these connectors are worth every penny! Actually, they're probably going to set you back about $50. (If you're a professional musician, chances are you're already an expert on MIDI and you've long since skipped to the next section.)

Uhh . . . Is This Microphone On?

Your ears are not the only lucky body parts to benefit from a sound card — your mouth also gets to enjoy itself. With a microphone attached to your sound card, you can take advantage of computer applications like these:

 ✔ **Voice recording:** The simplest application for a microphone is to help you record your voice and other sounds. You can create digital WAV files of sounds and attach these files to specific actions in Windows so that pulling down a menu, running a program, closing a window, and the like are accompanied by their own sound effects. You can also edit your recordings with a sound editor to add special effects, add these sound files to your Web page for Web surfers to enjoy, or just have a little fun with your dog. To try this out under Windows 2000 or Windows XP, choose Start➪All Programs➪Accessories➪Entertainment➪ Sound Recorder to run the Windows Sound Recorder program.

✔ **Voice command and dictation:** Imagine talking to your computer through a microphone to run programs, open and close windows, and even dictate into your word processor with a program such as Dragon NaturallySpeaking 8, from ScanSoft (www.scansoft.com). The idea has sort of a Buck Rogers or Luke Skywalker feel, doesn't it? You can even control some computer games these days with spoken commands. Thanks to the popularity of the PC sound card, these applications are available right now.

Note: You typically have to "train" your computer to recognize your verbal patterns, and these applications are nowhere near 100 percent accurate. However, this kind of technology is constantly improving, and it's a great help to computer owners who need special accommodations and those computer owners who might not feel comfortable with the keyboard.

✔ **Voice e-mail:** If you have an Internet e-mail client application that allows attachments, you can record your own voice as a digital WAV file and send it along with the text. Because of the large size of digital audio, however, voice e-mail applications record your voice at less than CD quality. Even so, attaching a human voice to an e-mail message still has considerable impact (especially when you haven't heard that certain voice in several weeks).

✔ **Internet telephone:** No doubt about it, Internet telephone programs are just plain neat. And if you call someone at long distance or international rates often, you can save a ton of money! An Internet telephone program turns your microphone and sound card into a telephone — but instead of talking over standard telephone lines, your voices are transmitted over the Internet as data. Therefore, the only cost that you incur is the online time from your Internet service provider (ISP).

Note: The person on the other end of the conversation must also have a computer, an Internet connection, and a copy of the same Internet telephone program that you're using. Some of these programs are so sophisticated that they have call screening and Internet telephone answering machines, too.

If you decide that an Internet telephone program is a good idea, look for one that supports full duplex operation. With a 32-bit sound card on both sides of the conversation, *full duplex* enables both of you to speak at the same time. If you're restricted to *half duplex,* you can talk only in turns, much like a CB radio.

You can find three basic types of computer microphones: the clip-on/stick-on model shown in Figure 9-3, the fancier boom microphone shown in Figure 9-4, and the headset microphone:

✔ **Clip-on microphones:** Designed to clip onto your lapel or collar, this type of mike is naturally better for capturing your voice. When not in use, this microphone fits into a holder that sticks to the front of your computer case.

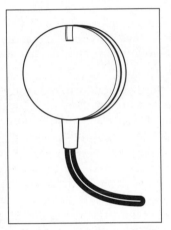

Figure 9-3:
A clip-on/
stick-on
microphone.

✔ **Boom mikes:** This kind sits on your desk or on top of your computer case. Boom mikes tend to pick up a little more background sound from around your computer.

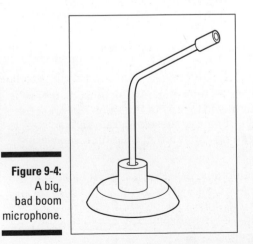

Figure 9-4:
A big,
bad boom
microphone.

✔ **Headset microphones:** You've typically seen these used by telephone operators. They enable you to use both hands while you talk, and they're the microphone of choice if you're using a voice command or voice dictation system. A headset microphone might come with or without stereo headphones.

Do you already have a microphone with a standard jack that you use with a cassette recorder? This type of microphone should work fine with your sound card. Just make sure that it has some sort of stand to hold it upright.

Speaking of Speakers

No matter what kind of sound card you have or what you choose to listen to, you can't hear anything without a speaker. External (add-on) computer speakers are another part of your system that might vary widely with your personal preferences. For example, some computer owners are happy with a set of headphones, which helps all family members maintain their sanity (especially if the computer room is located right next to the baby's room). In fact, if you have a portable stereo cassette player or FM stereo radio, you can use the headphones that came with it with your new sound card. And don't forget the internal speaker (also called the *PC Gnome*), which I mention in Chapters 3 and 4 — the internal speaker is really only useful for simple beeps, but it comes in handy when diagnosing problems when turning on your computer.

On the other end of the spectrum, some computer owners are as demanding about their computer speakers as they are about their stereo speakers. For these audiophiles, only the very best audio reproduction is acceptable, especially when they're battling slobbering purple dragons from Medieval Dimension X. Your preferences in audio quality determine whether you spend $10 or $200 (or even more) on your computer's speaker system.

Speakers are connected to your system in one of three ways:

✔ **A traditional analog line out jack and plug:** Every sound card has a line out or speaker jack — in fact, your speakers connect to your PC exactly like the headphones on your personal CD or cassette player.

✔ **A digital jack and plug:** Today's sophisticated stereo systems and high-end amplified speaker systems can accept a digital signal through an optical SPDIF output jack.

✔ **A universal serial bus (USB) connector:** If you've invested in a set of digital speakers, you'll use one of your USB ports. These speakers often don't require an AC adapter because they draw electricity directly through the USB port. Because these speakers require USB support, you should be using Windows 2003 Server or XP.

Unless you have a definite reason why you prefer using headphones, I strongly recommend a set of speakers especially designed to be used on a computer. Computer speakers come in all shapes and sizes — some are even integrated into your computer monitor — but a multimedia monitor is typically much more expensive than a regular monitor and a separate set of speakers. Speakers are best placed on either side of the monitor, about a foot away from your ears.

When you shop for a set of speakers, look for these features:

- **Amplified power:** If you're looking for a little more power and better sound, select a speaker set that has its own built-in amplifier. The downside is that the built-in amp needs power; depending on the size of your speakers, you need to provide C or D cell batteries. If your speaker set comes with its own AC wall adapter, you don't need batteries.

- **Magnetic shielding:** A traditional CRT monitor is highly susceptible to distortion from magnetic sources. Because larger speakers use larger magnets, the more powerful the speaker set you choose, the greater the chance that they can interfere with your monitor. To guard against this interference, most computer speakers are magnetically shielded so that you can place them next to a monitor without causing problems.

- **Speaker controls:** If your sound card has a volume control (and you can control the volume of your speakers from within Windows), why do you need separate bass, treble, and volume controls on your speakers? I prefer speaker controls because they're much more convenient. If you need to adjust the volume for a particular game or a Web site with audio, you can do so without opening another window, launching another program, or having to reach around to the back of your computer.

- **Flat-panel design:** Some people feel that flat-panel speakers are a little funny looking — they're not much thicker than a CD case — and other techno-types consider them cool. Most flat-panel speakers produce the same quality of sound as a standard speaker. Although they can save space on your computer desk, they're typically a little more expensive than traditional computer speakers.

The Subwoofer: Big Dog of Computer Speakers

If you enjoy your computer games — I mean *really* enjoy your computer games — I should mention one other speaker enhancement. A computer *subwoofer* provides the deep subsonic bass punch that adds realism whether you're flying a jet or playing an old arcade classic such as Asteroids. You'll feel every explosion! Figure 9-5 shows a standard subwoofer.

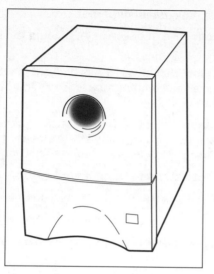

Figure 9-5:
A sub-
woofer can
deliver
an extra
measure of
realism to
games.

You can buy a subwoofer separately or shop for a speaker system that includes one. (It's no accident that high-performance sound systems sold for home theaters include a subwoofer.) A subwoofer is about the size of a loaf of bread, and one will typically set you back around $50 to $100, depending on the power that it can handle.

Unlike the rest of a computer speaker system, a subwoofer is best placed on the floor to cut down on vibration — unless, of course, the idea of your computer desk rattling like a tin roof in a hailstorm appeals to you. (Plus, your PC will avoid dancing the Shimmy, which could in fact be bad for your PC's hard drive.)

Putting Together Your PC Sound System

So you've bought a new sound card, speaker system, and microphone for your PC, and all your audio accoutrements are unpacked and ready. In this section, I show you how to install each piece of hardware (in sequence, no less, starting with your sound card). After you're finished, you can sit back and enjoy anything from Mozart to Metallica!

Installing your sound card

So you're ready to delve into the world of digital audio. Keep your sound card's manual handy because you may have to perform a little jumper surgery during the testing phase. Follow these steps:

1. **If your computer chassis is plugged in, unplug it.**

2. **Remove the cover from your case (if necessary), placing the screws in your parts bowl.**

   What's a parts bowl? You know, that covered plastic bowl, shoebox, or coffee can that holds all the small computer parts. You can't be a techno-wizard without a parts bowl.

3. **Finished dusting your antiques? You had better touch a metal surface before you install your card to discharge any static electricity that you might have picked up before it can damage a computer component.**

4. **Select an open PCI adapter card slot for your sound card.**

   For more information on PCI cards and PCI bus slots, see Chapter 4.

5. **Remove the screw and the metal slot cover adjacent to the selected slot.**

   Don't forget to stick the screw and slot cover into your parts bowl (or box, or can).

6. **Line up the connector on the sound card with the slot on the motherboard.**

   The card's metal bracket should align with the open space that remains when you removed the slot cover.

7. **Apply even pressure to the top of the card and push it down into the slot.**

   If the card is all the way in, the bracket should be resting tightly against the case.

8. **Add the screw and tighten down the bracket.**

Connecting your speakers

Before you can test the operation of your sound card, you need to connect your speakers. Follow these steps and see Figure 9-6, which illustrates the business end of a typical sound card:

1. **Locate the speaker jack on the sound card.**

   Usually the speaker jack is labeled Speakers or Spkr, although some cards also use the stereo term Line Out. If you need help identifying which jack to use, check your sound card manual.

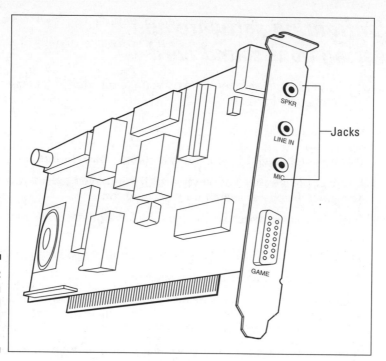

Jacks

Figure 9-6:
The jacks on
a typical
32-bit sound
card.

2. **Insert the audio cable plug from your speakers into the sound card's speaker jack.**

3. **If your speakers are amplified, add the required batteries.**

   If your speaker set uses an AC adapter or power cord, plug it into a nearby wall socket and plug the connector into the power connector on one of the speakers.

4. **Set the volume controls on all parts.**

   If your speakers are amplified, they probably have their own separate volume control. To avoid waking the neighbors and to prevent permanent hearing loss, make sure that all volume controls are set at less than the halfway point.

5. **If your speakers are amplified, turn them on.**

Configuring software and testing your sound card

Time to install the software required by your sound card, configure it, and test your new audio hardware.

Follow these steps:

1. **If you've unplugged your computer, plug it back in now.**

2. **Connect the monitor and keyboard (if you haven't already done so) and push the power switch on your monitor.**

3. **Push the power switch on the front or back of your case and allow your computer to boot.**

   The familiar face of Windows should eventually appear on your screen.

4. **Run the sound card installation software.**

   Insert the installation software into your CD-ROM drive and follow the instructions onscreen or in your sound card manual to install the driver. The installation program will probably make changes to your system files.

5. **After the software is installed, reboot your computer (if necessary).**

6. **Run the diagnostics software supplied with your sound card.**

   Your sound card should come with a diagnostics program that lets you test its operation. Typically, these diagnostics programs play digital audio effects and MIDI music from both speakers, individually and together. For example, you might be asked whether you hear a sound effect from the left speaker, from the right speaker, and then from the "center" channel. If you can't find the diagnostics software, try installing a game that has support for your sound card to see whether the card is working correctly.

If you've scavenged a sound card but didn't get any of the bundled software, don't despair! Digital audio players, MP3 players, sound editors, and text-to-speech conversion programs are available for just about every platform. Try connecting with the manufacturer's Web site or searching the Internet for shareware programs that will work with your scavenged card.

Adding a microphone

Follow these steps to add a microphone only after you've tested your installation and know that your sound card is working properly. If you need to remove your sound card to change some jumper settings, you have to disconnect only your speakers:

1. **Locate the microphone jack on the sound card.**

   On most cards, the microphone jack is labeled `Microphone` or `Mic`, although some cards also use the stereo term `Line In`. If you need help identifying which jack to use, check your sound card manual.

2. **Insert the audio cable plug from your microphone into the sound card's microphone jack.**

3. **If your microphone has an on/off switch, turn it on.**

4. **Adjust (or affix) your microphone.**

   If you're using a clip-on/stick-on microphone, remove the paper backing and stick the holder on your case. Make sure that the microphone and its cable don't obscure or block any switches, lights, or openings on the front of your computer. If you're using a boom microphone, place it on top of your case or to one side of your monitor.

For best operation, your microphone should be no more than one or two feet away from your chair. Of course, clip-on microphones work best attached to your person, and headset microphones will work correctly only when worn.

Installing a subwoofer

Follow this procedure to install a subwoofer only after you've tested your installation and your sound card is working properly.

Unless your subwoofer is part of a speaker set, you have to disconnect your speakers. The subwoofer plugs directly into your sound card, and the speakers then plug into the subwoofer.

1. **Find the speaker jack on the sound card.**

   Usually the speaker jack is labeled `Speakers` or `Spkr`, but some cards also use the stereo term `Line Out`. If you need help identifying which jack to use, check your sound card manual.

2. **Insert the audio cable plug from your subwoofer into the sound card's speaker jack and connect your two speakers to the subwoofer.**

3. **Plug the power cord for your subwoofer into the wall socket.**

4. **Set the subwoofer's volume control at less than the halfway point.**

5. **Turn on your subwoofer and then crank up your favorite audio CD to test it out.**

   I recommend Devo or George Thorogood and the Destroyers. (My editor leans towards the Talking Heads, specifically, the soundtrack album *Stop Making Sense!*)

Chapter 10

Modems and the Call
of the Internet

More than any other computer part, the modem has become a true household word — it's the major star of the Internet show. For most of us, the modem is our ticket to the Web. If you want to venture into the online world, the least expensive way to connect to the Internet is to add a dial-up modem. Just a scant decade ago (right before the Internet became a media sensation), modems were second-class computer citizens, behind printers and scanners. But because getting online is the reason why many people get a computer in the first place, the modem has arrived at center stage.

Would you like to join the online crowd? You could choose a *broadband* connection — typically, a cable or digital subscriber line (DSL) link to the Internet — but not everyone needs a high-speed Internet connection. In fact, if all you do on the Internet is occasionally visit a Web site, read your e-mail, or use instant messaging, you really don't *need* broadband — and the higher cost of such a connection. (I dive into the pros and cons of broadband in Chapter 13.)

If you don't need (or can't get) high-speed Internet access, stay right here! In this chapter, I show you how to select a modem with the features that you need. You then find out how to install the modem, either inside or outside your computer case. You might want to celebrate your new modem by sending a few faxes to your friends and co-workers — without ever touching a fax machine!

A Modem Primer for Real People

Exactly what is a modem? I could give you the lengthy techno-nerd description or the explanation favored by those who'd rather do something else with the next thirty minutes of their lives. Here's the abridged version: The word *modem* is short for *mo*dulate-*dem*odulate, which are the terms usually used for digital-to-analog and analog-to-digital conversion processes. A modem is a device that translates (or modulates) the *digital* language of computers (zeros and ones) into an *analog* signal (variable waves, like a human voice), which can travel over a telephone line. This analog signal doesn't sound anything like a human voice, but it can carry data. The receiving modem then translates (or demodulates) the incoming signal from analog back to digital, which the receiving computer can then use. Figure 10-1 gives you an idea of what's happening.

Figure 10-1:
Two modems strut their stuff, transferring data over a telephone line.

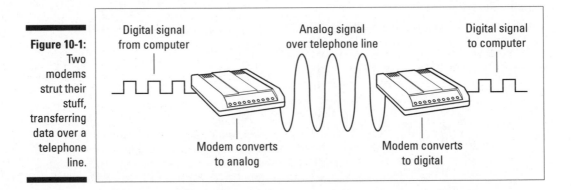

Digital signal from computer

Analog signal over telephone line

Digital signal to computer

Modem converts to analog

Modem converts to digital

Modems are *serial* devices, meaning that they send data one bit at a time over the same wire — in this case, your telephone line. In the past, serial devices connected to — you guessed it — a PC's serial port. Today, however, virtually all external modems connect to your computer's universal serial bus (USB) port. Or, if you select an internal modem adapter card, that card comes with its own serial port. If all this talk of internal cards and ports is foreign, don't worry; I cover the different types of modems in detail later in this chapter. (Curious about serial and USB ports? Chapter 5 covers the installation of all types of ports.)

If you can afford a high-speed DSL or cable connection to the Internet, you'll experience "the Web without the Wait." If you're going to spend two or three hours a night on the Net, I strongly recommend that you invest the money in a high-speed connection — if it's available in your area. (Find out more about DSL and cable Internet connections in Chapter 13.)

A bit of quaint modem history

Modems existed long before PCs and e-mail became popular — in fact, I bought my first 300 bps modem in 1983. Since then, an online world of some type has *always* existed.

In the beginning, *cyberspace* (a fancy term that refers to the online community as a whole) consisted of a number of individual computer techno-wizards who connected with each other over telephone lines to transfer programs and chat, much like ham radio operators. Mainframe computer centers also used modems to connect remote businesses and offices to the central computer.

The arrival in the early 1980s of the automated computer bulletin board system (BBS; one of the older abbreviations in this book) provided the first community-based online service, whereby callers in the same town could leave messages, play games, share files, chat with each other, and even participate in worldwide conferences through the Fidonet message network system. Most BBSes are still free to this day, and most are ready for calls 24 hours a day. Although BBSes have lost much of their popularity because of the Internet, many thousands of them are still in operation around the world because they offer a local online community that you don't find on the Internet. For a little historical cyberspace fun, you can visit my Batboard BBS, which has been online since 1984! (Boy, I'm getting old.) In fact, you can use your Web browser to call the BBS instead of connecting directly; just type `www.mlcbooks.com` to visit my Web browser, and click the Visit My Classic BBS link. The Batboard is free, and you'll find a number of popular online games!

Most of the online world is now centered around the global network called the Internet (especially the portion of the Internet called the *Web,* which is short for *World Wide Web*). Originally, the Internet served as a military and scientific information system, and people used it to search for information and files. The Internet is still a tremendous tool for researching almost any topic, although it has become increasingly commercial and is now considered by many to be one heck of an entertainment value.

The whole speed thing explained

In days of old, you practically had to have a degree in advanced quantified thakamology to buy a modem. You had to consider modem standards, whether you needed fax technology, actual *throughput* (the speed at which data is sent and received), and so on. As more and more people jumped on the online bandwagon, however, shopping for a modem became easier. Today you need to concentrate only on the modem's speed and the standards that the modem supports. (So much for that Ph.D. in advanced quantified thakamology.)

You usually see speed advertised as *bps,* which is short for *bits per second.* (A *bit* is the smallest subparticle of computer data; it's either a zero or a one. Different combinations of zeros and ones represent letters, numerals, and

When speeds differ

You might be wondering what happens if you have a 56 Kbps modem and your friend has an older 33.6 Kbps modem. For example, if the two modems are transferring data at different speeds, how do they communicate? The answer is that the faster modem in a connection always falls back to match the best speed of the slower modem. This process is *handshaking,* and each modem connection that you make begins this way: Both modems compare top speeds and standards and then automatically choose the fastest possible speed and standard supported by both modems.

other characters that make up words, numbers, and even entire computer programs.) When you transfer data across a telephone line with a modem, you're actually sending a long stream of bits between the two computers.

The first modems generally available to the public sent 300 bps. This speed was fine for simply reading text from a BBS. (The characters would appear on your monitor at about the rate of a fast typist.) As programs became larger and people wanted to do more online (and with less waiting), modems moved through a number of speeds: from 300 to 1200 bps, 2400 bps, 9600 bps, 14,400 bps, 28,800 bps, 33,600 bps, and now 56,000 bps. (Whew!)

Modem speeds in the tens of thousands are typically abbreviated. For example, 28,800 bps is usually expressed as 28.8 Kbps (kilobits per second).

The fastest possible telephone modem available today can *theoretically* reach speeds of 56 Kbps.

Check with your Internet service provider (ISP) to determine its top modem speed (and what modem standards it supports) before you buy or scavenge a modem.

Behind-the-scenes stuff: Modem standards

All modems sold in the past decade included a form of *error control,* which makes sure that none of the data is lost or changed by noise on your telephone line. Modems also use some form of *data compression,* which lets the modem send more data in a shorter time. These features are specified by international standards — every modem around the world that supports the same standard as your modem can automatically transfer data at the fastest possible speed.

You don't really need to remember what standards your modem supports to use it, although you should consider modem standards while shopping. The following standards determine the maximum speed at which your modem can connect to your Aunt Mildred's system in Wassaugh Falls, for example. Other factors that influence modem speed include the clarity of the telephone connection, the top speed of both modems, the overall performance of both computers, and even the type of data that you're transferring.

Here's a quick list of the standards that you'll encounter while shopping for a modem:

- **v.92:** An update to the v.90 standard. No speed increase here over the v.90 standard, but these modems do provide features such as *quick connect* (which cuts the handshaking time in half each time that you connect to your ISP), *PCM upstream* (which reduces the time required to upload larger files to the Internet), and *modem-on-hold* (which allows you to answer a voice call while you're connected to the Internet). If you're buying a new modem, chances are that it's a v.92 model.

- **v.90:** The international standard approved in 1998, which can provide transfer speeds as fast as 56 Kbps. All modems now sold support the v.90 standard.

- **56K x2:** One of two 56 Kbps pseudostandards that emerged before the v.90 standard was finalized. (A *pseudostandard* is a proprietary standard offered by one hardware manufacturer that isn't adopted by the rest of the civilized world.) These modems connect at up to 56 Kbps but only with other modems that support the same x2 standard. If the other modem doesn't support the proprietary x2 standard, the modems fall back to 33.6 Kbps. The x2 standard was developed by U.S. Robotics.

- **56K KFlex:** The other 56 Kbps pseudostandard that appeared while v.90 was in development. These modems connect at as much as 56 Kbps but only with other modems that support the same KFlex standard. If the other modem doesn't support the proprietary KFlex standard, the modems fall back to 33.6 Kbps. Lucent Technologies and Rockwell developed the KFlex standard.

- **v.34 extended:** An improved version of the v.34 standard. The v.34 extended standard allows for transfer speeds as fast as 33.6 Kbps.

- **v.34:** The most common modem standard in the early 1990s; provides transfer speeds as fast as 28.8 Kbps.

- **v.32bis:** Delivers a maximum speed of 14.4 Kbps.

- **v.42/v.42bis:** The original error control/data compression combination (and probably the oldest standard that you'll encounter in a scavenged modem). These modems usually transferred data at a maximum of 9600 bps.

A bit of clarification is necessary for the 56 Kbps modem specifications:

✔ Do you have an older, proprietary 56 Kbps modem that uses one of those pseudostandards that I mentioned? Unless it's upgradeable, you won't be able to connect at the highest speed with a standard v.90 modem. If you buy one of these proprietary 56 Kbps modems, check with the manufacturer to determine whether it can be upgraded.

✔ You're more likely to encounter an African wildebeest wearing a hula skirt in your living room than to connect at a full 56 Kbps with *any* telephone modem, no matter *what* the specification. Your telephone line has to be crystal clear, and conditions must be perfect. In fact, I have never received a full 56 Kbps. And, coincidentally, I've never seen a wildebeest, either.

In essence, 56 Kbps is the fastest modem speed available, but the most that you can squeeze from a standard telephone line is a respectable 49.3 Kbps connection. This restriction is due to the conversion process between digital and analog that the modem must perform and the less-than-perfect conditions provided by an analog telephone line.

This speed limit doesn't apply to DSL or cable Internet, which are broadband connections. A broadband Internet connection couldn't care less about even the fastest dial-up analog modem, which it considers strictly horse-and-buggy. If you are a speed racer, are not afraid to spend money, and want all the facts on a *really* fast connection, zip directly to Chapter 13.

If you're shopping for a modem (no matter what the speed), buying an upgradeable model is worth the extra money. These modems can be reprogrammed with the latest standards. Look for models advertising *flash ROM* or *upgradeable firmware* (fancy terms for upgrading your modem). For Windows XP users, the manufacturer should supply a modem information file (INF file) so that Windows can control your specific brand of modem. Your modem support should be installed automatically when you run the modem installation software for your particular operating system; if not, follow the directions provided in your modem's manual for your operating system.

If you've chosen a well-known modem brand, Windows will probably recognize your modem automatically when you install it. Your manual should tell you whether you need to install a new control file.

Will That Be a Card or a Case?

You can uncover plenty of pros and cons for both internal and external modems, so determining which type is right for you is generally easy. Here's a list of the clouds and their accompanying silver linings:

✔ **Cost:** Internal modems don't need their own case and separate power supply, so they're generally 20 to 30 percent cheaper than their external brethren.

✔ **Status lights:** As you can see by the example shown in Figure 10-2, external modems have lights that let you monitor how your call is proceeding. If you know something about what the lights mean, they can be a valuable tool in figuring out whether your modem and computer are cooperating (or whether your modem has sprung a leak). Internal modems have no lights and live inside your computer's case, so it's hard to tell exactly what they're doing.

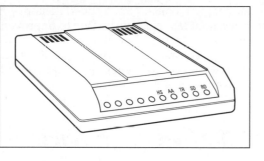

Figure 10-2: A typical external modem, complete with light show.

✔ **Portability:** If you have more than one computer (or if you need to carry your modem between work and home), an external modem is worth the extra cost. An internal modem, on the other hand, isn't very portable. Because it's buried deep inside your computer case, you have to open the case if you want to move the modem to another computer.

✔ **Security:** It's harder for an internal modem to "walk off" in an office environment.

✔ **Less clutter:** If you have limited desk space, an internal modem means one less box cluttering up your computer desk.

✔ **Overcrowding:** If you've already filled all the slots in your computer with various goodies, such as a separate video capture adapter and a FireWire card, you don't have room for an internal modem. This is another reason why many technoids have external modems.

✔ **Easy to install:** A USB modem is about as easy to install as your keyboard or mouse!

If you've scavenged an external modem with a serial connection, make sure that you also pick up the proper modem serial cable. Most modem cables use a 9-pin connector on the computer side and a 25-pin connector on the modem end. But many serial adapter cards with two ports have one 9-pin and one

25-pin serial connector. If your mouse is connected to your 9-pin serial port, you have to connect your modem to the second serial port.

While shopping for your serial modem cable, avoid buying a *null modem* cable. These special cables are designed to hook together two computers with a direct serial connection; they usually bear some sort of printing proclaiming their identity. A null modem cable will *not* work with your modem.

Time to Face the Fax

Back when a 2400 bps modem was considered a speed demon, you could choose a modem with or without fax technology. Due to improvements in technology and chip manufacturing, however, all new modems sold today have built-in fax support, for the same price. In fact, even if you decide on a broadband connection to the Internet, you might find that you still need a dial-up modem to use as your dedicated fax hardware.

The good and the bad on fax/modems

Just what exactly can you do with a fax/modem? Actually, just about anything that you can do with a real fax machine, and a whole lot more to boot! Naturally, you can use a fax/modem to send and receive faxes from other fax machines or other computers. You can also build a telephone directory, automatically send faxes at night, allow other fax machines to poll your computer for new documents, send broadcast faxes to multiple destinations, and design your own cover sheets, just like you can with an expensive fax machine. With a fax/modem, you can even send programs and data files to other computers with fax/modems.

Before you decide to take on the business world with a fax/modem, however, I must tell you about two drawbacks to faxing with a computer:

✔ **The document must be stored on your computer:** You can send only documents that you've created on your computer, which includes just about any word processing document, spreadsheet, image, or whatever you could normally print. However, you can't fax a photograph from today's newspaper or a recipe from Aunt Bertha's *Hometown Hash Handbook*. Anything existing on paper is called *hard copy* by both the press and computer tech types — and the only way that you can send hard copy with a fax/modem is to first scan it into your computer (with a scanner or all-in-one printer that has a built-in scanning feature). If you're interested in scanners and how you can capture digital images of a hard copy, flip your hard copy of this book to Chapter 14.

✔ **You gotta leave your computer on:** Your computer must be on 24 hours a day if you're serious about using it as a fax machine. Leaving your computer on enables your modem to answer fax calls while you're away and send faxes at the times that you specify. If you leave your fax program running under Windows XP, you can still take care of your work while your fax/modem lurks in the background, ready to pounce like a fierce jungle cat on any incoming call.

Leaving your computer turned on isn't as bad as it sounds because a computer uses less power than you might think. Your monitor is the real power hog in your computer system, and most people who run their computers constantly simply turn off the monitor unless they need to use the machine. Other PC owners use the built-in power-saving setting in Windows XP, which allows a computer to "awaken" automatically when an incoming ring is detected.

If you decide to use your new computer as a part of a home office, I strongly suggest that you have a second telephone line installed especially for your computer. Otherwise, anyone trying to send you a fax while you're on the phone ordering pizza is going to get an irritating busy signal. You can also use a separate telephone line for voice mail, as described in the section "Let Your Modem Speak," a little later in this chapter.

Can't add a second telephone line for your computer fax? Then you should consider adding *distinctive ring* service to your existing line. This neat feature from the telephone company lets more than one telephone number use the same physical telephone line to your home. The telephone rings differently for each number, so you can tell which calls are for you and which are for the computer. Today's crop of fax/modems and fax software can distinguish calls and can be configured to answer only a certain ring pattern. If you want to use this feature, make sure that your modem supports both distinctive ring and *adaptive answer* (which enables the modem to automatically switch to fax mode when necessary).

More good fax facts

"Okay, Mark, that's all well and good, but what can I really *do* with a fax that I've received?" That's part of the magic of a fax/modem. If you want, you can simply save the faxed document as a file on your computer and then view it onscreen whenever you need it (complete with rotation and zoom). If you want to get fancy, though, try these features on for size:

- ✔ **Print it:** If you don't have a plain-paper fax machine, you can print a fax on your system printer. (No more of that flimsy thermal stuff that turns yellow — we're talking *real* paper here.)

- ✔ **Send it as an e-mail attachment:** If friends or co-workers are connected to the Internet, you can attach the document in an Internet e-mail message to them, and they can load it just as though they had received it over the phone. This is an easy way to send a fax anywhere on the Internet.

- ✔ **Import it into a document:** If your fax software includes OCR (short for a real whopper of a term, *optical character recognition*), your computer can actually "read" the words on the fax and insert them as text into your favorite word processor. Although this recognition isn't 100 percent accurate, it's good enough to save you lots of time that you would have spent retyping the document.

- ✔ **Turn it into an electronic document:** If you've invested in Adobe's Acrobat software, you can turn that fax into a PDF document, which can be opened on just about any computer running these days. (Alternately, you can usually convert a fax document into an image file in TIFF or JPEG format, which are also common "legal tender" among different types of computers.)

- ✔ **Edit and resend it:** Most fax programs enable you to add your own text or even draw on the original fax and then resend it. This function is great for correcting errors or making suggestions during the development of a hard-copy document such as a contract or lease.

If you're shopping for a fax/modem, it's usually hard to tell which features are supported by the software that's included with your modem. If the fax software that you get doesn't support these features, invest in a full-featured fax or communications program such as WinFax PRO or Procomm Plus (both at www.symantec.com).

Let Your Modem Speak!

Have you ever called a business and tried to contact someone who was out of the office? You likely encountered *voice mail,* with which you can leave a verbal message for a specific person. If you think that this kind of technology is too expensive for your home office, think again. With today's voice modems, callers are presented with a professional telephone answering service for your business. The cost is usually only $50 or so more than a regular fax/modem.

Voice modem hardware and software provides a number of individual, personal voice mailboxes. (The number of mailboxes and the features available for each mailbox vary with the modem and the software that comes with it.) A caller can store a voice message for you by pressing keys on the telephone, which sends numeric commands to your computer. Most voice modems allow you to pick up your voice mail from a remote telephone, so you don't even need to be at your computer to check your messages.

Most voice modems also provide other amenities. For example:

- **Speakerphone:** One of my favorite voice modem features, the speakerphone can be used to dial the phone and talk to someone through your PC's microphone and speakers — no telephone handset necessary! (You can read more about microphones and speakers in Chapter 9.)

- **Personalized mailbox:** If you have more than one message mailbox, your voice modem should enable you to store an individual voice greeting for each mailbox.

- **Caller ID:** If you're curious about the origin of a call, make sure that you get a voice modem with caller ID support, including an onscreen display of the caller's telephone number. (You also need to sign up for caller ID service through your telephone company.)

- **Dual transmission:** The best voice modems enable you to transmit both voice and data in the same connection simultaneously. For example, you can talk to other players during multiplayer online games or talk to someone while sending that person a spreadsheet file.

- **Mail alerts:** Some voice modems can even dial your pager to tell you when you've received voice mail. (Personally, I don't ever want to be *that* tightly wired to my computer.)

You can choose a combination voice, fax, and data modem — or if the voice features aren't attractive, just a fax and data modem. The choice that you make depends on how you plan to use your computer and the price you're willing to pay for a modem. Although voice technology is neat, it's certainly not a requirement when connecting to the Internet or sending a fax.

Installing an Internal Modem

Installing an internal modem has been compared favorably with wrestling an enraged tiger with your bare hands — but often this observation has more to do with trying to shoehorn an internal modem into an existing computer, where several devices have already claimed serial ports.

For those who are scavenging an internal modem, you might need to change jumper settings on the modem if another component in your computer is already using the default COM port (another term for *serial port*). For example, if your mouse is using a serial port, it's likely connected to COM1, so you need to configure your modem as COM2. The installation software for your modem provides you with possible settings for the COM port.

Follow these instructions in order to install an internal modem, and you should come out unscathed on the other side:

1. **Did you just brush the family dog? You'd better touch a metal surface before you install your card!**

   By touching a metal surface before you touch any components, you release any static electricity that you might have picked up.

2. **If your computer chassis is plugged in, unplug it and remove the cover from your case.**

3. **Select an open PCI adapter card slot for your modem.**

4. **Remove the screw and the metal slot cover adjacent to the selected slot.**

   Don't forget to stick both these parts in your parts bowl.

5. **Line up the connector on the card with the slot on the motherboard.**

   The card's metal bracket should align with the open space created when you removed the slot cover.

6. **Apply even pressure to the top of the card and push it down into the slot.**

   If the card is all the way in, the bracket should rest tightly against the case.

7. **Add the screw and tighten down the bracket.**

8. **Plug the telephone line from the wall into the proper jack on the back of your computer.**

   If you have two jacks on the back of your modem, your modem accepts both the telephone line and a standard external telephone, so you can call others with the telephone when the modem isn't using the line. Check your modem manual to see which jack should receive the telephone line from the wall; it's typically marked Linc or has a picture of a wall telephone jack next to it. If you want to use a separate telephone, connect the cord from the telephone to the other jack (usually marked Phone).

Now jump to the section, "Installing Software and Testing Your Modem."

Connecting an External Serial Modem

As I mentioned earlier, I strongly recommend an external modem that uses a USB connection. (Your old serial modem makes a great target — hang it on the wall and throw darts at it. I never miss.) Anyway, pay heed to this Mark's Maxim:

If you're installing an external modem, embrace your USB port!

However, if you've scavenged an older external serial modem, make sure that you have an open serial port on your computer and a modem cable with the right connectors, and then follow these steps:

1. **Locate the 9-pin serial port on the back of your case.**

   The serial port is a small connector, as shown in Figure 10-3.

   If your mouse is already using your 9-pin serial port, don't worry. Simply connect your modem to your second serial port, which is usually set as COM2. You will, however, need a cable that matches the connector for your second serial port, which is typically a 25-pin port. Most computer stores sell little converter things that can turn a 9-pin connector on the end of a cable into a 25-pin connector.

Figure 10-3:
A 9-pin
serial
connector.

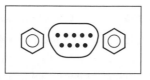

2. **Align the connector on the end of your modem cable with the serial port.**

   The angled edges on the connector are designed to make sure that it goes on only the right way.

3. **After the connector is correctly aligned, push it in firmly.**

4. **If you want, you can tighten the connector by turning the knobs on the connector clockwise.**

   If the connector uses screws instead, you need a small screwdriver. If the connector is already tight enough, you can leave it as is.

5. **Connect the power cord from your modem to the wall socket.**

6. **Plug the telephone line from the wall into the proper jack on the back of your computer.**

   Most external modems have two jacks, which means that you can also plug in a standard telephone and use it when the modem isn't using the line. Your modem manual should tell you which jack should receive the telephone line from the wall; it's usually marked Line or has a picture of a wall telephone jack next to it. If you want to use a separate telephone, connect the cord from the telephone to the other jack (typically marked Phone).

7. **Turn on your modem.**

Now jump to the section, "Installing Software and Testing Your Modem."

Connecting an External USB Modem

Bully for you — you've made the right choice for connecting an external modem! Follow these steps to install an external USB modem:

1. **Locate one of your computer's USB ports.**

2. **If necessary, connect the USB cable to your modem.**

   Some modems have USB cables that are permanently connected.

3. **Connect the power cord from your modem to the wall socket.**

4. **Plug the telephone line from the wall into the proper jack on the back of your computer.**

   Most external modems have two jacks, which means that you can also plug in a standard telephone and use it when the modem isn't using the line. Your modem manual should tell you which jack should receive the telephone line from the wall; it's usually marked Line or has a picture of a wall telephone jack next to it. To use a separate telephone, connect the cord from the telephone to the other jack (typically marked Phone).

5. **Turn on your modem.**

6. **Align the connector on the end of the modem's USB cable with the USB port.**

   The USB connector goes in only one way.

7. **After the connector is correctly aligned, push it in firmly.**

Windows automatically recognizes that you've added a USB modem, and you'll probably be prompted to load the CD-ROM from the modem manufacturer so that Windows can install the modem's drivers. After the driver software is loaded, you're ready to go. You can connect or remove your modem from your PC at any time without rebooting because Windows XP and Windows 2003 Server both support the USB hot-swap feature. *That's* convenient — and it's one of the reasons why USB devices are so doggone popular these days!

Installing Software and Testing Your Modem

To configure and test your internal or external modem, you must install the software and communications program that came with it. Follow these steps:

1. **If you've unplugged your computer, plug it back in.**

2. **Connect the monitor and keyboard and push the power switch on your monitor.**

3. **Push the power switch on the front or back of your case, and then allow your computer to boot.**

4. **Run the modem installation software.**

   Insert the installation software into your CD-ROM or floppy drive and follow the instructions (onscreen or in your modem manual) to install the diagnostics software as well as any communications software that might be bundled with your modem.

   If you've scavenged a modem and you don't have any communications software, I would recommend a commercial program suitable for your operating system (such as Procomm Plus; visit www.symantec.com). Remember, you don't need special communications software to use Internet Explorer, Outlook, or Outlook Express.

5. **Run the diagnostics program.**

Today's communications programs are written for Windows XP or Windows 2003 Server. If you plan to use one of these programs, don't install the communications software until you've installed your new operating system. You can read all about different operating systems and their pros and cons in Appendix A.

Part IV
Adding the Advanced Stuff

The 5th Wave
By Rich Tennant

"Hey Philip! I think we're in. I'm gonna try linking directly to the screen, but gimme a disguise in case it works. I don't want all of New York to know Jerry DeMarco of 14 Queensberry, Bronx NY, hacked into the Times Square video screen."

In this part . . .

Here I describe the power-user peripherals often found on high-performance computers. You discover more about speeding up your PC with SCSI, building a simple network, using a digital scanner or digital still camera, and adding high-speed Internet connections such as cable and DSL to your computer. The advanced (and sometimes expensive) technology that you find in this part isn't a requirement for your average home or small-office PC, although these chapters serve as an introduction to the world of power-user computing.

Chapter 11

Attack of the SCSI Monster

• •

• •

*A*lright, quit laughing at the acronym (which, by the way, is pronounced *scuz*-zee and stands for *small computer system interface*). Perhaps you first heard of SCSI speed in casual conversation at your computer user group. Maybe a friend of yours who's a computer guru recommends it. Or your friendly hi-tech salesperson at the computer store sidles up to you and says something like, "You know, you could *really* speed up that PC of yours with a SCSI card."

No, you're not being flim-flammed . . . the salesperson is telling you the truth. A SCSI component such as a hard drive can transfer data much faster than standard enhanced integrated drive electronics (EIDE) drives — in fact, SCSI hardware is still faster than serial ATA (SATA) hardware. (For the scoop on EIDE and SATA drives, skip back to Chapter 7.) If you crave raw speed, SCSI is indeed the answer to your dreams. SCSI can also support seven devices on a single adapter card, including neat stuff such as scanners, CD and DVD recorders, tape backup drives, and removable cartridge drives.

However, as the adage says, "You can't get something for nothing." And when it comes to adding SCSI support to your computer, the process is definitely more difficult than adding an EIDE hard drive (as I cover in Chapter 7). I doubt that you'll need a bottle of your favorite headache medication, and you *probably* won't turn antisocial during the installation process — but make sure that you read in their entirety both this chapter and the manuals that accompany your SCSI hardware.

In this chapter, I show you how to properly install and configure your SCSI adapter card and SCSI devices.

Do 1 Really Need SCSI?

Before you decide to add SCSI, you need to take a hard look at your computer and its applications. Unlike your keyboard and mouse, SCSI is definitely *not* a requirement for a typical desktop PC (especially one meant for simple applications such as reading your e-mail or using Quicken), so you shouldn't add SCSI to your system without a darn good reason. With that in mind, here are the darn good reasons:

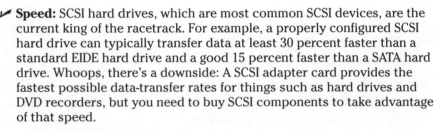

✔ **Speed:** SCSI hard drives, which are most common SCSI devices, are the current king of the racetrack. For example, a properly configured SCSI hard drive can typically transfer data at least 30 percent faster than a standard EIDE hard drive and a good 15 percent faster than a SATA hard drive. Whoops, there's a downside: A SCSI adapter card provides the fastest possible data-transfer rates for things such as hard drives and DVD recorders, but you need to buy SCSI components to take advantage of that speed.

Some peripherals that you wouldn't consider speedy (such as the most expensive high-resolution scanners) work faster and more efficiently on a SCSI system. The most common SCSI adapter cards can transfer data at anywhere from 20MB to 60MB per second, and more advanced variants of SCSI (such as UltraSCSI) can achieve a phenomenal transfer rate of up to 320MB per second. Figures like that, ladies and gentlemen, make a techno-wizard sit up and take notice. Blazing transfer rates also make network and Web site administrators take notice, which is why SCSI hardware is typically used on server computers that handle Internet traffic (as well as PCs built for uber-gaming or no-holds-barred video editing).

For many power users, this speed increase is reason enough to jump on the SCSI bandwagon. However, if you want to save money or you really aren't worried about squeezing that extra speed from your PC, a standard EIDE or SATA system is fine.

✔ **Expansion:** If you plan on hanging every *internal* device except the kitchen sink on your computer, a SCSI adapter card is a natural choice. When everything is configured correctly, a single SCSI adapter card can take care of seven devices. (The UltraSCSI variety can handle fifteen!) An EIDE or serial ATA controller card, on the other hand, can support a maximum of only four devices (two on the primary connector and two on the secondary EIDE connector). Your SCSI card automatically routes data to and from these devices, so you can even use them simultaneously.

You might be asking, "Why not use USB or FireWire rather than SCSI?" After all, universal serial bus and FireWire peripherals are a cinch to add to your system. However, both these connection types support only *external* peripherals, such as external hard drives, digital cameras, or scanners. Aha! — *there's* the rub. So you won't find an internal hard drive, DVD recorder, or tape backup unit that works with USB or FireWire.

✔ **Compatibility:** Some parts that require fast transfer rates use only a SCSI interface. For example, many digital audio tape (DAT, covered in Chapter 7) backup drives still use the SCSI standard and require a SCSI adapter because they need the fastest possible data transfer.

SCSI is recognized by a wide range of operating systems, including UNIX, Linux, and all versions of Windows. (See Appendix A for a comparison of operating systems.)

TIP

SCSI is available also as a built-in feature on many motherboards. If you're sure that your PC will include SCSI peripherals, you might want to pay the extra cash for one of these advanced motherboards. That way, you can save the card slot that would otherwise be occupied by a SCSI adapter.

SCSI adapter cards and devices are typically more expensive than their EIDE cousins. If you decide to walk the SCSI road, expect to pay the higher toll. On average, SCSI controller cards and peripherals cost about 20 to 25 percent more than a similar piece of EIDE hardware.

Figuring Out SCSI

In theory, mapping out the internal workings of a SCSI card and the various parts attached to it sounds no more difficult than figuring out how to pour a bowl of cereal. Most SCSI adapter cards enable you to connect as many as seven devices, so you can attach all sorts of neat toys, such as scanners, super-fast hard drives, and DVD recorders. Internal peripherals fit on one nice cable, and external peripherals connect directly to the external SCSI port on the adapter card. It couldn't be simpler: Your SCSI adapter card identifies each device attached to it by a unique number, called a *SCSI ID.* Pass the milk, right?

Wrong. You must take care of a couple of other requirements before everything will work:

✔ **Identify your devices:** Your SCSI adapter must be properly configured so that it doesn't argue with the other SCSI parts in your computer. You must assign a unique ID number to each of your SCSI devices. For example, if you assign the same SCSI ID to your SCSI hard drive and your SCSI CD-ROM drive, these components argue and fight over who gets the ID number and neither drive works. Read how to set these ID numbers in the following section, "More about SCSI ID numbers."

✔ **Terminate your device chain:** Each SCSI device connected to your SCSI card forms a link in a chain (made from cables rather than from metal), and the two ends of that chain must be correctly terminated to indicate that no more devices are left for the SCSI adapter to access. The combination of a SCSI adapter card and at least one SCSI component is often called a *chain*. If your SCSI components (including the SCSI adapter itself) aren't properly terminated, your computer will be unable to recognize them. Read more about chaining and termination in the upcoming section, "More about SCSI terminators."

If you keep these important requirements in mind when you install your SCSI card and devices, your SCSI chain will be easier to configure.

More about SCSI ID numbers

Each SCSI device on your SCSI chain (the adapter card as well as the SCSI peripherals) must have a unique SCSI ID number that identifies it to your computer. SCSI-2 cards use a range of ID numbers from 0 to 7, with ID number 7 typically reserved for the adapter card itself (which leaves seven ID numbers for your SCSI components). If you're unsure which default ID number your SCSI controller card uses, check your manual.

Suppose that you've decided to add a SCSI hard drive and a SCSI internal DVD recorder to your computer so that you can record your own audio CDs and DVD movies. That's a total of three ID numbers. If your SCSI card reserves ID number 7 for itself, you could assign ID number 1 to the SCSI hard drive and ID number 3 to the CD recorder. Figure 11-1 illustrates a simple SCSI chain.

Figure 11-1:
A simple SCSI device chain, showing the unique ID for each component.

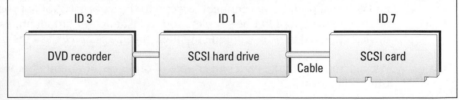

This scenario is all fine and dandy *if* those ID values happen to be unique *and* they're the defaults for each part. In fact, this is sometimes the case if you're adding just a SCSI adapter card and one or two devices. Once again, check the manuals for your SCSI components to determine what number the various devices use for ID number defaults.

Multiple SCSI cards for the techno-wizard

I know that many of you are sticking up your hand with a question, and I'll bet that question is, "Can I install more than one SCSI card in my computer?" Yes, you can install more than one SCSI adapter card in your system, but unless you use plug-and-play (PnP) SCSI adapter cards, you'll be facing a serious round of configuration before everything works. Unless you know a techno-wizard with an extremely powerful

computer, you'll find that a PC with multiple SCSI cards is about as rare as a white tiger.

Virtually all SCSI installations involve a single SCSI card by itself or perhaps a single SCSI card added to an existing computer that's already using EIDE hard drives and devices. Enhanced IDE and SCSI coexist pretty well in the same machine.

When adding a SCSI adapter card or SCSI devices to your PC, keep updated records on what devices use what numbers!

If you're really lucky, the controller card and peripherals will have ID numbers that are already unique. If so, you can joyfully jump to the following section, "More about SCSI terminators." Otherwise, grumble to yourself about Murphy's Law and change the matching SCSI ID numbers until each of them is unique.

You can use one of these three methods to set SCSI ID numbers on SCSI adapter cards and devices:

✔ **Spin the wheel:** Your device might have a thumbwheel on the bottom, which you can use to change the ID number. The ID number appears in a little window, as shown in Figure 11-2. To change the number, turn the thumbwheel until you see a number that's not already assigned to another SCSI peripheral or the SCSI adapter card.

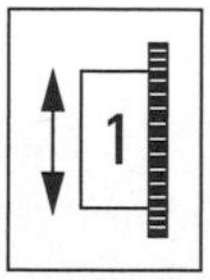

Figure 11-2:
A SCSI ID
thumbwheel.

✔ **Set the jumper:** Your SCSI adapter card or device might have a series of jumpers, which you move to set the correct ID number. Figure 11-3 shows a typical *jumper* (a plastic-and-metal crossover that you can move to connect different sets of pins). To change the ID number on a device that uses jumpers, pull the jumper off the pins and move the jumper to the correct pins. For example, you might have to move a jumper that connects pins 1 and 2 to pins 3 and 4. Check the part's manual for information about configuring the jumper. A pair of needle-nose pliers or tweezers makes a good tool for moving jumpers.

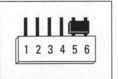

Figure 11-3: A SCSI ID jumper block.

✔ **Let the device set its own ID number:** That's right — some components set their own SCSI device IDs automatically. These devices require a SCSI adapter card that supports SCAM (a tacky acronym that stands for SCSI configured automatically). All devices on the SCSI chain must also be SCAM compliant.

More about SCSI terminators

The other requirement for a successful SCSI installation is the proper configuration of terminators. If *terminator* makes you think of Arnold as a big walking robot with a bad temper and a bazooka, forget it — in the SCSI world, a *terminator* is a stop sign for your SCSI adapter card. All SCSI hardware (including SCSI adapter cards) can be terminated.

The terminator tells your SCSI adapter card that the SCSI chain has ended and that no other SCSI devices are remaining on the chain. Without a terminator, your SCSI card continues to look for devices farther down the SCSI cable. On the other hand, if you terminate the chain too early and another SCSI peripheral is connected farther along the cable, your SCSI adapter card will never recognize that part. Either way, it's no picnic.

Suppose that you want to add a SCSI adapter card and a SCSI scanner to your PC. You need only two SCSI ID numbers, but you must also indicate to your SCSI adapter card that one (and *only* one) SCSI peripheral is on the chain. This SCSI configuration is the easiest type to figure out: Because both these components mark an end of the SCSI chain, both need to be terminated. Figure 11-4 illustrates a simple SCSI chain.

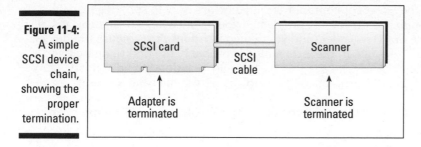

Figure 11-4:
A simple
SCSI device
chain,
showing the
proper
termination.

When you introduce another SCSI peripheral, things get trickier. To illustrate, suppose that you have a SCSI adapter card with a SCSI hard drive and a SCSI internal DVD recorder. Figure 11-5 shows a properly terminated chain.

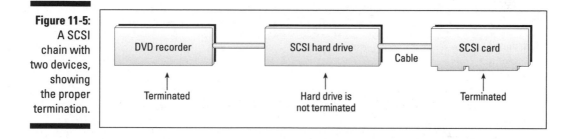

Figure 11-5:
A SCSI
chain with
two devices,
showing
the proper
termination.

Figure 11-6 illustrates what happens when the SCSI adapter card is improperly terminated: Your adapter card doesn't recognize your CD recorder, and you can't use it.

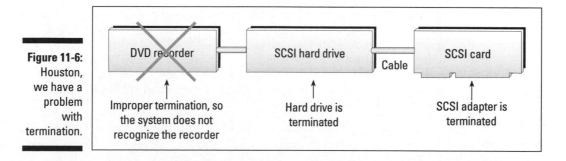

Figure 11-6:
Houston,
we have a
problem
with
termination.

Because the effects of improper termination are easy to spot, it's usually pretty simple to correct this problem. If you install a device (such as a SCSI hard drive or CD recorder) and your computer doesn't recognize the device or you can't operate it, the termination is probably the first thing that you should check. Your SCSI adapter card should include a SCSI diagnostics program; running this program might help you determine what's wrong.

You can use one of three methods to set termination on SCSI adapter cards and peripherals:

✔ **Insert the resistor pack:** As you can see in Figure 11-7, a *resistor pack* is an electronic plug that typically looks like a silicon caterpillar. To terminate a SCSI device with a resistor pack, simply plug in the resistor. Your device manual should show you where the resistor socket is located.

Figure 11-7:
A SCSI terminator of the resistor pack variety.

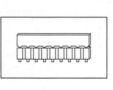

✔ **Set the jumper:** Older SCSI devices might have a jumper, which you can move to enable or disable termination (according to the instructions in your device manual). To change the termination, move the jumper to the correct pins. Check your device manual for information about configuring the jumper. (Also see the earlier section, "More about SCSI ID numbers.")

✔ **Set the DIP switch:** DIP (dual inline packaging) switches are commonly used to select the configuration settings for a hardware device. Use a pointed object to slide the tiny switches, as specified in your device manual. The switches can be either on or off. (Generally the on direction is noted on the DIP switch itself, as shown in Figure 11-8.) One series of on and off will equal termination and the other will disable termination (as specified in your manual).

Figure 11-8:
A SCSI terminator of the DIP switch variety.

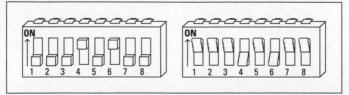

External SCSI

If you're using an external SCSI device (such as an external DAT backup drive) on your SCSI adapter card, that component still needs a unique ID and the proper termination. Your SCSI adapter should provide an external connector, which is usually on the back of the card. Because it has 50 or 68 pins, your SCSI port is typically easy to locate. Figure 11-9 illustrates a common external SCSI port.

Figure 11-9: The exotic curves of an external SCSI port.

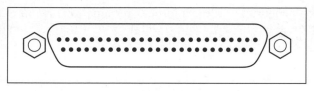

 Unfortunately, you can find a number of variations on the cable connectors for a SCSI external device, so it's a good idea to buy the cable after you've both installed your card and bought the device.

You can attach to your PC multiple external SCSI devices, such as an external DVD multi-drive unit and an external SCSI tape backup — a process that old, burned-out hackers who date back to the days of the Atari and Commodore 64 (like myself) call *daisy chaining*. When two external SCSI devices are daisy chained, you connect the two peripherals with a short *SCSI cable* — in effect, continuing the chain through the devices. (And yes, it is just like the daisy chaining that you can perform with USB and FireWire devices. Go figure . . . a good idea has staying power.)

 If you're connecting an external SCSI peripheral to a SCSI card that's already connected to internal SCSI devices, remember that your SCSI adapter card should no longer be terminated. In effect, the SCSI card is now in the middle of the SCSI chain, with devices on either side.

If you do install multiple external SCSI devices, you need to terminate only the *last* external peripheral in the daisy chain. For example, Figure 11-10 shows a typical external chain — adding an external DAT drive to your PC.

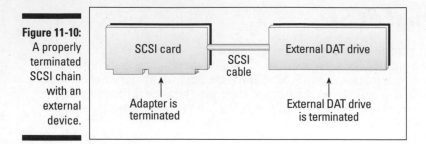

Figure 11-10:
A properly terminated SCSI chain with an external device.

As you can see in Figure 11-11, the improper termination of your SCSI adapter card (when it shouldn't be terminated) will prevent other SCSI devices from being recognized.

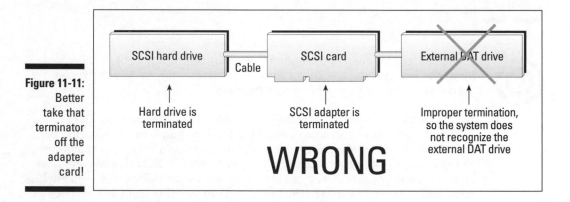

Figure 11-11:
Better take that terminator off the adapter card!

Your SCSI Shopping List

If you've decided to add SCSI support to your computer, be prepared to spend anywhere from $45 to $250 for your SCSI adapter card. With such wide price ranges, it makes sense to weigh the advantages of one card against another. While you're comparing SCSI adapter cards, keep these advanced features in mind:

- **PCI or bust:** If top transfer rates for your SCSI hard drives are your goal, buy a PCI (peripheral component interconnect) SCSI adapter card (or buy a motherboard with built-in SCSI support). (Get the scoop on PCI and ISA in Chapter 4.)

- **Plug and play:** As with other adapter cards, if your motherboard supports *plug and play (PnP),* you save a great deal of time and trouble if you buy a PnP SCSI adapter card. PnP enables your computer to automatically configure your SCSI adapter card.

✔ **Bus mastering:** *Bus mastering* is a data transfer protocol that greatly increases the efficiency of multitasking operating systems such as Windows XP and Linux. When you reduce the technology to terms that mere mortals can understand, bus mastering enables your SCSI card to move different files smoothly to different places at the same time.

✔ **Upgradeable firmware:** Your SCSI adapter card has its own basic input/output system (BIOS), so it really doesn't need the help of the BIOS on your motherboard to recognize SCSI peripherals and hard drives. However, just like the BIOS on your motherboard, your SCSI BIOS should be upgradeable; a card with this type of BIOS can be reprogrammed with bug fixes, new features, and support for new devices. Some SCSI cards call this feature *flash ROM*.

✔ **Cache memory:** SCSI adapter cards with onboard cache memory are typically used whenever your SCSI hard drive (or drives) must transfer data at the fastest possible speed, or when your computer will be accessing a large number of files simultaneously (for example, a network or a Web server). These SCSI cards have their own random access memory (RAM) onboard, which holds data that the CPU accesses frequently, so your SCSI drive doesn't have to reread that data over and over. Some cards can even anticipate the data that your computer will need. For example, SCSI cards with cache memory can load the contents of a multimegabyte file into RAM, where the drive can later access it. The larger the RAM cache, the better (and usually the more expensive the SCSI adapter card).

Installing Your SCSI Card

The typical SCSI installation will have to share your computer with an existing EIDE or SATA hard drive. However, you can install SCSI by itself and ignore the passé world of EIDE; if you've decided on a SCSI-only system, don't forget to strut your SCSI stuff at the next technoid get-together!

If your motherboard has SCSI built-in, you can ignore the card installation instructions in steps 4, 5, 7, 8 and 9 — simply ground yourself (as shown in step 1), open your case (steps 2 and 3), check termination (step 6), and attach the SCSI ribbon cable to the SCSI connector on the motherboard (step 10). Oh, and feel free to gloat.

1. **You've just been kidnapped by aliens and returned, and you want to install a SCSI adapter card? In case you picked up any static electricity, you'd better touch a metal surface before you install your card.**

2. **If your computer chassis is plugged in, unplug it.**

3. **Remove the cover from your case.**

4. **Select an open PCI adapter (32-bit) card slot for your SCSI card.**

5. **Remove the screw and the metal slot cover adjacent to the selected slot.**

   Don't forget to stick both these parts in your parts box.

6. **Check your SCSI adapter for proper termination.**

   If your SCSI card needs to be terminated (because it's at one end of the SCSI chain), you'll find that setting a jumper or adding a resistor pack is much easier *now* than after you've installed the card. *Remember:* Your SCSI adapter will need to be terminated if you have only internal SCSI components to add, with no external peripherals (and vice versa). Because you're installing your SCSI adapter card first, the default SCSI ID number (typically 7) is okay. (You'll find more on ID numbers earlier in this chapter in the section "More about SCSI ID numbers.")

7. **Line up the connector on the card with the slot on the motherboard.**

   The card's metal bracket should align with the open space that's left when you removed the slot cover.

8. **Apply even pressure to the top of the card and push it down into the slot.**

   If the card is all the way in, the bracket should be resting tightly against the case.

9. **Add the screw and tighten down the bracket.**

10. **Attach the SCSI ribbon cable to the proper connector on the card.**

    Your adapter card manual can help you locate the SCSI cable connector.

 For any ribbon cable, pin 1 on the male connector must always match the hole for pin 1 on the female connector. In almost every case, pin 1 on the male connector is the pin in the upper-left corner of the connector on the device. Every ribbon cable has one wire that's painted red, or somehow marked; that wire is wire 1, and you should always connect it to pin 1.

Adding an Internal SCSI Device

After you install a SCSI adapter, you can then add internal SCSI components, such as a DVD recorder, a hard drive, or a tape backup drive. If you're adding a new internal SCSI peripheral to an existing SCSI chain, remember that this installation usually involves a change to your current termination configuration. You might have to change the termination on either end of the SCSI chain. If you forget to set the proper termination, your SCSI adapter card might not recognize your new peripheral. Even worse, an existing SCSI part that's been working flawlessly for months will suddenly stop working, too.

To install an internal device, follow these steps:

1. **If your computer chassis is plugged in, unplug it and remove the cover.**

2. **You've been rubbing a birthday balloon on your head, and now you want to install a SCSI component? Don't forget to touch a metal surface to discharge any static electricity.**

3. **Check the termination and SCSI ID number on your new device and configure these settings properly.**

   If your new part will be connected closer to the end of your SCSI cable than any existing SCSI components on the chain, the new device should be terminated. For more information on terminating your SCSI hardware, see the section "More about SCSI terminators," earlier in this chapter. For details on setting the SCSI ID number, see the section "More about SCSI ID numbers," earlier in this chapter.

   If you've forgotten the SCSI ID numbers for other SCSI components you've previously installed, you can use the SCSI diagnostics or utility program that came with your SCSI adapter to determine the ID numbers without disassembling your computer.

4. **Select an open drive bay for your new component.**

5. **From the front of the case, slide the device into the bay and attach it to the side of the bay.**

   Slide the component back and forth until the screw holes in the side of the bay line up with those on the side of the device. Then secure the part using the screws that came with it.

6. **Connect one of the power cables from your power supply to the power connector on the device.**

   Note that the connector fits only one way.

7. **Connect the ribbon cable coming from your SCSI adapter card (or your motherboard if it has a built-in SCSI adapter) to the back of the device.**

   If you're installing the first internal SCSI peripheral on your SCSI chain, use the first open device connector on the cable. If you're installing an internal SCSI peripheral on an existing SCSI device chain, use the next open connector on the cable. On the ribbon cable, the wire with the markings is on the side with pin 1. If you're unsure which pin on the device's connector is pin 1, check your manual. The connector should fit snugly, so press it all the way on after you align it correctly.

Connecting an External SCSI Device

If you're adding a new device to an existing SCSI chain, you'll probably have to change your current termination configuration. You might need to change the termination on either end of the SCSI chain. If you forget to set the proper termination, your SCSI adapter card might not recognize your new part.

To install an external device, follow these steps:

1. **Set the correct termination and SCSI ID number for your external peripheral.**

   For more information on termination, see the section "More about SCSI terminators," earlier in this chapter. For details on setting a SCSI ID number for your new external peripheral, see the section "More about SCSI ID numbers," earlier in this chapter.

2. **Locate the external SCSI port on the back of your case.**

   The SCSI port is a flat, thick connector with 50 or 68 pins (refer to Figure 11-9). If you're installing a new external SCSI peripheral on an existing external daisy chain, plug the cable from the new device into the secondary SCSI port on the external device that's now last on the chain. (To understand daisy chaining, see the earlier section in this chapter, "External SCSI."

3. **Align the connector on the end of your SCSI cable with the SCSI port and push the connector in firmly.**

   The angled edges on the connector are designed to make sure that it goes in only the right way.

4. **Tighten the connector by snapping the wire clips toward the center of the cable, as shown in Figure 11-12.**

5. **Connect the power cord from your external device to the wall socket.**

Figure 11-12:
External SCSI connectors typically use wire clips to ensure that the cable stays on.

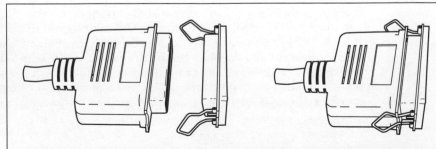

Installing Software and Testing Your SCSI Adapter

To install the software required by your SCSI card and to test your new SCSI chain, follow these steps:

1. **If you've unplugged your computer, plug it back in now.**

2. **Connect the keyboard and the monitor (if you haven't already done so) and turn on the monitor.**

3. **Push the power switch on your computer case and allow your computer to boot.**

4. **Run the SCSI card installation software.**

   Insert the installation software into your CD-ROM or floppy drive (as appropriate) and follow the instructions onscreen (or the instructions in your SCSI card manual) to configure your SCSI management software.

5. **If the installation program prompts you to reboot your computer, do so.**

6. **Run the diagnostics software supplied with your SCSI card.**

   Your SCSI card should come with a diagnostics program that lets you test its operation. Typically, these diagnostics programs also enable you to check for proper recognition of devices on the SCSI chain.

Troubleshooting Your SCSI Devices

So you've installed a SCSI device and . . . nothing. Your computer doesn't recognize your new peripheral. Brothers and sisters, I've been there, and I feel your pain. Believe me, this situation is the definition of the word *hassle*. Before you take a chain saw to your computer, here's a quick checklist of possible causes for the problem:

- **Are your ribbon cable connections correct?** Pin 1 on the male connector must match hole 1 on the female connector — this applies to both the adapter card and the device. (External SCSI peripherals don't have this problem.)

- **Termination, termination, termination!** This is the classic problem when adding a new SCSI component: The last device on the internal SCSI cable should be terminated. If you have one (or more) external SCSI peripherals, the last of those peripherals should be terminated. If you don't have any external components, your SCSI adapter should be terminated.

✔ **Does the device have a unique SCSI ID?** Without a unique ID, two SCSI peripherals will fight to a standstill like drenched cats, and neither of them will work.

✔ **Is your SCSI device receiving power?** Don't forget to plug in an external SCSI peripheral. Internal SCSI components should be connected to one of the power cords leading from your computer's power supply.

✔ **Do you need to install a device driver?** Although your SCSI card might recognize your new SCSI component, don't forget to install any manufacturer-specific software drivers that might be required for the peripheral.

✔ **Is the device conflicting with existing SCSI components in your PC?** Run the SCSI diagnostics program that came with your adapter card to determine whether your new peripheral is recognized by your computer; if it is, the problem is probably not caused by a SCSI device conflict. If the new part isn't recognized (and both termination and SCSI ID numbers are okay), it's probably time to call the manufacturer's technical support hotline.

Chapter 12

So You Want to Add a LAN?

*A*mong the many revolutionary concepts that have rocked PC design for more than two decades, the most important has been the desktop computer network. On a local area network (or LAN, for short), your desktop PC can share programs and data with other computers in your home or office. With the right equipment, your networked PCs can run programs and use shared hardware that resides on a central server computer. You can use a network to share a broadband digital subscriber line (DSL) or cable Internet connection, too. In fact, with network software called *groupware,* you can participate with others in officewide projects, where everyone works and communicates together. Networks can be as small or as large as you like: They can link desktop computers in an entire building or an office with ten computers, or you can simply connect two or three PCs in your home to share the same printer and exchange e-mail.

Gamers, don't feel left out because the business types get to have all the fun. Networks also enable several players to compete in the same game, with each player using a different PC. These first-person graphic multiplayer battles began with the first version of Doom, the classic shoot-'em-up game. But now just about every game that arrives on the store shelf features network play. You can race cars, build empires, pilot star fighters, or deliver a cyber karate chop to your boss. (If you're a real gladiator, you can even set up a network at home just for gaming.)

Adding network support isn't for everyone. If you have access to only one computer or you have no pressing reason to add your computer to an existing network, you can stop reading here and jump to the next chapter.

Feel like connecting? Then read on!

Adding the Network Advantage

If you use several PCs in your home, you might want to connect them through a network. By doing so, you can share data between your computers — everything from a shared family calendar to your kid's artwork. In addition, with a network you can also look forward to the following benefits, which I call the *four Cs*: convenience, communication, cooperation, and contact.

Convenience

Imagine being able to load a document into your word processing application directly from someone else's hard drive — no running back and forth with a floppy disk. (Most techno-types call the archaic floppy disk method a *sneakernet.*) If your PC is connected to a network, you can transfer files, run programs, and access data on the other networked computers, just as though those programs and files resided on your local hard drive (that is, the drive that's physically in your own PC).

The convenience of a network doesn't stop with just data, though. You can also share peripherals. For example, on a network, you can share a printer, a DVD-ROM jukebox, a fax/modem, or a tape drive, which is a great way to cut expenses for a small business that has just a handful of employees. Instead of buying a printer for each PC, everyone can share the same printer.

With software such as Procomm Plus (from Symantec, at www.symantec.com), you can even access your network from a remote site by using a modem connection. For example, you can use the modem on your home computer to connect to a modem server on your office network. After you successfully *log on* (enter your username and the correct password), you can retrieve files or answer e-mail.

Communication

One of the primary uses for a small office network is interoffice electronic mail. E-mail software is built into Windows XP and Windows 2003 Server, although you can find e-mail *clients* (applications that let you read e-mail) for DOS and

Linux as well. E-mail can contain more than mere text messages; you can include attachments such as data files, voice and video clips, or even entire programs.

Unfortunately, you can also share a virus with the outside world through a LAN connection or e-mail attachments. *Get yourself a good antivirus program,* such as Norton AntiVirus (www.symantec.com), *install it, and keep it updated!*

With an antivirus program running while you're using your computer, you're protected — just in case.

Standard 100 Mbps (or even 1000 Mbps, or *gigabit*) networks with fast trans-fer rates can support videoconferencing between computers on the network. Because everyone involved needs a video camera, videoconferencing isn't widespread yet, although it could eventually replace the telephone for those with a high-speed Internet connection.

Cooperation

For businesses of every size, the answer to office cooperation is a *groupware system.* A typical groupware system such as Lotus Notes from IBM (www.lotus.com) includes e-mail and an electronic public message base (where you can leave messages of general interest, such as announcements), along with a common word processor, spreadsheet, and database program that everyone uses. Each of these common applications shares the same documents, so anyone can use and update those documents. Groupware enables users to discuss, change, and revise data on a project, often simultaneously. For exam-ple, in a small office, Bill can add a note to a proposal for a new product while Jane makes a change to the product's dimensions. (Even Microsoft has joined the groupware bandwagon. For example, you can also work with the same type of cooperative documents using Microsoft Office under Windows 2003 Server.)

Using groupware also enables you to coordinate numerous schedules when you want to organize a meeting or an office event. By using a shared calendar, for example, family members can specify when they're available during any given week, thus allowing anyone who's planning a family event to keep track of upcoming soccer games or music lessons.

Contact

The final benefit, contact, refers to contact with the Internet. If your com-puter has access to an existing office network, that network might already have a fast, dedicated connection to the Internet. With a network connection on your office PC, your file transfers and Web surfing will be many times faster than they would be over a modem connection.

Yes, home office types can also distribute a single Internet connection amongst the entire network gang! As I mention earlier in this section, both Windows XP and Windows 2003 Server allow you to share a broadband Internet connection among all the computers on your network. Or, if you like, you can allow everyone on your network to access the Internet connection by using a hardware device called an *Internet router* (also called an *Internet gateway* or *Internet sharing device*).

Do you need to connect to a network to access the Internet? Definitely not! A majority of home computer owners still connect to the Internet through a dial-up connection (Chapter 10 tells you all about using a modem) or one of the high-speed connections (as I describe in Chapter 13). Although the Internet is actually a huge network of smaller networks, you do *not* need your own network to use it.

Deciding Which Network Architecture Is Best for You

This section explains the basic terms that you need to know when discussing networks. I show you the fundamentals of network *architecture,* which is the structure in which you string computers together. Read on to find out how to construct a basic network with the smallest investment in time and money.

You could go full-bore and network all the PCs in your entire neighborhood, but that's not what this book is about. For you home users and small-business owners, this section gives you the basics on constructing a small network of two to five computers, called *nodes* in network terms. For more detailed information on building a network, I suggest that you check out *Home Networking For Dummies,* 3rd Edition, by Kathy Ivens (Wiley).

Comparing client-server and peer-to-peer networks

Desktop networks fall into one of two mysterious categories; you continually hear them mentioned if you hang around a networking techno-nerd. Rather than force any well-adjusted human being into hanging around such a social derelict, let me explain these terms up front:

✓ **Client-server:** This term is one of the more popular buzzwords in use by the computer elite these days. Luckily, *client-server* turns out to be simple.

On a network, a *client* is simply a computer that uses the network's resources. Usually, a client computer is the computer on your desk.

The other half of the name, the *server,* refers to a computer dedicated to providing a resource for the client computers on the network. For example, a *file server* provides the other computers on the network with the fastest access possible to a set of files, which reside on the server instead of the individual client computers. Other servers, such as dedicated CD/DVD servers, printer servers, and modem servers, allow everyone on the network to use the same hardware and access the same data.

A *client-server network* is a network that includes one or more server computers, no matter what the function of the server. Although file servers and printer servers are the most common shared resources, any server transforms your network into a client-server network.

✔ **Peer-to-peer:** For once, the name means what it says. A *peer-to-peer* network has no servers — all computers are connected to each other. (In fact, every computer is as good as its peers.) You save the cost of an expensive server computer, but it's harder for computers to share the same information. A peer-to-peer network is best for the home user or for an office in which everyone simply wants to exchange e-mail and files or use a common printer. Windows XP and Windows 2003 Server both include simple peer-to-peer networking, which is suitable for file and printer sharing.

Comparing network configurations

Wait — don't breathe yet! Now that you understand the difference between client-server and peer-to-peer, you should know something about the three popular configurations of desktop computer networks:

✔ **Simple Ethernet:** *Ethernet* was the first widespread network topology used with PCs. (*Topology* is a 50-cent word for *network structure.*) Ethernet is still the most popular network topology by far, and it works equally well as client-server or peer-to-peer. Traditional Ethernet networks without a switch transfer data more slowly and less efficiently than a star Ethernet network (which I describe in the following bullet).

On an Ethernet network, each computer's network card is assigned a unique identifying electronic number. Packets of data are broadcast across the entire network. The computer that matches the number collects the packet and processes it; computers that don't match the packet ignore it. If two computers attempt to broadcast packets at the same time, the entire network is basically placed on hold until the conflict passes. This on-hold delay accounts for the relative inefficiency of an Ethernet network without a switch.

✔ **Star Ethernet:** The *star* Ethernet network topology is the king of the hill in PC networking, with the best performance and highest efficiency.

A star Ethernet network is built much like a modern railroad switching station: Each computer sends data packets to a central switch, which routes the data to the proper receiving node. Because each node is separately connected to the switch, a star network enables each computer to send data packets at the same time, and no conflicts arise that might reduce the efficiency of your Ethernet network. The switch simply keeps up with each packet and suspends those it can't send immediately (rather like an airport control tower placing an airplane in a holding pattern). When the receiving node is ready to accept the data, the switch gives the packet "clearance to land," and the packet is allowed through the switch. Figure 12-1 illustrates a star Ethernet network.

Most home and small business PC owners who want to install a network should stick with the star Ethernet topology: It's cheap, easier to install, and supported by Windows 2003 Server and Windows XP. Hey, you're now a network techno-genius — you understood the buzzwords! Better go look in the mirror and see whether you've grown a beard or suddenly sprouted a pocket protector full of old ballpoint pens. (Suspenders are a dead giveaway, too.)

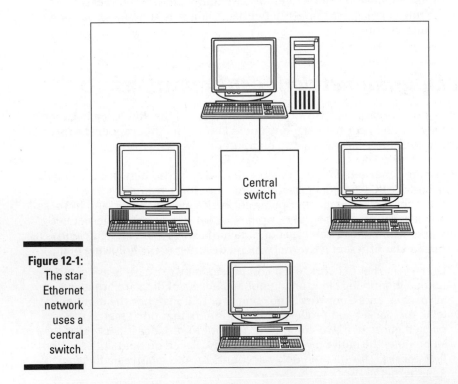

Figure 12-1:
The star
Ethernet
network
uses a
central
switch.

Anyway, an Ethernet network with a switch best fits the requirements of quick, easy, and cheap. In fact, many Ethernet networking do-it-yourself packages are now available, such as the Linksys EtherFast 10/100 Network in a Box (www.linksys.com), which sells for around $50 online; it features two network cards, all the cabling that you need, and a five-port switch. (More on switches later in the chapter.)

Shopping for an Ethernet kit? It should include most of the required hardware and software, but note that many of these packages still require you to buy your own cable and connectors. On the positive side, they can be installed by mere mortals (or a brand-new techno-wiz like you). If the PCs you want to connect already have built-in 10/100 network hardware, you don't need a kit — just a switch and cables.

Selecting a network operating system

If you're familiar with networking under Windows XP, you already know that you can use the built-in Ethernet networking support offered in both Windows XP and Windows 2003 Server.

As I discuss in Appendix A, Windows 2003 Server and its older sibling, Windows 2000, have become the operating systems of choice for larger networks that use a server. For peer-to-peer networking in the home or a small office, Windows XP is a better choice than UNIX and Linux; UNIX and its progeny work best as servers, and UNIX is more difficult to set up and maintain than Windows XP.

Collecting What You Need for an Ethernet Network

As you can tell, I like the "everything's included" approach, and I always recommend a networking kit for those setting out on the Ethernet voyage for the first time. However, if you're buying your network supplies from different places or you've scavenged an adapter card or two, you need to make sure that you have the proper hardware. Here's a quick checklist of what you need:

✔ **Network interface cards:** You need a network interface card (NIC) for each computer that you plan to connect to your network. I discuss these cards in the next section. (If the PCs on your network use motherboards with integrated NIC hardware, you won't need separate cards, and you have my admiration.)

✔ **Cabling:** Today's Ethernet networks use *twisted-pair cable,* which resembles telephone wire. This option is usually chosen for a home network and is far more popular today than coaxial cabling (although coax is still often used in networks installed within the walls of a home or an office). Twisted-pair cable has a connector (an RJ-45) that looks very much like a telephone wire, as you can see in Figure 12-2. With twisted-pair cabling, each computer is connected to the switch. Figure 12-3 shows a typical twisted-pair star Ethernet configuration.

Figure 12-2:
A twisted-pair cable and connector, ready to rock.

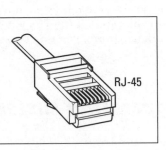

RJ-45

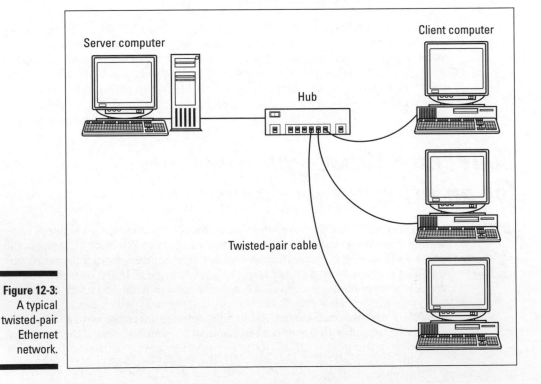

Figure 12-3:
A typical twisted-pair Ethernet network.

You *can* connect two computers using twisted-pair cable without using a switch, but three or more computers on a twisted-pair network require a switch. If you're connecting just two computers for multiplayer games, file transfers, or printer sharing, ask your local computer store for a *twisted-pair crossover cable*.

✔ **Software:** If you're running any flavor of Windows 98 or later, the software that you need for a peer-to-peer network is built in. (Thanks, Microsoft!)

✔ **Switch:** A switch makes the maintenance and upgrading of your network much easier because all your network computers are connected to a single box. As I stated earlier, a switch also provides the best performance and highest efficiency for an Ethernet network — it's A Good Thing indeed.

More stuff about network interface cards

As I mentioned earlier, if your motherboard has network hardware built-in, you can skip this section with a smile.

The most expensive part of an Ethernet network is the network interface card required for each computer. A typical network card uses a PCI slot — or, if your motherboard includes integrated Ethernet networking hardware, you can save that slot and avoid buying a separate network card.

Like every other adapter and part you can stick in your PC, some cards cost more than others. The following checklist tells you what important features are offered by a good network card:

✔ **Light emitting diode (LED) status lights:** The status lights on a network adapter card help determine what's gone wrong if you experience problems. For example, a green light usually indicates that the adapter is correctly receiving a broadcast signal from the cable.

✔ **Certified:** How can you tell whether the network interface card that you've chosen will work with your flavor of Windows? Look for interface cards carrying the manufacturer's certification that the card works with your chosen network software. The certification process involves testing by both the software manufacturer and the card manufacturer, ensuring that the card performs without problems. Most certified network cards advertise their compatibility, but if you need reassurance, you can always check with the card manufacturer.

✔ **Automatic or software configuration:** No one wants to bother with setting jumpers to configure a network card. The best network cards automatically configure themselves after you've connected them to your network.

✔ **Full driver support:** Check the manufacturer's Web site or technical support department to make sure that the card comes with the necessary drivers for your operating system. Those drivers should also be available for multiple operating systems because you never know when you might have to hook a computer running Linux to your network.

More stuff about cables and connections

Installing the cables and connecting everything is the most time-consuming chore involved in setting up a traditional cabled Ethernet network. Keep these guidelines in mind when you shop for cables and connectors (and also while you crawl around under desks):

✔ **Making cables is no picnic:** I can't stress this enough, so it's Mark's Maxim time.

Unless you've created your own network cables before, buy them ready-made!

Building your own cables from scratch is roughly akin to crafting a grand piano from a bowl of jelly — with a pair of chopsticks. I'm not going to discuss how to create cables in this chapter: a number of different varieties are available, each of which is rated to handle specific network speeds. It's much easier to walk into your computer store or call your favorite mail-order outlet and ask for a premade network cable (sometimes called a *patch cable*). Ready-made cables come in several standard lengths and already have the connectors on both ends, too. You don't waste time or money trying to learn how to cut cable, and you can be sure that the cable works.

✔ **Always buy extra cable:** No matter how well you plan your network and how closely you measure the distance between your computers, something's going to come up that demands more cable or more connectors. Buy cables at least a foot longer than you *think* you need.

✔ **Get help:** Enlist the aid of someone to hand you things, prepare cable, and listen to your epithets.

✔ **Just Say No to exposed cable:** Although running cable behind a desk or along the baseboards docs work, avoid exposed cable whenever possible. You'd be amazed at how clumsy people can be (even if you've taped your cable under a rug) as well as how a cat's gnawing teeth can lead to lost data and a lost network connection.

If your cable has to cross a hallway or corridor and your building uses a suspended ceiling, you might try routing the cable above the ceiling tiles. For a solid ceiling, the molding used by electricians to cover exposed cables works well.

There Are Always Exceptions!

After you become familiar with the virtues and requirements of a traditional star Ethernet network using twisted-pair cable, guess what? You can toss all that to the four winds! What if I told you that I can install a network without running a single piece of Ethernet cable or a pesky network interface card?

It's true: Thanks to the arrival of four alternative network technologies, you're no longer tied down to your grandfather's LAN, and these technologies work with any network software that uses a standard Ethernet connection. All four are compatible with Windows XP and Windows 2003 Server, too.

However (isn't there always a *however* whenever it comes to computers?), these new networks also have their own limitations, so let's take a look at all four. After you've finished this section, you can decide whether to stick with the tried-and-true twisted-pair cable Ethernet network or whether to strike out on your own with a new breed of home network.

Use your telephone wiring

Alexander Graham Bell would have never conceived that his invention could carry network packets, too. (Of course, he had very little training in computer hardware.) With a home phoneline network (HomePNA for short, at www.homepna.org), your Ethernet hardware uses existing telephone wiring in your home or office to transmit network data packets. To connect a new PC to the network, you install a special network interface card, locate the nearest telephone jack, and (snap!) plug in a cable. The jack can be located anywhere within your home.

Unlike a dial-up connection to the Internet through your modem — which rudely claims your telephone line and presents a busy signal to the world — a HomePNA network allows you to use your telephone normally for answering and dialing voice calls.

On the downside, a HomePNA network is slower than a standard cabled Ethernet connection, although it should be fast enough for multiplayer gaming and sharing an Internet connection. Most cabled Ethernet networks run at 100 Mbps (and some expensive hardware can reach 1000 Mbps), but current HomePNA networking hardware is limited to about 10 Mbps. Also, the hardware is a bit more expensive than a typical Ethernet kit, running approximately $100 for a two-PC HomePNA kit. You should also consider how many telephone jacks are spread throughout your house. Because most homes have only a handful, you're somewhat limited with this option.

Use your AC wiring

Come to think of it, there's another network of wiring within the typical house — but can AC current and computer data coexist? You bet! You simply plug a *powerline* adapter plug (which acts as a network card) into any AC wall socket in your home and connect the other end of the cable to your computer's network interface card (or USB port). You probably have an AC outlet in just about every room of your home, so this system is a little more adaptable than a HomePNA network.

As you might expect, speed and cost are again the issues: A powerline network is somewhat slower than a home phoneline system, and it's much more expensive than a basic twisted-pair Ethernet kit. I'd recommend this option for those who want only basic file and printer sharing because it's not really fast enough for multiplayer gaming or for sharing a DSL or cable Internet connection.

Use your USB port

If you don't mind cabling things together, the USB port — the jack-of-all-trades of the PC world — can act as a network portal for your computers. Like a powerline network, this option doesn't require network cards, and you don't have to remove the case on your computer. One end of each cable connects to the USB port on each PC in your network, and the other end of each cable connects to a black box called a *USB hub*. The hub both connects the cables and — surprise — acts as a switch in a traditional Ethernet network.

A USB network is about the same price as a standard Ethernet network kit, so it's cheaper than a home phoneline or powerline network. At 10 Mbps, it's also faster than a home phoneline network but far slower than a full-fledged twisted-pair 100 Mbps Ethernet network.

Unfortunately, the downside for a USB network is tied to the length of the cable. There can be a maximum of only 10 meters between computers on a USB network — which, coincidentally, is also the maximum length of a standard USB cable. Anything longer, and your network signal fades between computers. Of course, this isn't a problem if all your computers are in the same room, but I don't think that the Brady Bunch will be using a USB network.

Go wireless

If you eschew any type of wiring, hop on board the wireless Ethernet bandwagon! For this option, each PC in your network needs a wireless network adapter card (or built-in integrated wireless hardware). You also need a stand-alone piece of hardware called a *wireless base station* or *wireless access point,* which acts as the switch of your network, transmitting and receiving data from the computers. The two common wireless networking standards to choose from follow:

✔ **802.11b:** This is the most common wireless standard, more popularly called *Wi-Fi.* It can reach about 10 Mbps, and the signal can be received up to 75 to 100 feet away, depending on the intervening walls and any electrical devices such as cordless phones and microwave ovens that might interfere with the signal. 802.11b hardware should be good enough for sharing a broadband Internet connection wirelessly.

✔ **802.11g:** Don't ask me who decided on the name, but 802.11g is much faster, allowing maximum connection speeds around 54 Mbps. (802.11g hardware is much more expensive than 802.11b stuff. Go figure.) Anyway, this new faster standard is backward compatible with any "antique" 802.11b hardware that you might pick up. 802.11g is a better choice than 802.11b for network applications that demand faster data transfer, such as copying and moving large files of 250MB or more between your laptop and your home network or for playing today's latest network games. (Just to be confusing, many folks call this faster standard "Wi-Fi" as well. Go figure.)

Okay, okay. There's one more (albeit "orphaned") wireless standard on the market: 802.11a, which also does 54 Mbps. However, I strongly recommend that you give 802.11a the widest berth possible because it's not backward compatible with 802.11b, and PC manufacturers are already dismissing it in favor of 802.11g. Remember, *g* is better than *a!* (Don't you just love engineers?)

Both Windows XP and Windows 2003 Server can handle wireless connections with aplomb, maintaining the proper security so that your next-door neighbors don't use your Internet connection for free.

For a comprehensive look at wireless connectivity in your home, check out *Wireless Home Networking For Dummies,* by Danny Briere, Walter Bruce, and Pat Hurley (Wiley)

Installing Your Network Interface Card

Ready to install your first PCI network interface adapter? Make sure that every computer on your network that needs a network card has at least one PCI slot open. Follow these steps:

1. **Just finished polishing the silverware? Touch a metal surface before you install your card to discharge any static electricity on your body.**

2. **If your computer chassis is plugged in, unplug it.**

3. **Remove the cover from your case.**

4. **Select an open card slot for your network card; then remove the screw and the metal slot cover adjacent to the selected slot.**

5. **Line up the connector on the card with the slot on the motherboard.**

   The card's metal bracket should align with the open space left when you removed the slot cover.

6. **Apply even pressure to the top of the card and push it into the slot.**

   The bracket should be resting tightly against the case.

7. **Add the screw and tighten down the bracket.**

8. **Connect the network cable to the corresponding port on the card.**

   Your adapter card manual can help you locate the network cable connector on your card.

9. **Install the network adapter card driver software.**

   Check your card's manual for information on how to load the driver software for your particular operating system.

Connecting a Twisted-Pair Cable

If you've ever plugged a telephone cord into a wall or a modem, you've probably performed a twisted-pair connection before:

1. **Push the male connector into the female connector until it clicks.**

   The connectors fit only one way. Figure 12-4 illustrates the connection. The connection is the same for both cable-to-switch and cable-to-network cards.

2. **There is no Step 2.**

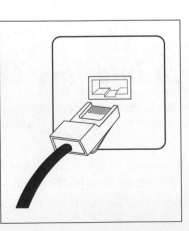

Figure 12-4:
Folks, it doesn't get any easier than connecting a twisted-pair cable.

Turning Things On

After you install the network adapter cards in all your computers and connect your cables, all that remains to get things running is to install the driver software on each computer and "flip the networking switch" inside Windows XP.

The exact steps and the order to follow in the network driver installation process vary according to the version of the software, the operating system on the computer, and the options that you select. Therefore, the generic steps coming up might not match what you see onscreen. Luckily, the card's installation program should display complete instructions, so you should always follow the onscreen directions when things vary.

To install the software, follow these steps:

1. **If you've unplugged your computer, plug it back in now.**

2. **Connect the keyboard and monitor (if you haven't already done so) and push the power switch on your monitor.**

3. **Turn on your computer by pushing the power switch and then allow your computer to boot.**

4. **Run the driver installation software provided by your network adapter card manufacturer.**

   Insert the install software into your CD-ROM or floppy drive and follow the onscreen instructions. You'll likely have to provide an identifying name for this PC on your network.

5. **Allow the installation program to reboot your computer. Watch the network start-up messages and write down any error messages that appear.**

   These error messages and possible solutions should be listed in the card's manual.

After you install the drivers on the PC, you can use the Windows XP New Connection Wizard to automatically configure the computer as a good network citizen. To run the wizard, choose Start➪All Programs➪Accessories➪ Communications➪New Connection Wizard, which displays the dialog box that you see in Figure 12-5.

Figure 12-5:
The
Windows
XP New
Connection
Wizard
helps
maintain
your sanity.

Follow the wizard's prompts (which appear as a series of honest-to-goodness, understandable English questions), and Windows XP will configure itself for you. (If you feel the urge to hug Bill Gates afterwards, that's normal.)

Chapter 13

Life in the Fast Lane with Broadband

*B*roadband Internet connections represent a dream come true for telecommuters and Internet junkies. Imagine transferring data over existing telephone lines with throughput anywhere from 640 Kbps to 8 Mbps. Think about smooth, real-time videoconferencing that doesn't look like a bad silent movie from the 1920s. Picture an Internet connection that lets you receive a Web page and talk to someone on the telephone simultaneously. Huzzah! You just *have* to have a broadband connection, right?

As my favorite Western star, John Wayne, used to drawl, "Hold on there, pard-ner." Yes, you can do all that with broadband (think *high-speed Internet,* as compared with an old-fashioned analog dial-up modem). But a high-speed broadband connection, like digital subscriber line (DSL) or a cable Internet connection, definitely isn't for everyone, although many techno-nerds want you to believe that. (After all, if broadband were *that* essential, everyone would already have it, like a toothbrush or a pair of cheap sunglasses.)

In this chapter, I cover all the advantages *and* disadvantages of broadband, such as its expensive hardware and higher subscription rates compared to a dial-up connection. In fact, DSL and cable access are still not available in some areas of the United States, and the rate that your telephone or cable company charges for access might be outrageous.

In short, I present you with a fair and honest picture of your high-speed Internet options. You can decide for yourself whether you just have to have broadband.

Figuring Out Whether You Need Broadband

Before you go any further in this chapter, you should decide whether you need a broadband connection to the Internet. For example, there's no reason to even consider the expenses involved in cable or DSL if all you do is connect to the Internet for a few minutes a day to check your e-mail. Of course, you don't have to meet any certain criteria to add a broadband Internet connection to your system, but it really isn't cost effective to use it for only a few minutes a day.

Choosing cable or DSL could be a winning proposition if you fit one of these descriptions:

✔ **Internet junkie:** I'm talking heavy-duty Web surfing here — at least three or four hours a day of Internet access. If your primary activities on the Internet are file transfers using file transfer protocol (FTP) or Web surfing, a broadband connection will be great for you. However, if you use the Internet for only an hour a day — or if your primary Internet applications are e-mail, newsgroups, instant messaging, or Telnet — I recommend sticking with a 56 Kbps analog modem. (See Chapter 10 for more about modems.)

✔ **Telecommuter:** If you need high-speed access to your office network from your home, DSL is a good choice. You can connect to the network at your office and log on normally, just as though you were sitting at a computer at work. (Take my word for it: If you work from a home office using your computer, broadband is a must-have. Heck, perhaps your employer will pay for it.)

✔ **Conferencing wizard:** A broadband connection is practically a requirement for high-quality videoconferencing, such as over a local area network connection or over the Internet. If you've tried conferencing over an analog modem, you'll be amazed at the difference. Broadband provides the fast data-transfer rates for audio and a larger screen as well.

✔ **Multimedia lover:** Looking for the best sound from Internet radio stations? Do you crave online music downloading from services such as Apple's iTunes Music Store? Or perhaps you love to download those trailers for upcoming movies? Then sign up for broadband because a dial-up connection just won't cut it.

What about ISDN?

Integrated Services Digital Network (ISDN) is certainly a name chock-full of healthy buzzwords, but the important piece of the name is the *digital* part. (For those of us who have been running bulletin board systems and using the Internet long before it became fashionable, the abbreviation has subtly changed. If you've been waiting for the arrival of digital networks for several years now, like I have, ISDN has come to mean *It Still Does Nothing*.) ISDN was the first arrival on the high-speed Internet scene, and we all know what happens to the first generation of just about any technology, right?

Although an ISDN connection is similar to a DSL connection in some ways — for example, ISDN uses the same physical telephone line as your traditional analog connection, like DSL —

I heartily recommend that you give ISDN the cold shoulder for three big reasons. First, ISDN is considerably slower than DSL, which cuts down on the *broad* in *broadband*. Second, ISDN isn't an always-on connection like DSL. Heck, you actually have to *dial* the ISDN number to reach your ISP, just like you would with a standard dial-up connection using a modem! (How *mundane.*) Third, ISDN is virtually extinct now because of the popularity and convenience of DSL service. In other words, it's the first big loser in the broadband technology wars.

Actually, make that four big reasons because ISDN is much harder to install and configure than a DSL connection, and the equipment necessary to add an ISDN connection is more expensive, too.

Comparing Communications Technologies

For many years, people wondered whether 28.8 Kbps was the fastest transfer rate that could be squeezed out of an analog modem over a typical telephone connection. (You get the gist in Figure 13-1.) Notice that I said *typical*. Because a crystal-clear analog modem connection is a rare jewel indeed, it pays to remember that analog lines are probably only 85 percent noise-free. Modem manufacturers then squeezed a little harder, and lo and behold, suddenly the top possible transfer rate was 33.6 Kbps. Everyone shook their heads with finality and said, "Surely that must be the fastest possible speed!"

Figure 13-1:
A slow, tired analog signal.

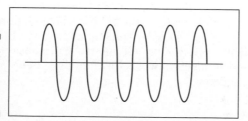

Nope. Modem manufacturers have again proved the techno-types wrong. The v.90 and v.92 international standards now provide a top data-transfer rate of 56 Kbps (with compression). Will these faster dial-up speeds forestall the eventual doom of the dial-up analog connection?

The answer is "Definitely not!" If you fit the mold of the typical broadband customer that I outlined previously, the advantages of DSL or cable far outweigh the money that you save with a simple analog modem connection. The nearly perfect quality of the DSL line means virtually no interference. Both cable and DSL will still be superior in raw throughput.

Analog dial-up technology just can't keep up. You'll need a nearly perfect analog v.92 connection to get anywhere near the top throughput of 56 Kbps on an analog modem, and that just doesn't happen often in the real world. (You'll more likely end up with anywhere between 36 Kbps and 43.2 Kbps throughput.) Your throughput will vary from call to call. (For more information on high-speed modems and their mating habits, jump to Chapter 10. I'll wait for you here.)

On the other hand, Figure 13-2 illustrates a *digital* signal, which is basically a long string of zeros and ones, or on and off states (the same digital vocabulary spoken by your computer and your audio CD player). That means no interference and approximately the same connection throughput at all times. Plus, most cable and DSL systems remain connected to the ISP (and therefore the Internet) at all times, so you need never listen to those screeching dial tones again.

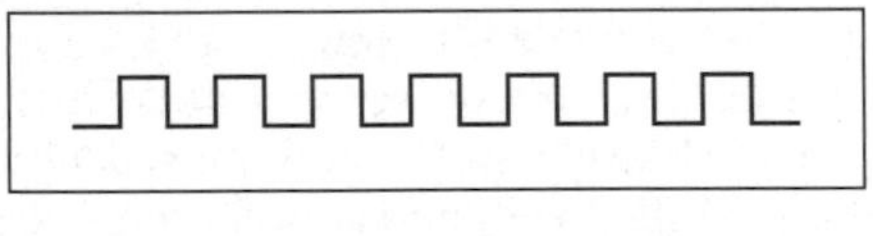

Figure 13-2:
A spunky digital signal, full of vim and vigor.

However, a 56 Kbps analog modem connection will have an effect on the popularity of broadband for some time to come. The higher cost of a broadband connection, the higher ISP subscription prices, and the extra hassle involved with setting up a broadband connection will keep millions of people satisfied with a high-speed analog modem.

"So, Mark, what's the difference between DSL and cable connections? And what other higher-speed connection options do I have?" I'm glad you asked!

- ✔ **Cable modems:** With a cable modem and an enhanced cable network (which must be capable of two-way communications), your cable company suddenly becomes an ISP and can supply you with a digital Internet connection of 500 Kbps or faster. Cable modem service is now available to most cable subscribers. With the nearly universal access of cable, this type of broadband connection could well turn out to be the long-awaited, high-speed connection for the common person. (Unfortunately, a cable modem connection forces you to share bandwidth with all the other cable Internet subscribers in your area. Therefore, your top speed depends on the time of day and the current number of connections to your cable provider.)

    Cable service has other advantages: A high-speed cable modem connection doesn't interfere with your cable TV service. And if your house is already wired for cable TV, it's a cinch to expand that service to a cable modem. Your telephone suddenly reverts to the job it had originally: handling voice (and sometimes fax) calls, blissfully free of busy signals and modem noise! Finally, your cable Internet service is always on.

    Most cable Internet providers include a cable modem as part of their service. This "black box" looks like a regular analog modem, but it connects to your coax cable on one end and to a network card installed in your computer on the other. If your computer doesn't have a network interface card installed already, your cable company will probably provide one and install it as well.

- ✔ **DSL:** Like cable modems, DSL was once another "could be big in just a year or so" technology. Like cable Internet access, it was about as available as sunshine in Carlsbad Caverns. Recently, however, DSL has become a power player as local telephone companies expand and improve their DSL coverage, with top speeds around 4 to 10 Mbps for received data (depending on the flavor of DSL being installed) and as much as 2 Mbps for transmitted data.

    Like its ancestor ISDN, DSL uses a digital signal, and it works over the standard copper telephone line in your home, so all you need is — you guessed it — a DSL modem (which is usually supplied by your local phone company) and a network interface card for your computer. (Depending on the service that you receive, you might also need a splitter to separate the regular phone signal from the higher-frequency DSL signal.) Like a cable modem connection, most DSL connections are always on, so you don't have to dial your ISP, and you can use your voice telephone and place regular calls at the same time you're connected to the Internet! Most DSL connections require you to have an Ethernet network card in your PC, but some ISPs offer USB DSL modems for computers without a network port.

Do you want a WAN?

If you've installed an Ethernet network, you can use your broadband Internet connection to create a WAN (a ridiculous sounding acronym that stands for *wide area network*). This procedure is one method of tying together more than one network; you connect the two networks through your Internet connection using virtual private networking (VPN). Suddenly your home network can become a part of your office network — share the same files and access the same e-mail server with aplomb! Creating a WAN is no easy matter, and there are security concerns (such as hackers trying to access your network through the Internet), so it's best to seek professional help in tying your home network to an outside network.

Whether you can obtain DSL service also depends on your distance from the telephone switch. In most areas, your home or office can't be farther than 18,000 feet from a switch or local cable loop that supports DSL, so it's nigh impossible to obtain DSL service in your mountain cabin.

✔ **Multilink modems:** A *multilink* analog connection using two telephone lines and a special modem can deliver data at up to 112 Kbps. Modem manufacturers such as 3Com are offering "doubling" modems. A bonded analog connection uses standard telephone lines (which are nowhere near perfect), so don't expect 112 Kbps with every connection. Windows XP and Windows 2003 Server Edition provide support for multilink connections. I wouldn't recommend a multilink analog connection unless you simply can't get faster Internet access in some other way; the hassle of two telephone lines for a relatively small increase in speed just doesn't compare with cable or DSL.

✔ **Satellite Internet connections:** In Chapter 15, I discuss satellite Internet connections in detail. They're fast, but they usually require you to continue to use your analog modem connection — and most Internet junkies don't want anything to do with those "antique" 56K analog modems anymore. However, if you can spend the money, you can get a *two-way* satellite Internet connection that doesn't require a phone line or modem — and that might be the only viable alternative for that mountain cabin I keep mentioning.

Figuring Out Those Connection Charges

The biggest expense in going broadband isn't the hardware that you add to your computer, which is usually covered by your cable or DSL provider as part of your subscription. Rather, it's the installation charges and monthly access fees levied by your local telephone company.

Installation charges for a broadband connection differ widely across the globe, and every local telephone and cable company has a different pricing plan. Some telephone companies make it as easy to install a DSL line as a standard analog line. They offer telephone ordering for DSL service and Web sites with helpful instructions; some will even charge a flat monthly rate. Other telephone companies offer no presale help for DSL users (forget the Web site) and charge an hourly rate that will leave you pounding your head against a wall when the bill comes in. It all depends on where you live.

The important thing to remember is that you need full support from your telephone or cable company before you begin your broadband quest. Installing a cable modem is not a fun project that you can do yourself, and DSL connections are usually installed professionally, so I won't go into the setup or configuration of a broadband connection here. (In fact, it's important to note that you can't follow the same procedure that you would use to set up a dial-up Internet connection because DSL and cable Internet subscribers are effectively connecting through a local area network. They don't dial to connect to the ISP.)

What's an average rate for broadband service? Installation costs an average of $25 to $50, although you might get free installation if you're on the ball. Monthly broadband ISP charges typically range from $35 to $50.

Locating an Internet Service Provider

After you decide to go broadband, you have another bridge to cross: You need to find an ISP that offers the service that you want. (From this angle, broadband callers are no different from callers using analog modems. You still must have an ISP to link you to the Internet.)

You might be limited to only one ISP for your cable or DSL connection: namely, your cable company or local telephone company. However, some larger cities offer more than one choice for your broadband provider. Here's a quick checklist of possible sources for local ISP information:

- **Your telephone book:** Like any other business, the Yellow Pages likely lists the ISPs in your area.
- **Friends, relatives, and neighbors:** Ask those around you for the name of their ISP. You can also find out whether they're satisfied with the quality of service that they receive from their ISP (and whether their connection slows down during peak hours).

✔ **Local computer stores:** Computer stores are always a good source of information.

✔ **Computer club or user groups:** You'll get a chorus of possibilities from club members.

✔ **Local bulletin board systems:** If you're already calling a local bulletin board system (BBS), leave a message addressed to everyone about their ISP recommendations or ask the BBS sysop (*system ope*rator).

Use the Net to find an ISP

Do you already have Internet access ... perhaps at work? If so, check out ISPs.com at (you guessed it) www.isps.com. This Web site has information and links to thousands of ISPs in the United States, Canada, and around the world (so that even you readers in Djibouti or Liechtenstein can find an ISP easily). Use these resources to find out which ISPs in your area offer DSL, what type of 56K modem standard they support (see Chapter 10), and what the ISP charges for broadband installation and monthly access.

Chapter 14

Input and Output: Scanners, Cameras, Video Capture, and Printers

*1*f you have lots of artistic talent, your computer can be a wonderfully cre-ative tool. Just ask anyone who makes a living as a computer desktop pub-lisher, graphics designer, or 3-D rendering wizard. With the help of today's powerful software, you can use a computer to produce a convincing image of an oil painting or create a fleet of 3-D spaceships so real that you'd swear that they really exist.

But what if you're like me? I learned long ago that I failed finger painting in first grade for good reason — I can't draw even a stick figure. Thanks to today's scanners and video capture devices, though, anyone can convert a kid's drawing, a photo of a ball team, or a small business logo into a digital image. (And don't forget that you can print your digital images with an inkjet or a laser printer.) You can even use a digital camera to snap your own origi-nal digital images or use a Webcam to record digital video.

Although these peripherals aren't requirements for assembling a PC, they *are* requirements for joining the world of digital photography and digital video — and just try creating a hard copy of your resume without a printer! Therefore, consider yourself warned: You'll likely be choosing up at least one or two of these toys within a few months after you've finished building your computer!

The Wide, Wonderful World of Scanners

Are you looking for images to add to your desktop-publishing project or your personal Web page? If you're searching for graphics and you're not having much luck, cheer up — you're probably sitting in the middle of a gold mine. With the help of a *scanner,* which converts a printed page to a digital image, you can digitize graphics from books, magazines, cereal boxes, CD covers, your children's doodlings, and even the daily newspaper. Anything that you can legally copy (and lay flat) is fair game for scanning. I write more about copyrights in the sidebar "The lazy person's guide to copyrights," elsewhere in this chapter.

A decade ago, a top-quality, high-resolution color scanner would set you back at least $1000, but today (thanks to the wonders of modern manufacturing, good clean living, and the worldwide popularity of digital scanning), a color scanner with the same specifications will cost you less than $200, making it an affordable addition to your PC. In this section, I discuss the various types of scanners on the market and what you should look for while shopping.

For a comprehensive look at scanners (including basic image editing, maintenance, troubleshooting, and a huge repository of scanning tips and tricks), I invite you to pick up a copy of another of my books, the bestselling *Scanners For Dummies,* 2nd Edition (Wiley).

Recognizing scanners in the wild

Scanners come in four flavors these days:

✔ **Flatbed scanner:** "Yessir, this here's your Cad-ee-lac of scanners. Ain't she a beaut?" In fact, the flatbed scanner looks more like a copy machine than a luxury car. But now that flatbed models have dropped so dramatically in price, they're the clear choice for most shoppers. The large scanning area of a flatbed enables you to spread out an entire magazine or a book page. Flatbed scanners typically offer higher resolutions and better color depth than sheetfed scanners (which I discuss in the following bullet). Even 8 x 10 glossy photographs are no problem. In other words, images scanned on a flatbed scanner offer greater detail and more true-to-life colors. The Hewlett-Packard Scanjet (www.hp.com) and the Microtek ScanMaker series (www.microtek.com) are two well-respected models of flatbed scanners.

Figure 14-1 shows a typical flatbed scanner. Older flatbed scanners typically used a small computer system interface (SCSI), which (at the time) provided the fastest possible scanning speed. Most late-model flatbed scanners now use a USB (universal serial bus), SCSI, or FireWire connection. If your PC has USB connectors, a USB scanner is the easiest route for connecting a scanner. And, coincidentally, I discuss these ports in Chapter 5.

A flatbed scanner is your best choice!

✔ **Sheetfed scanner:** A typical sheetfed scanner looks similar to a fax machine and takes up less space on your desk (as shown in Figure 14-2).

With a sheetfed scanner, you feed in letter- or legal-size sheets of paper, which the scanner draws in automatically. Unfortunately, this process limits sheetfed scanners to source material no larger than a sheet of paper. And unlike with a flatbed scanner, you have to tear a page out of a book or magazine (or photocopy the page first) to scan it. Also, if your source image is smaller than a page, you might need to tape the image to a sheet of paper for the sheet feeder to pull the image in. (You can also use a clear plastic sleeve to hold smaller items for scanning.)

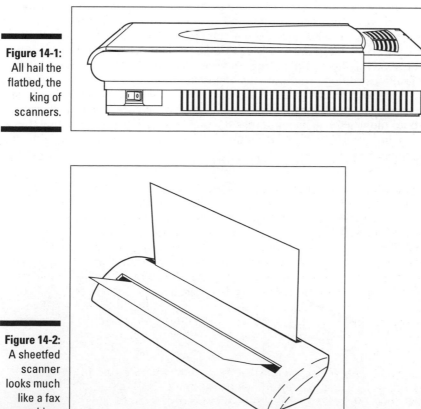

Figure 14-1:
All hail the flatbed, the king of scanners.

Figure 14-2:
A sheetfed scanner looks much like a fax machine.

✔ **Photo scanner:** Photo scanners are a relatively new breed of image scanner. They're available as external USB peripherals that you can carry with your laptop. These scanners scan individual pictures (or even small printed items, such as business cards or a driver's license). Most people use photo scanners to digitize prints that they've taken with a regular film camera. Because a photo scanner can't accept any original wider than a photograph, however, the size of the material that you can scan with one of these devices is limited. (Photo scanners should not be confused with *negative/slide scanners*, which are mondo expensive; they produce incredibly high-resolution scans of film negatives and slides.)

On the other hand, photo scanners are automatic and fun to use — just feed the picture in and the scanner slowly spits the picture back out as it reads the image. Photo scanners generally offer the same scan quality as a sheetfed scanner, and they run on any PC with a USB connection. Unless you're sure that your scanning needs will be limited to film prints, consider a flatbed scanner, which is far more versatile.

✔ **Handheld scanner:** In olden times, when flatbed scanners were too expensive for most computer owners, handheld scanners were the cheap alternative. To use one, you run the scanner across the material that you want to scan. A handheld scanner can read a strip only about four inches across, so if your source graphic is larger than that, you need to scan the entire picture in multiple strips and then "paste" the strips together using a graphics editing program. This *almost* sounds like fun, but in real life, most people I know with handheld scanners have never been able to successfully merge strips together. Plus, if you're not careful and deliberate about moving the scanner across the picture, you end up distorting the scan and have to start over. Figure 14-3 shows a traditional handheld scanner.

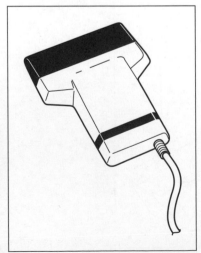

Figure 14-3:
A typical
handheld
scanner —
do *not* buy
this object.

The pen is mightier than the handheld

Unlike an antique handheld scanner, a pen scanner like the Logitech io 2 digital pen (www.logitech.com) is a cutting-edge piece of technology: In real time, the io 2 can scan handwritten notes and sketches while you write and draw. The io 2 is also great for those who enter appointments and action items into Microsoft Outlook because the pen scanner records them while you're writing them down — and then you can automatically import your new data into Outlook! At about $200, the io 2 is an easy investment to make, but there is one downside: You have to buy a special type of paper to use the pen, as well as custom paper inserts for things such as your Day Planner.

Because of their low resolution and all the hassle (and the fact that flatbed scanners are so much more affordable today), handheld scanners are antiques. Give 'em a wide berth.

Diving into color depth

Most scanners advertise 24-, 36- or 48-bit color, which is a measure of how many colors that a scanner can record in the electronic version of an image. Color depth is important because you want the electronic image to include the full range of colors found in the original. For example, if you're creating a Web site featuring famous paintings, you would probably rather offer images with 16.7 million colors (which is about the maximum that the human eye can discern) than 16 colors (which would produce masterpieces that resemble paint-by-number pictures).

Any scanner on the market these days will be capable of a minimum of 24-bit color. If a scanner is advertised as *true color,* it's probably a 24-bit model. A 30-bit scanner can record images in as many as 11 billion colors, and a 36-bit scanner can deliver more than 68.7 billion colors.

This same 24-bit color figure comes up again when computer folks discuss their video adapters. In the world of video adapters, 24-bit color is equivalent to the 16.7 million colors that a modern video adapter card can display on a super video graphics array (SVGA) monitor. (You can find more about video adapter cards and monitors in Chapter 6.)

Please pass the image

Another feature that you should look for in a color scanner is single-pass scanning. A *single-pass* scanner makes only one scanning trip across the source material and captures the entire image at one time. On the other hand, you can still find a handful of *triple-pass* scanners, which must make three trips to scan the same image. If the scanner must make three passes, you introduce three disadvantages:

- ✔ **Shaky scan:** There's more chance for a slight movement in the original material, which can cause distortion in the final image. Any movement of the scanner (even a tiny bump) can affect the image. Of course, closing the cover on your scanner helps, but if you're scanning a book or something that's not completely flat, it's hard to keep your material perfectly motionless. (For this reason, never scan material while on a Ferris wheel or any other moving surface.)

- ✔ **Boring:** A triple-pass scanner typically takes three times as long to scan an image.

- ✔ **Memory drag:** A triple-pass scanner must store three separate images and combine them by using software, which usually means that your computer will need more memory and more temporary hard drive space to produce the final image.

For these reasons, pick up a single-pass scanner. Trust me.

Resolving the right resolution

Many people tend to base their purchase of a scanner solely on the advertised resolution (usually in *dpi,* short for dots per inch). The higher the resolution, the better the quality of your scanned image. Most scanners available to normal human beings like you and me have these standard raw (or *optical*) resolutions:

- ✔ **600 x 600:** Appropriate for the kids and their school projects

- ✔ **1200 x 1200:** Good for scanning snapshots and photographs from books or magazines; images for Web sites

- ✔ **2400 x 2400:** The standard resolution for a good-quality scanner

- ✔ **4800 x 4800:** Suitable for graphics artists who need high-resolution detail at a higher price

It's true that the higher the raw resolution, the better the scanner. However, some manufacturers also advertise the interpolated resolution for a particular model. What's the difference between raw and interpolated resolution?

The answer is in the software: The *raw resolution* value is the actual optical resolution at which the scanner reads an image. The *interpolated resolution* (the value of which is always higher) is calculated by the software provided with the scanner. In fact, the interpolated value adds extra dots to the scanned image without reading them from the original material.

Technoids would tell you that the interpolation step uses an *algorithm* (a mathematical formula) to improve the quality of the image. In layman's terms, that's the equivalent of the imaging software inserting new dots by using an intelligent guess — but it's still a guess. (Call me old-fashioned.)

When you're shopping for a scanner, judge it by its optical resolution and forget about the interpolated value. If you don't see the raw or optical resolution in a scanner's advertisement, check with the manufacturer to get that crucial bit of information first . . . before you buy.

Scanners and . . . Mark Twain?

Buying a TWAIN-compatible scanner is a good idea. *TWAIN* is commonly thought to stand for *technology without an interesting name* — at last, a group of techno-types with a sense of humor — but it actually refers to a line from Kipling, "and never the twain shall meet." Anyway, trivia aside, TWAIN is a standard that ensures that your scanner will work with the image-capture software and other graphics applications on your system. If both the hardware and the software are TWAIN compatible, it doesn't matter who manufactured either piece. (Pretty refreshing, eh?)

Figure 14-4 illustrates my favorite TWAIN-compatible, image-editing software, Paint Shop Pro, acquiring an image from my Webcam. I heartily recommend Paint Shop Pro. You can download the shareware version of this great program from www.corel.com.

Because TWAIN compatibility makes such good sense, just about every scanner made today supports TWAIN, although it never hurts to make sure before you buy.

Most scanners come bundled with various software programs, which should include the image-acquisition software that you need for scanning. You might also receive other software, such as an image-editing program, a desktop-publishing application, or an optical character recognition (OCR) program. OCR software can "read" the contents of a printed page that you've scanned and enter the text from the page right into your word processor, just as though you had typed the text yourself. Although OCR technology isn't perfect and you might need to correct some errors, you don't have to manually retype the entire contents of a page into your word processor.

See the sections at the end of this chapter for the lowdown on installing a scanner.

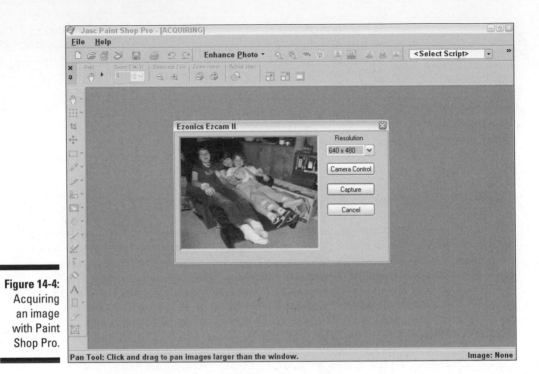

Figure 14-4:
Acquiring
an image
with Paint
Shop Pro.

Digital Camera Details

Until the arrival of digital cameras, getting original photographs into your computer as images was a laborious chore. You had to take the exposed film to your friendly photo lab to get the pictures developed, and then you sat down at your expensive flatbed scanner and slowly digitized each of the finished prints into your computer.

If you need a large number of original digital images and you want to avoid the drudgery of scanning them, look no further than the digital camera. Like scanner technology, the digital camera has been around for some time, but until recently, the typical digital camera was so expensive that you needed a bodyguard to carry one. Prices for digital cameras have now dropped to less than $200 on some models, although the higher-priced models with more features still hover around $500 to $1000 (or more). Popular brands include Casio, Hewlett-Packard, Canon, Nikon, Minolta, Kodak, and Olympus.

You might be wondering where a digital camera stores the pictures and how you "develop" them. The images that you take are stored in *flash RAM,* a form of memory with the neat ability to store information after you turn off the camera. More expensive digital cameras have more flash RAM onboard, so they can store more pictures. (Not every digital camera uses flash RAM.

Some use removable cartridges, others have tiny hard drives, and some models of digital cameras even use standard 1.44MB floppies or mini-CD discs.)

Loading the pictures from a digital camera into your PC couldn't be easier: You simply connect an appropriate cable between the camera and your PC's USB (or FireWire) port, run the camera's software, and the pictures download right from the camera into your computer. (I explain how to add these ports to your computer in Chapter 5.) The cable is usually furnished with the camera.

Figure 14-5 shows an image taken with a typical digital camera (and displayed in Paint Shop Pro). The picture was taken with a Casio digital camera, which stores a maximum of 96 24-bit images. Ignore the strange guy with the vacuum cleaner; I couldn't crop him out of the picture.

Figure 14-5: A very strange person photographed by a digital camera.

Most digital cameras look similar to their film-based cousins (including accessories such as a flash and that useless wrist strap). Point-and-shoot digital cameras are typically just as easy to use as the simple point-and-shoot 35mm film cameras available in any drugstore. Here's a list of features that can help you spot a better digital camera while you're shopping:

✔ **LCD viewfinder:** Now *this* is a feature I really like! An LCD (liquid crystal display) viewfinder can help you see what your picture will look like before you take it. Most digital cameras that offer this feature also let you review your picture immediately after you take it, so you can judge the results immediately and retake the shot if necessary. "Whoops, little Sparky wasn't smiling in that one, was he? We'll just take it again from the top."

✔ **Photo management:** This feature gives you the ability to review and delete your pictures from the camera itself. For example, if you're out in the field taking shots of houses for your real estate company and you suddenly run out of RAM for new pictures, you can flip through your images and delete those that you don't want. Deleting the unwanted images frees up additional RAM, and you're back in business. *Note:* Some older digital cameras require you to hook your camera up to your computer to delete shots, or you have to delete all your pictures at once.

✔ **Removable flash RAM:** Although more expensive cameras have more built-in flash RAM elbow room, the ultimate is a removable flash RAM card system. If you have one of these cameras, you can simply buy another flash RAM card and swap the cards for more storage whenever you need it. The card that you remove stores the images you've already taken until you can get them loaded onto your computer.

✔ **Higher resolution:** Just like a scanner, a digital camera has a resolution rating. In fact, many digital cameras can take pictures at more than one resolution. It's important to remember that the higher the resolution for an image, the more space the image takes in RAM. Therefore, cameras with multiple resolutions give you a choice. (You can have either a smaller number of higher-resolution pictures or a larger number of lower-resolution pictures.)

Unless you spend a fair chunk of change on a digital camera (read that as $500 or more), you're not going to get anywhere near the fine detail of a 35mm film camera (even the cheaper point-and-shoot models). If you need to save money but you still want high-resolution images, you might decide to stick with the tried-and-true method of scanning film prints. In general, a higher-resolution flatbed scanner is still much less expensive than a higher-resolution digital camera. (If you plan on scanning lots of photographs, check out the photo scanner information in the section "Recognizing scanners in the wild," earlier in this chapter.)

✔ **Compression:** Digital cameras can compress your images so that they take less space in memory. These images are similar to the highly compressed JPEG-format images common on the Web. Although you lose some detail when you use compression, it's usually not noticeable. These cameras can pack many more images into their memory, so your "roll" of digital film can carry twice (or even three times) the number of pictures. A camera with variable compression might enable you to turn off compression, too. (If a digital camera saves images in the TIFF format, you'll get better quality, but you'll get fewer images on a memory card because TIFF images are larger.)

✔ **Zoom:** The more expensive digital cameras have the same zoom feature found on standard film cameras. Zoom enables you to magnify your subject for more detail. The higher the optical zoom offered by a camera, the more expensive it usually is.

> ✔ **Special effects:** Many cameras now offer onboard special effects, just like the familiar special effects on a typical video camcorder. Typical effects include automatic color palettes (which give your images a special look, such as sepia tone or pastel) and negative imaging (in which the image looks like a photograph negative).

Digital Video Capture: Its Time Has Come

PCs have the ability to *capture* digital video; that is, you can display synchronized video and audio on your computer (or save it on your hard drive for playback later). With the right hardware, you can record and store video from any source, including a standard camcorder, your VCR, or a PC videocamera (often called a *Webcam*). You can use digital video in numerous practical ways on your computer, including videoconferencing, video clips for the Web, business presentations, and even multimedia programming for games.

Making sure your PC can handle digital video

If you're taking full advantage of an advanced video card, DVD-ROM drive, and the raw power of the Pentium 4 and Athlon CPU families on the market today, you can easily work with digital video on your PC. At the time of this writing, Pentium 4 and AMD Athlon 64 chips are the best choice for digital video. Also, digital video takes up a lot of bytes, so make sure that you have a roomy hard drive to handle all your clips.

At a minimum, your PC needs a Pentium 4 processor — for the AMD crowd, an Athlon 64 processor should do the trick. You'll also need a video card with at least 64MB of RAM, and your PC should have at least 10 gigabytes of free space to handle the digital video files.

Getting other gadgets for digital video

No matter how powerful your processor, your PC can't do digital video all on its own. You need to add other gadgets and software as well so that you can capture the video and then edit it on your PC.

You can use two general methods to capture video clips and still photos on your personal computer:

✔ **Capture new video in digital form:** For this you need a digital video (DV) camcorder or Webcam. Webcams are perfect for videoconferencing, capturing simple video clips, or taking still images of you and the kids — these cameras usually look like a little ball or a small box sporting a camera lens. They sit on top of your monitor and connect to your USB port. (More expensive models connect to your FireWire port; FireWire transfers data at a much faster rate for smoother and better-looking footage.)

✔ **Convert other video sources into digital video:** For this, you need a video capture device that can produce digital video from an analog source. Such a capture device attaches to your computer in many ways; most are internal adapter cards, and others are USB or FireWire based. After you install a capture device, you can plug a VCR, laser disc player, or analog camcorder into it as the source. Like a computer videocamera, a video capture device can capture continuous video clips or just snap still images.

With a video capture device, you can also take all those home movies that you've taped on bulky videocassettes and transfer them to recordable CDs or DVDs. (See Chapter 8 for more about CD and DVD recorders.)

After you capture video, you'll want to edit it. With the recent improvements in hardware speed and video quality, a ton of commercial and shareware video-editing programs are on the market today, such as Adobe Premiere Pro (www.adobe.com). With Premiere, you can add digital effects and WAV-format digital sound to your AVI video clips. Video capture hardware typically comes with bundled software, which might include a video-editing program and a multimedia studio (such as Macromedia Director; www.macromedia.com).

While you're editing video on your newly assembled PC, you'll quickly run head-on into The Big Question: What digital video file format should you use to save your finished classics? The two most popular formats for digital video these days are *AVI* (the Microsoft standard supported in Windows XP and Windows 2000) and *MOV* (the Apple QuickTime format, which originated on the Macintosh but is now available also for the PC). Another popular format that you encounter often on the Web is the *MPEG* standard, which is highly compressed and more suitable than AVI or MOV files for downloading. I prefer MPEG because it's recognized in just about any video-editing application (and MPEG is the standard format for DVD movie discs, too).

Both Windows XP and Windows 2003 Server include support for playing DVDs. (For more about DVD video, check out the DVD discussion in Chapter 8.)

Reducing the size of video clips

After you start using your new PC for digital video, you'll soon realize that even highly compressed digital video can take up a tremendous chunk of hard drive territory. Don't be surprised to see ten seconds of high-quality, high-resolution video occupying 10MB of hard drive space. However, you can adjust a number of settings to reduce the size of a video clip after you've recorded it:

✔ **Color depth:** Of course, video looks best in 24-bit true color, but you can reduce it to 256 colors and thus reduce the size of the file.

✔ **Frame rate:** A *frame* is an individual image, like the single images that make up a roll of movie film. Although a greater number of frames makes for a smoother video, you can reduce the frame rate to shrink the size of the video file.

✔ **Size of the video:** Traditionally, reducing the onscreen size of a video clip has been the solution most people take when working with digital video, which is why video clips were typically three inches square a few years ago. The smaller the onscreen size of the video, the smaller the size of the file.

One Word: Printers, Printers, Printers!

If you ask computer owners what one peripheral gives them the most value and fun for their money, most would probably say a modem or a printer. The printed page is still useful in today's world (at least for now), and the latest inkjet and laser printers can produce everything from T-shirts to transparencies, from greeting cards to stickers, CD and DVD labels, glossy photos, banners, and paper airplanes. Calendars, business cards, coloring books . . . you can see just how useful a printer can be, especially if you have kids.

In this section, I discuss what's available in a printer these days for less than $500 and how you can choose the right model for your needs.

Will that be laser or inkjet?

You have two breeds of computer printer to choose from these days:

✔ **Laser:** A *laser printer* uses heat to bond a fine powder (toner) to the paper to form characters and images. Although laser printers were once very expensive, the technology has dropped in price. Many black-and-white low-end models are now available for around $100; color laser printers hover around $300.

✔ **Inkjet:** An *inkjet printer* shoots ink onto the paper. Inkjet printers (also known as *Bubble Jet printers*) are the most popular personal printers around these days. Inkjets can produce images ranging from standard black text to quality photographs. In fact, inkjet technology is used in high-resolution photo printers and in *multifunction printers* (which combine a fax, copier, and printer in one unit).

✔ **Dot matrix:** A scavenger might encounter a *dot matrix printer,* which creates characters by pushing tiny pins through an ink ribbon (rather like an old-fashioned typewriter). The days when dot matrix was king are behind us. These printers are noisy, prone to jamming, and don't print graphics very well. Plus, they print only in black. However, you can still find dot matrix technology in limited use whenever the job demands forms with multiple carbon copies because inkjet and laser printers can't print carbon copies.

The lazy person's guide to copyrights

Just because you can capture a video clip from a VCR or scan an image from a magazine doesn't mean that you can use it. Be careful when you're choosing material for your documents or your Web site. Although I'm not a lawyer, I can provide you with a few pointers that might steer you clear of original copyrighted material. Keep these guidelines in mind:

✔ **Beware the hidden copyright:** Under current law, copyright is granted immediately upon creation of an original work, and copyrighted text or images can be protected by copyright regardless of whether a copyright notice appears with the material.

✔ **Make sure permission is granted:** You must obtain permission to copy any original copyrighted work, even if the author has previously granted you permission for other work. For example, just because you obtain permission to use one of a series of pictures on your Web page does *not* mean that you can use the entire series of images: You must obtain permission for each individual image.

✔ **The source is important:** Most people think that images they receive from an Internet newsgroup or copy from a Web site can be copied, but it doesn't matter where you obtained the material. If it's copyrighted, sticking the text or image on a newsgroup does not make it *public domain* (intellectual property that's not protected by copyright because it "belongs to the community at large"). You still need permission from the author to use the copyrighted material.

✔ **Alterations mean zip:** Another common misconception is that "If I draw a mustache on this picture of Mr. Spock, it becomes my original work." Altering the original material does not reset or clear the copyright, and you still need permission.

✔ **A change in media means nothing:** If you scan a copyrighted image from an original on paper, the electronic image or document doesn't suddenly become your original work. (If it did, I would have claimed the works of Shakespeare, Edgar Allan Poe, and Mark Twain a long time ago.) You guessed it — the copyright still remains valid, and you need permission from the author to use the material.

✔ **Consult your lawyer:** Above all, if you're uncertain whether you can legally copy something, *ask your lawyer!*

You should look for a number of features if you're shopping for either an inkjet or a laser printer: Your new printer should be able to print legal- and letter-size paper, envelopes, and labels. The bigger the paper capacity, the better. The printer that you select for your system should also be able to handle at least 150 sheets of paper. And any printer that you consider should also come with additional software, such as a printing kit for kids (with software and blank paper) or a business printing kit, as well as the driver software you need for your particular operating system. (See Appendix A for more about operating systems.)

If you're buying a parallel port printer, don't forget to buy a *bidirectional parallel printer cable* at the time you purchase your printer. Printer cables are typically not included with the printer.

Other features are specific to the type of printer, so it's time to examine the advantages of both inkjet and laser printers.

Advantages of inkjet printers

Inkjet printers offer these advantages:

- **Less expensive to buy:** Inkjet printers range from $45 on up, and the least expensive laser printers typically start at about $100. I should note, however, that laser printers produce a better looking black-and-white page for less money than a typical inkjet, and they can handle heavier printing loads. If you're looking for a heavy-duty monochrome printer with good quality for an office, a laser printer ends up costing much less in the long run when it comes to supplies.

- **Cheaper ink:** Ink cartridges for an inkjet printer are somewhat less expensive than a toner cartridge for a color laser printer. You can also refill your used black ink cartridges to save even more.

- **Cost-effective color printing:** Although laser printers also offer color, you can expect to pay at least $500 to a whopping $1000 for a color laser printer (depending on the quality and speed of the output). Most inkjet printers use a *dual-cartridge* system (both cartridges are loaded side by side). One ink cartridge contains black ink, and a separate color ink cartridge contains at least three colors of ink. Some inkjet printers use five or more separate ink cartridges for printing true-color, 24-bit images, which deliver really amazing results. (They can actually match photoprint quality.) However, to get the best results with these special cartridges, you'll need special glossy inkjet paper.

If you crave color on a budget, stick with a more expensive inkjet printer that has a higher resolution of 1440 x 720 or 4800 x 1200. You'll still spend less than $200.

✔ **Higher resolution:** A printer's resolution is measured in dots per inch (dpi). Most laser printers can produce 600 x 600 or 1200 x 1200 dpi resolution, but today's inkjet models under $200 can do much better, at 4800 x 1200 dpi. These printers are better choices for high-resolution graphics.

In general, inkjet printers are better suited to the home or to an office requiring quick color printing.

Advantages of laser printers

Thinking about a laser printer? Laser printers offer these advantages:

✔ **Faster printing:** Laser printers can hit anywhere from 12 to 30 pages per minute, which is faster than an inkjet's average of 8 to 12 pages per minute.

✔ **No smearing:** Because laser printers bond the toner to the paper, your documents are reasonably safe from water. The ink used to print pages on an inkjet printer usually smears if it gets wet.

✔ **True black:** Even a dual-cartridge inkjet printer can't deliver the true black of a laser printer, especially in graphics with large areas of black.

✔ **More pages per cartridge:** Black toner cartridges are more expensive than black inkjet cartridges, but they last much longer: You'll generally get about double (sometimes even triple) the number of pages from a black laser toner cartridge. Toner cartridges can also be refilled, thus saving you quite a bit of money over a new cartridge.

Laser printers are a better choice for offices of every size and any situation where the best-quality black print is required.

Installing a Printer with a Parallel Port Interface

The process of installing a scanner or printer with a parallel port connection is the same. Follow these steps:

1. **Locate the 25-pin parallel port on the back of your computer case.**

   Figure 14-6 shows a standard parallel port.

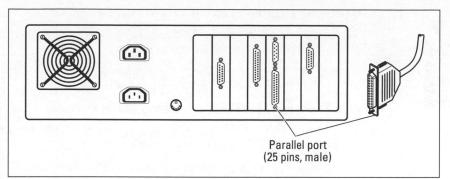

Figure 14-6:
A parallel
port
connector.

Parallel port
(25 pins, male)

2. **Align the connector on the end of your parallel cable with the parallel port and push it in firmly.**

   The angled edges on the connector are designed to make sure that it goes on only the right way.

3. **If you like, you can tighten the connector by turning the knobs (or screws) on the connector clockwise.**

   If you feel the connector is in firmly, you can leave it as is.

4. **If you're installing a printer, connect the other end of your cable to the printer.**

5. **Connect the power cord from your printer to the wall socket, turn the peripheral on, and restart your PC.**

If you're using Windows XP, your PC will automatically recognize the new device during the boot process. Depending on the age and type of peripheral, Windows might prompt you to insert the driver disk that came with the device. Or, if the driver was included on the Windows CD-ROM, you might be prompted to load your Windows CD-ROM so that the computer can locate the driver. (Check the manufacturer's Web site for driver software if you've scavenged a printer and didn't get any drivers!)

If you're adding a parallel port printer to your system, a new icon for your new printer should now appear in your Printers folder.

Installing a Scanner, Capture Device, or Printer with a USB Connection

If you're using a scanner, capture device (such as a Webcam), or printer with a USB connection under Windows XP, follow these steps:

1. **If necessary, connect the USB cable to the device.**

   Some USB peripherals have their own cables permanently attached, and others accept standard USB cables.

   It's always a good idea to check to see whether you need to buy a USB cable for your new device before you leave the store!

2. **Plug in the peripheral's power supply and turn it on.**

3. **After you've booted Windows normally, plug the USB connector on the cable into a USB port on your computer.**

   Windows should recognize that you've added a USB device. (If not, check again to make sure that the peripheral has been turned on. If the device is indeed receiving power and it's on — and Windows still doesn't recognize that it's been plugged in — check the connections from your PC's motherboard to your PC's USB ports.)

4. **When prompted, load the manufacturer's CD-ROM that came with your device so that Windows can install the correct drivers.**

   You might also be prompted to load your Windows CD-ROM. If you're adding a USB printer to your system, a new icon for your new printer should now appear in your Printers folder.

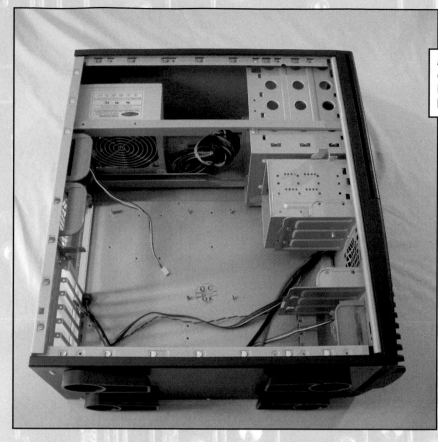

A standard ATX PC case, right out of the box. The power cables for internal devices (yellow, red, and black) are at the top center.

What's the first thing you always do before working on your PC's innards? That's right, ground yourself by touching the metal chassis before you touch any electrical components.

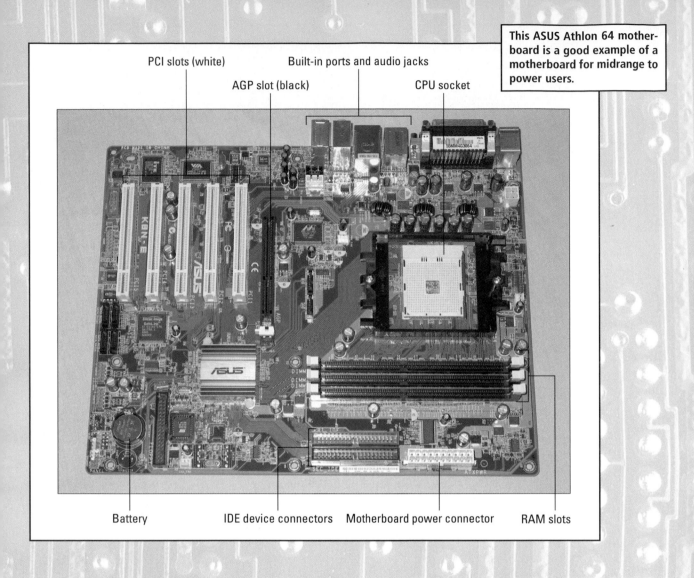

PCI slots (white)

AGP slot (black)

Built-in ports and audio jacks

CPU socket

This ASUS Athlon 64 mother-board is a good example of a motherboard for midrange to power users.

Battery

IDE device connectors

Motherboard power connector

RAM slots

On the left, the Athlon 64 CPU is ready for insertion in the ZIF socket. The fan/heat sink assembly clips on after the processor is installed, as shown on the right. The tube of thermal compound is applied between the heat sink and the CPU.

Connecting the CPU fan to the motherboard. Most of today's motherboards include a software utility that displays and monitors your CPU temperature.

Aligning a DDR RAM module with a RAM socket on the motherboard. Note the notch on the module connector matches the spacer in the socket only when everything is lined up correctly.

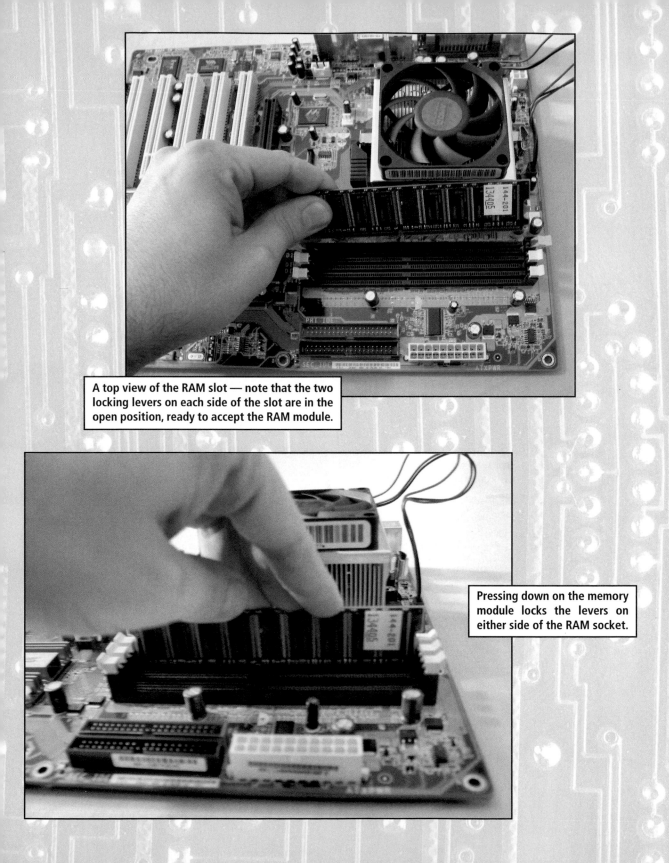

A top view of the RAM slot — note that the two locking levers on each side of the slot are in the open position, ready to accept the RAM module.

Pressing down on the memory module locks the levers on either side of the RAM socket.

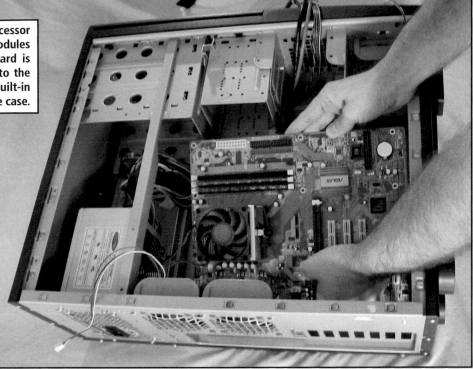

With the AMD 64 processor assembly and RAM modules installed, the motherboard is ready to be installed into the case. Note that the built-in ports face the rear of the case.

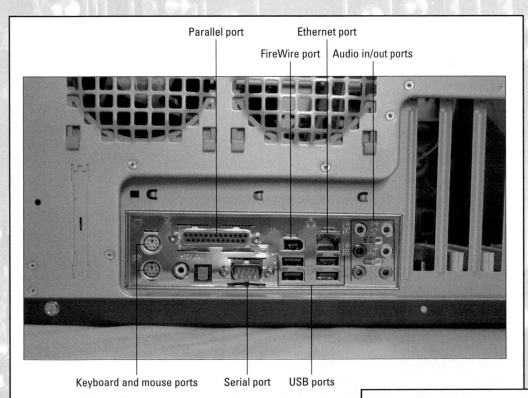

Parallel port

Ethernet port

FireWire port   Audio in/out ports

Keyboard and mouse ports   Serial port   USB ports

After an ATX motherboard is installed, the ports appear through the back plate of the case.

The motherboard is installed, with all the slot covers open and ready to accept adapter cards. Note the power connections made to the motherboard for the various fans.

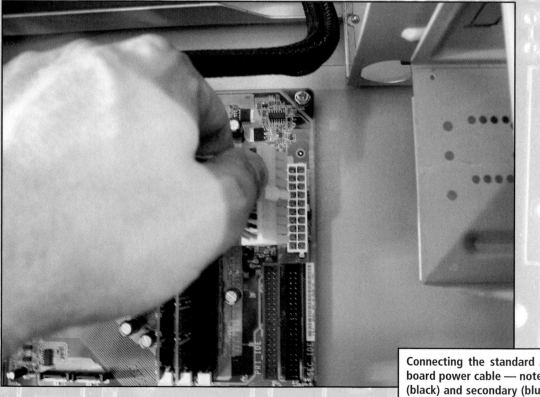

Connecting the standard ATX motherboard power cable — note the primary (black) and secondary (blue) EIDE/PATA connectors, situated right next door.

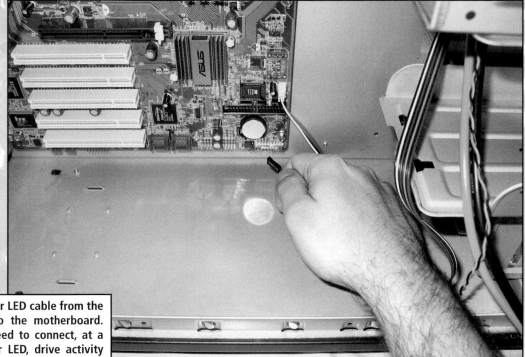

Connecting the power LED cable from the front of the case to the motherboard. Typically, you will need to connect, at a minimum, the power LED, drive activity LED, and reset button cables.

A typical AGP video card — in this case, an ASUS GeForce 6600 model with 128MB RAM. This card is a good high-end choice for gaming. Note the notched hook that appears at the end of the bus connector; this hook must be inserted first when installing the video card.

An intimate view of an AGP video card slot. AGP and PCI-Express video card slots are usually a different color.

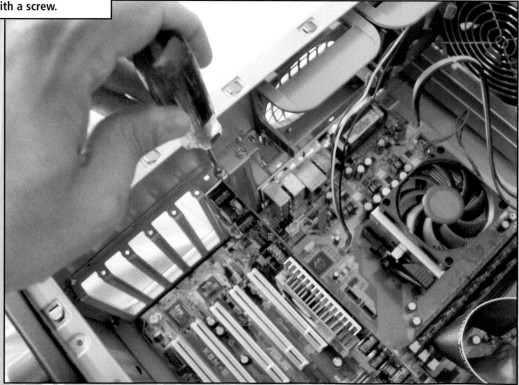

Fixing the AGP video card in place with a screw.

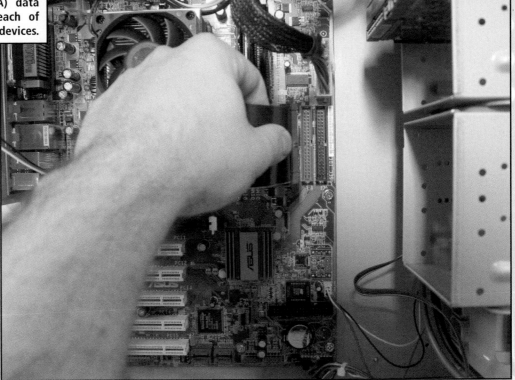

Most motherboards have two EIDE (or PATA) data cable connectors, each of which supports two devices.

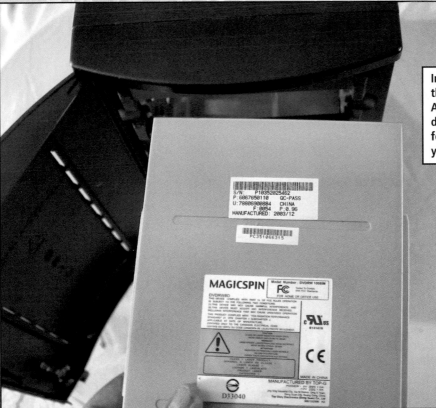

Installing an internal device — in this case, an EIDE DVD recorder. Align the device with the open drive bay and slide it inside. (Don't forget to attach the rails first, if your drive bay requires them.)

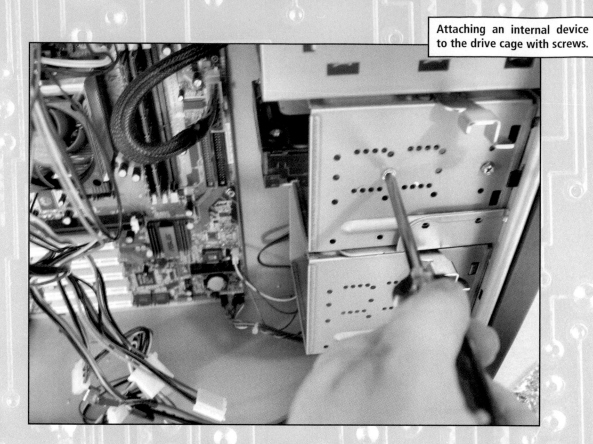

Attaching an internal device to the drive cage with screws.

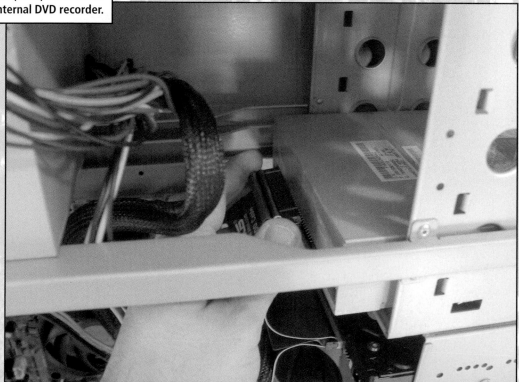

Connecting the EIDE (PATA) data cable to the back of the internal DVD recorder.

Remember, your internal device won't work without a power connection!

This close-up shows the primary EIDE cable and ATX power cable connected. Note that two of the three RAM sockets have been filled.

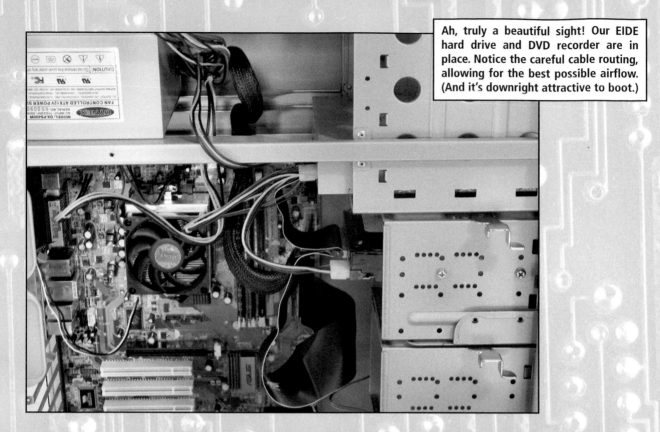

Ah, truly a beautiful sight! Our EIDE hard drive and DVD recorder are in place. Notice the careful cable routing, allowing for the best possible airflow. (And it's downright attractive to boot.)

After everything has been tested and is working, it's time to close the cover. This case has a clear side panel.

Connecting the keyboard to your new system. Note the second FireWire port, which uses a separate slot.

It's easy to feed a hungry PC — connect the power cable from your AC outlet. The master power supply on/off switch is next to the socket.

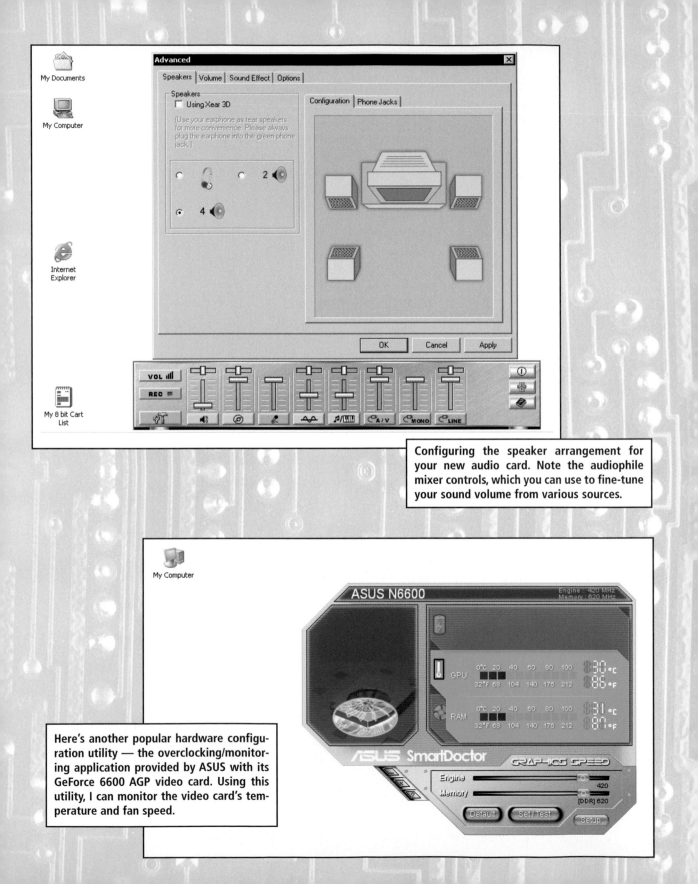

Configuring the speaker arrangement for your new audio card. Note the audiophile mixer controls, which you can use to fine-tune your sound volume from various sources.

Here's another popular hardware configuration utility — the overclocking/monitoring application provided by ASUS with its GeForce 6600 AGP video card. Using this utility, I can monitor the video card's temperature and fan speed.

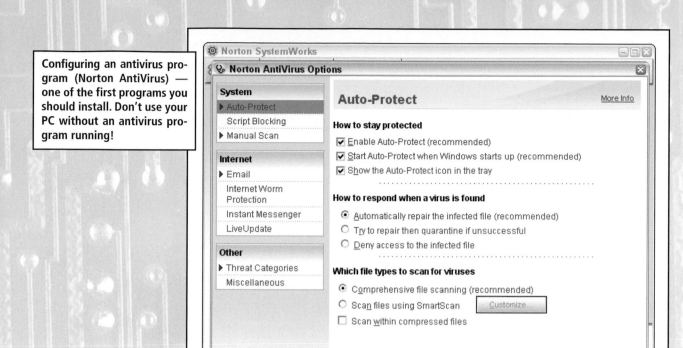

Configuring an antivirus program (Norton AntiVirus) — one of the first programs you should install. Don't use your PC without an antivirus program running!

Norton SystemWorks

Norton AntiVirus Options

System
▶ Auto-Protect
Script Blocking
▶ Manual Scan

Internet
▶ Email
Internet Worm Protection
Instant Messenger
LiveUpdate

Other
▶ Threat Categories
Miscellaneous

Auto-Protect

More Info

How to stay protected

☑ Enable Auto-Protect (recommended)
☑ Start Auto-Protect when Windows starts up (recommended)
☑ Show the Auto-Protect icon in the tray

How to respond when a virus is found

⦿ Automatically repair the infected file (recommended)
○ Try to repair then quarantine if unsuccessful
○ Deny access to the infected file

Which file types to scan for viruses

⦿ Comprehensive file scanning (recommended)
○ Scan files using SmartScan   Customize...
☐ Scan within compressed files

Default All   OK   Cancel   Page Defaults

XRouter Pro MainPage - Microsoft Internet Explorer

File   Edit   View   Favorites   Tools   Help

Back   ⬤   ✕ ⬜ ⬆   Search   Favorites   ⬜ ⬜

Address http://192.168.1.1/   Go

Xsense.com   **OnePage Setup**

Main Menu
• OnePage Setup

Advanced
• DHCP Settings
• Access Control
• Virtual Server
• Device Admin.
• Status Monitor
• Special App.
• DMZ Host
• RIP
• Static Routing
• PPPoE

Private IP Address

Private IP Address: 192   168   1   1

Subnet Mask: 255.255.255.0 ▼

Public IP Address

⦿ Get an IP address automatically

○ Specify an IP address   0   0   0   0

Public Subnet Mask: 255 255 248 0

Default Gateway IP Address: 0   0   0   0

Domain Name Server 1:   0   0   0   0

Domain Name Server 2:   0   0   0   0

Domain Name Server 3:   0   0   0   0

Internet

A typical configuration utility for an Internet router (often called a sharing device). With a networking device like this one, you can easily share one high-speed broadband Internet connection among all the computers on your network.

Our last color plate is a work I call "Storage through the Ages." It gives you an idea of how quickly things move in the high-tech world of computer hardware.

At the bottom of this pyramid is my first hard drive, an antique Radio Shack TRS-80 15MB external hard disk subsystem, which was state-of-the-art in 1987. (Yep, that's right, 15MB, and it had its own key locking system.) In the middle is my circa-2000 80GB FireWire external hard drive. And, at the top, my 512MB solid-state USB 2.0 USB Flash drive, which holds about thirty-four times as much as the TRS-80 drive, all in the size of a pack of chewing gum.

The moral of my story? Be prepared to upgrade that cutting-edge PC you've built because hardware marches on!

Chapter 15

More Power User Toys

I'm the first to admit that I'm fascinated by gadgets and toys. Most power users covet the smallest, newest, or fastest examples of computer technology, like the calculator watch that every techno-nerd wears all through high school. (I had two.) Although such technological marvels are rarely a requirement for your PC, power users crave these play toys anyway.

If you take a look at today's high-end computer gadgets, you'll find that most of these technological wonders are more than mere toys. They really *do* simplify your life by keeping track of data, speeding up the network and Internet connections you use every day, or reducing your computer to the size of your checkbook (or even your business card). Many of these toys are upgrades to features that are now considered necessities; for example, Windows XP has a built-in bare-bones firewall, but you can do much better by spending some of your hard-earned cash on a third-party firewall. (More on firewalls later in this chapter.)

In this chapter, I introduce some high-end hardware items, software programs, and services that you can add to your PC. The power user hardware and software products that I discuss in this chapter aren't necessary, although they can revolutionize the way that you use your PC.

Please note that this chapter is an informative overview, so I don't tell you how to install the hardware and software discussed here.

Live, Via Satellite: The Internet!

You might be asking, "Is there such a thing as an Internet connection that provides fast throughput without requiring me to install new telephone lines?" In fact, there is: A number of data communications companies offer satellite Internet links, using the same type of hardware commonly used for satellite TV service.

By connecting your PC to the Internet via a satellite connection, you can download files, Web pages, graphics images, sound or movie files — or whatever your heart desires — at blazing speeds of at least 500 Kbps (the download speed advertised for the Small Office VSAT Service, offered by Satellite Communication Services, at `scs-ems.com/home.htm`).

Compare that speed with the puny 56 Kbps for a single modem analog connection, 112 Kbps for a *multilink* analog connection (using two telephone lines to increase the speed of a single connection), or an average of 400 Kbps for a typical cable modem connection. You can see why the satellite system is no longer just a neat gadget.

To link your PC to the Internet via satellite, you might need both (or just one) of the following main links:

- ✔ **A modem connection:** Today's satellite subscriptions typically use VSAT (two-way) technology, so your PC actually both receives *and* sends data via the satellite — this way, you won't need an incoming telephone line and dial-up modem (or any type of cable connection) at all!

  However, beware those satellite connections that still need a regular modem and a regular Internet service provider (ISP). That's because the data that you send to the Internet needs to travel out over a standard analog dial-up connection. This data might include commands to display a Web page, search requests that you submit to a search engine such as Google or Yahoo!, outgoing e-mail, or files that you send from your computer.

- ✔ **A satellite connection:** Data that you receive from the Internet is typically transmitted at 500 Kbps from the satellite to your receiving antenna on the ground. The data then travels over a coaxial (coax) connection between the ground antenna and a special card installed in your computer, or an external receiver. (Again, if you have VSAT satellite hardware, you'll also send your data to the Internet by transmitting it back to the satellite.)

Figure 15-1 illustrates the elements in the less expensive PC/Internet link, which still requires a modem and telephone line.

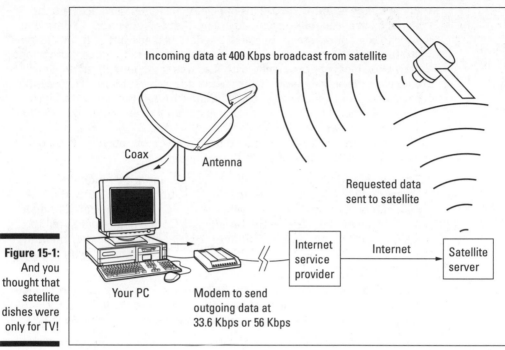

Incoming data at 400 Kbps broadcast from satellite

Coax

Antenna

Requested data
sent to satellite

| Internet service provider | Internet | Satellite server |

Your PC

Modem to send
outgoing data at
33.6 Kbps or 56 Kbps

Figure 15-1:
And you
thought that
satellite
dishes were
only for TV!

If you're using a receive-only satellite system, sending (or *uploading*) a large file to another site on the Internet using file transfer protocol (FTP) or e-mail takes just as long as it would on a standard Internet modem connection. All outgoing information (your e-mail, files that you send to a friend, or your commands to view Web pages) goes through your modem and a regular phone line. This speed bottleneck is removed with a two-way VSAT satellite connection.

If you consider how most people use the Internet, a satellite system (which gives you blazing reception speed) is a highly efficient way to browse the Web. For example, almost all my online time is spent waiting for my PC to receive a Web page, e-mail, an FTP file, or the text of a newsgroup message, rather than transmitting requests to those sites. (The Web didn't earn the nickname *The World Wide Wait* for nothing!)

What comes with an Internet satellite system?

In this section, I outline what you get with a typical satellite Internet system:

✔ **Proprietary adapter card:** This specially designed card accepts the signal from the satellite dish and converts it to conventional data that your PC can understand. Because the data is transmitted from the satellite to your dish antenna in an encrypted format for security, the adapter card also decrypts the signal; within a two-way connection, the card encrypts the signal before it's transmitted to the satellite. The adapter card also provides power to the antenna through the cable that links them together. This adapter card is installed like any other standard PC adapter card, which I discuss in Chapters 4 and 5. (Note that some services may provide you with an external converter/receiver instead of an internal card, but they both do the same job.)

✔ **The satellite dish:** Figure 15-2 illustrates a standard 24-inch dish, which looks much like the dish used to receive satellite TV broadcasts. The dish can be mounted on your roof, a wall, or a pole. The satellite dish must be aligned to receive the broadcasts from a particular satellite, which usually takes about 30 minutes of trial-and-error experimentation (moving the dish back and forth) to get the best signal. (If you decide on a professional installation, someone does this for you.)

✔ **LNB:** (That's short for *low noise block,* for some strange reason.) This black box mounts on your antenna; it receives the signal from the satellite and sends it along the cable to the adapter card in your PC.

✔ **Coaxial cable:** Standard coaxial cable connects the different components to the adapter card in your PC. Although this stuff is considered weather resistant, it should be protected from the elements whenever possible. If you bury your cable, I recommend that you route it through PVC pipe to your antenna.

✔ **Software:** Your PC requires special software to recognize the adapter card. This software is provided as a part of the package.

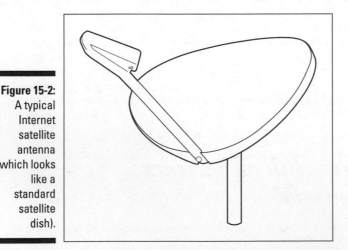

Figure 15-2:
A typical Internet satellite antenna (which looks like a standard satellite dish).

How expensive is a satellite Internet connection?

The price you'll pay for your connection depends on the source of your service and whether you choose a send/receive or receive-only system. A basic satellite package typically doesn't cover installation. However, if you're comfortable installing an adapter card in your PC, mounting the antenna, and routing the cable, you shouldn't have any problems with the installation process. It typically takes only a day for two people to install the system.

The buck doesn't stop with installation charges. You still have to pay a basic rate for the connection (based on either a flat monthly fee or a fixed rate per megabyte downloaded) that starts at about $50 a month. If you choose a receive-only system, you also still need to maintain a standard dial-up Internet account with a local ISP so that you can send your e-mail data files and upload your Web browser commands.

Okay, it's neat, but . . .

Does a satellite Internet connection make sense? If you want smoking download speed and the other types of broadband access aren't available in your area, you can still make use of satellite technology.

However, the real determining factor is whether you truly need the raw speed delivered by this system. Most casual Internet Web surfers will be satisfied with a 56 Kbps connection or perhaps even a multilinked 112 Kbps connection. Only people with a need (and the money) for the fastest connection and who are unable to connect by using another type of broadband technology need to be interested in satellite technology — for example, Internet junkies living in the country who spend more than four or five hours a day on the Web, telecommuters, and those who receive large files via FTP regularly.

Reading a Pesky Macintosh Disk

Programs that read Macintosh floppy disks or CD/DVD discs on a PC have been around for many years now, but the utility program MacDrive 6 (from Mediafour Productions, at www.media4.com) was the first one that reads (and even records) Mac disks transparently (meaning you don't have to do anything different than you would with PC media). After you install

MacDrive 6, you don't need to run a special program before you read Mac media; just stick that disk in your PC running Windows XP or Windows 2003 Server and read those Mac files to your heart's content. Although most people might consider a program like MacDrive 6 to be a useful tool, it also qualifies as a power user play toy because it's so doggone *neat*. Oh, and it's cheap, too: You can download a copy for only $50.

In addition to reading Mac floppies, CDs, and DVDs, you can actually format *and record* them on your PC, and you can also save and delete files from Mac media. (Older Mac-to-PC programs enable you to only read Mac media.) Again, the process is transparent to you. Just use any Windows function or application to write files to the Mac media, and your Macintosh can make sense of the result.

Conversing with Quake

I'll be the first to admit that I need another set of hands when playing the 3-D games Doom 3 or Half-Life 2 or flight simulators such as Falcon or Apache Longbow. Just because you're an ace typist doesn't make you better at fragging your buddies in a hot-and-heavy multiplayer game. You have to control your weapon with your mouse, trackball, or joystick, but moving around, selecting weapons, and using special commands normally entails a quick leap toward the keyboard! It's easy to get confused when you can't take your eyes off your monitor without being blown to your component atoms.

Although you can solve the problem with a programmable joystick, it's an expensive solution. You have to create a button configuration by hand for each game, and you'll spend more than a few days teaching yourself all those button assignments. There is an alternative: If you're like me, you'd rather use your voice to control your character! With the Game Commander 3 software (priced at $75) from Mindmaker (www.gamecommander.com), you can program as many as 256 keystrokes that your computer will automatically "press" when you speak a single command. To change to the next weapon in Quake, for example, you'd say, "Next," instead of reaching for the bracket key on your keyboard. Plus, voice commands in a game such as MechWarrior or Freelancer seem much more realistic than pecking at your keyboard. With a little imagination, you'll feel like you're talking to your ship's computer or your copilot! I've been using Game Commander 3 for several years now, and the program has helped increase my scores.

It's also easy to configure Game Commander for new games using templates that you can download for free from the Mindmaker Web site. These templates can be loaded within Game Commander 3 to provide you with a complete ready-made set of spoken command assignments.

To use Game Commander 3 under Windows, you need a full-duplex sound card (all modern sound cards made in the last three or four years are full duplex, but you can check the manual for your card to make sure) and a headset microphone. (More about sound cards and microphones in Chapter 9.)

Even People like You and Me Need Internet Security

Stories abound on the Internet, TV, and the movies about the lack of Internet security. Although it's unlikely, someone can intercept your electronic mail or discover personal information about you. You can take certain security measures, such as ordering products online only if your Web browser and the Web site can create a secure connection or using an encryption utility to encode the text within your e-mail messages. These procedures create a level of security for most Web surfers and casual Internet users.

However, large corporations make use of powerful firewall software to carry their Internet protection a step further. A *firewall* is a program or hardware device that constantly monitors the company's Internet connection to prevent unauthorized access to the company's Web server (or, even worse, the company's network itself). Firewalls are typically complicated beasts that cost hundreds (or even thousands) of dollars. A company without a firewall is a potential target for an attack by a computer hacker. Wouldn't it be nice if anyone could install a firewall, just to be safe?

Thanks to the good folks in Redmond, the Service Pack 2 updates to Windows XP now turn on the built-in XP firewall by default. However, this is bare-bones protection — you can't easily modify or customize the Windows XP firewall, for example, and there's not much feedback on what attempts, if any, have been made to compromise your PC.

If you're like me — on the Internet for hours at a time visiting Web sites and downloading files — you can use a third-party software firewall instead. For example, Symantec's Norton Personal Firewall (www.symantec.com) is an inexpensive firewall for protecting your machine while you're online — in fact, I'd recommend it for anyone, even the casual Internet user with a dial-up modem connection. Here's a quick list of the possible security violations that Norton Personal Firewall can monitor and prevent:

✔ **Guarding the cookie jar:** Personal Firewall alerts you to the use of Web cookies by a site and enables you to block them if you want. A *cookie* is a file that contains personal data about you, usually from a form that you filled out online. Cookies are often stored automatically on your hard drive without your knowledge.

✔ **Protecting your programs:** Personal Firewall monitors and controls which programs on your computer are allowed Internet access so that an unauthorized program written by a hacker can't automatically connect and transfer your personal information across the Internet without your knowledge.

✔ **Ad filtering:** Personal Firewall filters those irritating and bandwidth-hogging banner ads. Because you don't download them, you surf the Web faster.

✔ **Trojan horse denial:** Personal Firewall takes care of a problem that has already plagued many Internet users — *Trojan horse* Java applets and ActiveX controls that your Web browser runs automatically. Although these hostile Trojan horse programs are rare, they can destroy data or wreak havoc on your Windows system files. However, if you block all beneficial Java and ActiveX traffic, you can't enjoy many of the high-tech Web sites with animated graphics and interactive controls. Personal Firewall solves the problem because any potentially hostile applet that you receive is flagged before it runs.

Norton Personal Firewall runs under both Windows XP and Windows 2003 Server. For more information on this program, visit the Symantec Web site (www.symantec.com).

Hey, I Can Get TV and FM Radio on My PC!

Do you love your PC? I mean, really, *really* love your PC? If so, you might have a comfortable reclining chair in case you fall asleep in front of the keyboard. Or maybe one of those little refrigerators to keep your source of caffeine and sugar close at hand. (Considering a late-night burrito? I recommend that you keep the portable microwave a healthy distance away from both you and the computer.)

TIP

Bringing video to your PC

You can use TV tuner cards for more than just watching TV or listening to the radio on your PC. Most tuner cards also enable you to capture incoming video or audio to your hard drive, making captured video a cheap source of multimedia material for your next project. If you want to watch or capture a movie, you can also plug your VCR into most tuner cards.

Warning: Capturing copyrighted video or audio and distributing it yourself is illegal. For more information about copyrights, see Chapter 14.

Depending on the tuner card, you might also get bundled software that enables you to take individual still images from the incoming video. It's the perfect way to get a good image of Uncle Milton from that family reunion video.

The ultimate in PC mouse-potato technology, however, is the FM stereo/TV tuner adapter card. Install one of these tuner cards, and you can watch TV or listen to your favorite FM stereo station on your PC. These cards carry full-featured TV tuners and radio circuitry — but instead of using a separate TV tube or speakers, the display is shown on your monitor. Because the audio is routed with a cable from the TV card to your sound card, you hear the audio through your PC speaker system. Some TV/FM tuner cards, such as the AVerTV Go 007 FM Plus, from AVerMedia Technologies, Inc. (www.aver.com), can act as a personal video recorder as well. Sweetness. (See the sidebar "Bringing video to your PC" for more details.)

Most tuner cards provide an onscreen remote control that enables you to control the volume, change the channel or station, and choose the size of the TV display. If you're running another program on your PC, you can display the TV program as a picture-in-picture window or toggle it to full screen when it's time for that really important cartoon.

Backing Up to the Web

Sure, backing up your PC's data is important. In fact, backing up your data is the only way to guard against hardware failures or the occasional "Uh-oh!" (or worse), indicating that you just accidentally erased an entire folder on your hard drive. Many computer owners back up their data with tape drives, and others use removable media, such as Zip or DVD rewriteable discs. (In

Chapter 7, I discuss each of these backup methods.) An unfortunate few probably still back up on floppies, but my advice to them is to enter the twenty-first century, and soon.

Wait until you hear about the power user's dream backup method. No tapes to handle, and no time spent listening to your drive wind and rewind over and over again. Plus, you have the confidence of knowing that your data is stored safely offsite, so it's secure even if your house or office is kidnapped by aliens. I'm talking about storing your PC's data on an Internet site with the software service SwapDrive Backup (from SwapDrive, at `www.swapdrive.com`).

How does the service work? All you need is Windows XP or Windows 2003 Server, a copy of the SwapDrive Backup software, a subscription to the service, and at least a 56 Kbps connection to the Internet (of course, the faster, the better). SwapDrive Backup enables you to set up an automatic backup schedule, or you can perform a manual backup at any time.

At the scheduled time, the data that you mark for backup is read from your hard drive, encrypted to a military-grade standard, and sent over the Internet to the SwapDrive server. The company stores your data with your password in encrypted form until you need it.

SwapDrive charges $75 for a year's subscription with 100MB of online storage. After you subscribe, you can back up and retrieve your files as often as necessary.

Speaking of retrieval, your data can be retrieved and restored only with your account password, which introduces an additional layer of security.

Will You Move the Joystick, or Will It Move You?

The Logitech Wingman Force 3D joystick is a power user's play toy. What sets this piece of hardware apart from the pack is its ability to provide actual tactile feedback. In other words, when something happens in the game, you can feel an authentic sense, force, or impact through the joystick. For example:

✔ If you're flying a light plane with a flight simulator, you feel the stick resist your movements when you begin a turn and then relax gradually as the turn continues.

- ✔ If you're driving a tank, you feel the impact of each hit on your tank's armor as well as the recoil of each shot you fire.

- ✔ If you're playing a first-person shoot-'em-up (where you're immersed in a 3-D world), you feel your way around corners in the dark and recognize different wall textures.

- ✔ If you're bowling, you can tell whether your ball hit the lane too early or just right.

As a dyed-in-the-wool computer game fanatic, I can tell you that this kind of feedback adds that extra touch of realism. Much like how a sound card with 3-D support enhances the audio experience of a game, the Wingman Force 3D enhances physical sensations of your game-playing experience. After all, a game becomes much more realistic when your World War II fighter plane gets harder to control when you're dodging bullets with an enemy on your tail. The Wingman Force 3D reflects every hit on your plane as well as the force required to pull out of a power dive.

Like most of the more expensive joysticks on the market, you can program each button to perform a keyboard command. And the stick itself is specially designed for hours of hazardous flying through the enemy-filled skies of Planet SpeedBump without cramping your hand.

Before you tense your muscles to leap out of your chair and run to your local computer store for a Wingman Force 3D, don't overlook the downside:

- ✔ **Pricey:** Compared with a standard joystick that costs $15 or $20, the SideWinder Force Feedback Pro is significantly pricier at about $50.

- ✔ **Game-dependent:** The game that you're playing must explicitly support the Wingman Force 3D to enable the tactile-feedback feature. So, for older games, Wingman Force 3D becomes just another joystick.

Part V
The Part of Tens

The 5th Wave — By Rich Tennant

"I think you're just jealous that I found a community of people online that worship the yam as I do, and you haven't."

In this part . . .

1 provide you with worthwhile advice and tips (and even the occasional warning) concerning five topics, ranging from the assembly process to speeding up your PC. Each chapter includes ten tips. Consider "The Part of Tens" as a quick dose of experience (without the hard knocks).

Chapter 16

Ten Reasons Not to Buy a Retail PC

Buying a PC from a retail computer store or a big mail-order company is easy: Out comes the credit card, the boxes arrive at your house, and installation is as simple as plugging in the keyboard, mouse, speakers, and monitor. Even the most experienced PC hardware junkie will have to admit that a novice can save time and potential headaches by buying a retail PC.

Therefore, you might be asking yourself, "Why don't I just travel the retail PC route like most people? Why go to the trouble of building my own computer?" In this chapter, I give you several doggone good reasons why you should assemble your own machine.

It Just Plain Costs Less to Build Your Own PC!

The first and, for some people, the most important reason for building a computer is to save as much money as possible over the cost of a retail PC (especially if you're buying a PC from a local retail store, or if you're building a super-fast gaming system). If you build your own computer, you're not paying for all the overhead tacked on to the original price of a computer, including a storefront, advertising, and a salesperson's paycheck.

If you've been shopping for a PC, you already know that many retail PC packages don't include a monitor, so often the price that you see isn't for a complete system. And yes, you can save a hundred dollars or more over the price of a complete PC offered by a big mail-order company. As I explain earlier in this book, it's simply a matter of searching for the right companies that sell computer components at rock-bottom prices.

Using a Web site such as www.pricewatch.com can bring you — in just a few seconds — the best prices available *anywhere*!

Even if you have to buy every single component from your computer case to your mousepad, you're still likely to save a considerable amount of cash by assembling your own computer.

Recycle Used and Scavenged Hardware

If you have an older computer hanging around the house, does it make sense to throw it away or to sell it for a fraction of what you paid for it several years ago? Why not recycle what you can out of that machine (for example, the case, keyboard, modem, floppy drive, and monitor) and use those scavenged parts when you build your new PC? When you build your own PC, you can take advantage of used and scavenged hardware, and every part that you avoid buying means even more money that stays in your pocket.

The constant urge among techno-types to upgrade means that you'll likely find sources of used hardware right in your own office or school, and those parts are often only a couple of years old! My favorite example is "yesterday's" 3-D video card that has a "mere" 64MB of video RAM (shameful!) rather than the 128MB or 256MB that hard-core gamers desire. If you're not interested in playing the latest games in high resolution, that 64MB is a perfect choice for you.

Avoid the Monster Myth

If you're shopping for a computer in a retail store, you're likely to be told that you should "buy more computer than you need right now." I call this the monster myth: Buy a monster machine now, and you won't be sorry later. (Coincidentally, that more expensive and more powerful computer also earns the salesperson a higher commission — go figure.)

If you're going to be using your computer often and you know that you'll need more power and more features in the future, I won't argue that this line of reasoning is good advice. You'll avoid upgrading your computer several times in the long run. However, the large percentage of new computer owners have little experience on a PC, and they're not really sure what they're going to do or how often they'll use their PC. Why spend all that money on a monster machine if you're not sure that you and your family will *use* it?

You might find yourself asking, "Do I really need all this stuff just to read my Internet e-mail and keep an address book?" The answer: Definitely not. I know many computer owners who are still satisfied with older Pentium II and Pentium III PCs. Their machines run Windows 98SE, a browser, and an e-mail program — and that's all they need.

Too bad that most computer stores don't have a bare-bones PC that you can choose. But if you assemble your own computer, you can start out with an economy-class Intel Celeron or Pentium 4 PC and add functionality later as you gain experience. In fact, you can customize your computer to your specifications and avoid buying unnecessary hardware. (A number of big retail chains now boast that they allow you to build a custom PC, but the price for one of these custom machines ends up sky-high compared with a machine that you assemble yourself.) Some mail-order catalogs and Web stores are starting to get the idea, too, and are offering fairly low-cost machines, but you usually don't get to customize these inexpensive PCs very much. And don't forget to make sure that they're using brand-name components before you think about buying one!

Encourage Freedom of Choice!

If you build your own computer, it's much easier to select special components that don't fit the cookie-cutter mold of retail PCs. For example, don't expect to find specialized pointing devices such as trackballs on most retail PCs at your local computer store. If you buy a retail PC and you want to use a trackball rather than a mouse, you'll have to buy one separately (and then you're stuck with a mouse that you don't need). That might not seem like much of a hassle, but consider other specialized components, such as a high-end sound card with Dolby Digital support, a gamer's 3-D video card with 256MB of video RAM, or a TV/video capture card. Buying one of these adapter cards, removing the case, and substituting the adapter card that you *really* wanted in the first place becomes a big deal.

When you design and assemble your own computer, you buy precisely what you need, including any specialized hardware or peripherals. Even if the perfect computer that you were considering at the computer store doesn't have a FireWire port and a DVD recorder, you can certainly build a computer that does have these extras! If you're considering buying a PC from a direct vendor such as Dell or Gateway and you need special hardware, the vendor can usually supply it — although you'll pay substantially more for the vendor's version of the part than you would have paid for the part through a mail-order catalog. Having a custom PC is nice, but unless you build it yourself, you'll *always* pay more.

Enjoy the Learning Experience

What do you learn when you buy a retail PC? The answer: Not much. Sure, you get a crash course in removing Styrofoam and plugging in cables, but most owners of a retail PC are still afraid to remove the case from their computer. If you buy a retail PC, you'll be left in the dark when the time comes to upgrade your system to extend its useful life or replace a broken component.

On the other hand, if you build your own computer, you *know* what makes it tick — you'll suddenly blossom into a bona fide techno-wizard! With your assembly experience and your knowledge of PC hardware, you'll be better prepared to fix problems and upgrade hardware and peripherals. The technicians at your local PC repair shop will wonder what happened to you; perhaps you should visit them from time to time just to swap hard drive specifications.

Spare Yourself the Shipping and Repair Hassles

When you buy a retail PC from a store (or even from one of the big-name, mail-order companies), you'll probably be presented with a technical support number and assurances that your computer will be promptly repaired if it breaks. You'll find that the word *promptly* has many meanings: waiting several minutes (or even an hour) to speak to a technical support representative, finding out that you'll be without your PC and the data that you need for several weeks, or making an appointment with a service representative to eventually drop by your house and bring a replacement part. Oh, and don't forget that this coverage usually lasts for only a year, unless you paid big bucks for the extended service contract when you bought your PC.

When you build your own PC, you can buy parts locally — and, if a part breaks, you don't have to pick up the telephone and start waiting. You'll never find yourself repacking your computer to send it halfway across the country. Instead, you can bring the faulty component back to the store for an immediate replacement.

Dodge Bundled Software Costs and Get What You Want

Retail PC salespeople like to crow about the cool software that's included with their computers. You usually get a productivity suite (which includes a word processor, some sort of database application, and a spreadsheet program), a few Internet applications, and free hours on an online service. If you're lucky, you might also get a year-old game or two with your computer. Generally, these programs are stripped-down versions of larger packages. For example, although you might get Microsoft Works, most retail PCs sold in stores don't include Microsoft Office unless you pay more for it.

Unfortunately, this bundled software isn't free at all: You pay for it along with your hardware, the documentation is usually sparse, it's rarely exactly what you need, and you usually can't subtract it from the total price of your computer if you don't want it. Often, you won't even receive the original program CD-ROM, so you can't reinstall the software. In fact, many new computer owners end up uninstalling the bundled software to make room for the programs that they really want to run. If you build your own PC, you can select your own full versions of your favorite applications later and save additional money.

Avoid the Computer Sales Experience

Although used-car salespeople seem to rank the lowest on the social totem pole, computer salespeople aren't much better. Many salespeople that I've encountered in retail computer stores either consider the customer an idiot or have little idea of exactly what they're selling (making them the perfect target for a few well-placed techno-questions — nothing's funnier than an embarrassed clueless salesperson who treated you like a computer novice just a few seconds before)! Others try to pass off a computer that's been returned as near the quality of a brand-new machine. (Look closely for the word *refurbished* the next time you shop for a computer, and you might see this technique in action.)

By building your own PC, you can circumvent your computer retail store and all the techniques that salespeople use to try to talk you into a specific computer — and you end up with a better computer that is less expensive and *perfectly* suits your needs.

Select the Brands That You Prefer

Are you looking for specific brand-name components in your computer, such as a Western Digital Raptor SATA hard drive or a Sound Blaster Audigy 4 sound card from Creative Labs? If you buy a retail PC, you end up with whatever hardware the manufacturer deems satisfactory (and you'd be surprised by how many big-name manufacturers of retail PCs use no-name parts). Often the only way that you can determine what you're getting is to open the computer's case on the sales floor.

Even if you're buying a computer from a direct vendor that offers customized PCs, it's unlikely that you'll be able to ask for a specific brand for most of the components used to assemble your computer. Typically, these vendors do use brand-name parts but only those brands and models the vendor prefers. If you need a different model, you're no better off than you would be buying a computer in a chain store.

When you build your own computer, *you* select the parts required to build it, including any specific brand-name preferences.

Get the Full Warranty for Each Part

If you've found a retail PC at the price that you want and it includes many of the brand-name parts that you're looking for, you're not necessarily receiving the full manufacturer's warranty on each of those components. Instead, the brand-name components on many retail computers are covered by the computer company's warranty (typically a year for both parts and labor). If that name-brand hard drive breaks after two years in a retail PC, you might not be able to return it to the manufacturer for service or replacement (even though the drive has a three-year warranty if you buy it separately).

If you buy your own components and build your own PC, you're assured that each component is covered for the full length of the manufacturer's warranty.

Chapter 17

Ten Tools and Tasks for a Power User's PC

To me, a *power user* is a person who is perfectly at home at the computer keyboard. For example, a power user knows the keyboard shortcuts that can speed up a favorite Windows program. Experienced power users also know tips and tricks that can help make their computers run faster (such as defragmenting a hard drive), and they know how to diagnose problems with their computers. Power users are also more efficient, and this ability makes them more productive at work and at home.

You can become a power user even if your computer isn't the fastest or most powerful PC on your block. Most people would say that it certainly helps to start with the best computer possible, and that's true in general: Speed and capacity never hurt. However, I've sat down in front of many a top-of-the-line retail computer system and noticed many features that could be added or improved.

In this chapter, I name ten computer hardware and software extras that help make your life easier behind the keyboard. And although they're not necessarily expensive, each adds convenience, comfort, or efficiency to your computer.

If you are comfortable, confident, and productive with your computer — no matter *how fast it is* — you are a power user!

Forget Your Mouse

The mouse is now the most popular computer pointing device, but many power users favor other pointing devices. Power users dislike standard mice because they take up too much space on the desktop, they trail their cord "tails" behind them, and they get filthy after a few months of constant use. Mice are also terribly inefficient creatures because they require movements of your forearm, which often makes it necessary to pick up your mouse and relocate it to another area of your desk just to move the cursor all the way across the screen.

I heartily recommend that you select another pointing device instead of a mouse. These devices can include a touchpad, trackball, drawing tablet, or fingertip mouse. My favorite is the trackball, which offers precise control with movements of your thumb or fingers rather than your forearm. A trackball doesn't move across the surface of your desk, so it needs cleaning far less often, and it requires only a fraction of the desktop real estate necessary for a standard corded mouse. (For more information on these pointing devices, see Chapter 5.) Remember to try out your new pointing device at the store — like a keyboard, a mouse is a personal device, and what feels comfortable to one person feels like a plastic brick to another!

If you're absolutely set on using a mouse, consider an infrared *wireless mouse,* which at least eliminates that doggone tail.

Guard That Power Supply!

It never fails. The moment that you've finished the last chapter of your Great American Novel — you know, the one that you've been working on for the past 20 years — someone on your block decides to juice up a new electric car, and every transformer within three miles goes up in smoke. You get hit with a power failure, and the crowning chapter of your novel is suddenly headed to that home for unfinished classics in the sky.

What can you do? Unfortunately, the answer is a big "nothing." If you've saved your work often, you can at least back up to the last revision, although the loss of power might have resulted in lost clusters on your computer's hard drive. In the worst-case scenario, you might have been burning a CD or DVD on your computer; if the recording process is interrupted by a power failure, you've just created a dandy coaster for your cold drinks.

However, you can prevent such a catastrophe by adding an uninterruptible power supply (UPS) to your computer system. A *UPS* is essentially a giant battery that automatically provides power within a few milliseconds in case of a power blackout or brownout. A typical UPS provides your computer with another priceless 15 minutes or so of operation before it's fully exhausted, which should give you ample time to save your work and shut down your system normally (or finish recording that DVD movie). Believe me, it's a weird feeling to see your computer monitor alive and well with every other light and appliance in your home as dead as a doornail. (After you've finished saving your work, gather the family around for a computer game or two!)

Note that a UPS is different from a *surge protector,* which is essentially just an extension cord that self-destructs if it gets hit by a massive power surge. You don't get any additional power in case of a blackout with a surge protector.

A UPS is constantly recharged from your wall socket, so it's always ready. Most of these power supplies also filter AC line *noise* (small variations in line voltage caused by some appliances, such as vacuum cleaners and televisions) and provide some measure of protection against lightning strikes.

Back Up, Back Up, Back Up

Even if your computer is connected to a UPS, you can still lose data. Hard drives fail, viruses attack, and human error can result in deleted files. There's only one way to truly secure your computer from loss, so follow this Mark's Maxim to the letter:

Back up your data to tape or removable media — and do it on a regular basis!

As a consultant, I've seen individuals, small businesses, and even one or two larger companies hammered by the loss of sensitive or irreplaceable data because of hardware failure. The sad part is that the data could have been backed up to a tape cartridge or a DVD-RW in just a few minutes. If you have important data that would take time or money to replace, remember the power user's secret weapon: *Back up your data!*

How often should you back up? It all depends on how often you significantly change your data. At minimum, I back up my work in progress every week using DVD-RW discs, and many companies run automated backups of their entire network every night. If time is tight, back up only your user data (such as documents, graphics, and spreadsheet files). If I'm in on the road with my laptop, I'll even create a copy of an important document on my removable USB flash drive, just in case disaster strikes my laptop's hard drive. However, if you have the time, I recommend that you back up your entire system, including all your operating system files and application programs. This way, you avoid the hassle of reconfiguring Windows and reloading your programs on a new hard drive before you're back to normal.

Check Chapter 7 for more information on tape backups and how you can install one in your computer.

Back up your data! (Did I stress that enough?)

Diagnostics Software to the Rescue

Most power users have at least one diagnostics program because they understand that hardware and system problems can lead to a slower computer, lockups, or even lost data. Unfortunately, these problems usually aren't obvious, so you need a program capable of both locating potential glitches and eliminating them (or at least identifying them and providing a possible solution or two). Some operating systems come with a simple disk-scanning utility — for example, you can scan a hard drive for errors under both Windows XP and Windows 2000 — but these programs don't check for hardware problems and don't offer the range of features provided by commercial diagnostics software.

Probably the oldest and best-known diagnostics package for the PC is Norton SystemWorks, from Symantec (www.symantec.com). This suite of programs has been around since the days when DOS was king, and the Utilities have saved my neck more than once! The Utilities package includes one of the best disk defragmenters available, a system information and benchmark program, a Windows optimizing and troubleshooting program, and the comprehensive Disk Doctor that checks for just about every conceivable file error. I run the Disk Doctor at least once a day, so I know that the files on my hard drives are in good shape.

Stick Your Keyboard in a Drawer!

If you're going to remain comfortable at your computer, you need to consider ergonomics. Your keyboard should be at the proper height for comfortable typing, your wrists should be supported to avoid carpal tunnel syndrome, and your monitor should be close to your natural eye level to avoid cramping your neck.

One of my first additions to my desktop computer was a *keyboard drawer,* which is a metal case that holds a sliding drawer for your keyboard (as well as a place to store a pencil and paper clips). Your computer sits on top (or to the side) of the metal case, and you simply pull the drawer out and begin typing. The drawer keeps the keyboard at the proper height and saves desktop space that you would otherwise need for your keyboard. When you're finished at the PC, slide the keyboard back into the case. (Some drawers are designed to hold the keyboard and support the monitor instead, while the PC sits on the floor beneath the desk.)

If your computer's tower case sits on the floor (with only your monitor and pointing device on your desk), I recommend a keyboard drawer that attaches to the bottom of your computer desk. If you're shopping for a computer desk, it's worth it to spend a bit more for a keyboard drawer.

Stop the Spread of Viruses

The latest wave of e-mail viruses might leave you thinking that computer viruses are hovering outside your Internet connection 24 hours a day, just waiting to bite your computer like a rabid silicon dog. It never hurts to be prepared, especially if you receive lots of e-mail or try out lots of demo and shareware software on your PC. Every computer power user worthy of the title runs an antivirus scanning program constantly in the background.

The best-known virus scanning software for the PC is Norton AntiVirus, which includes regular virus data updates downloaded automatically over the Internet. These data files enable the program to recognize all the new viruses that have been identified since the last update. You can learn more about this great program (which should set you back about $50) at www.symantec.com.

Most virus-scanning programs identify viruses present in your computer's random access memory (RAM), on your hard drive's boot sector, and within files stored on your drive. Some scanners attempt to remove the virus from the program or data file, and other programs simply advise that you delete the infected file to guarantee that the virus is eradicated.

Be sure to update your virus signatures every week. Outdated virus protection is worse than no virus protection at all because you *think* you're covered and are likely to take risks, such as downloading and running software from the Internet!

If you do a lot of Web surfing, you should immediately install a spyware removal program. In my opinion, *spyware* is just one step below a virus: these programs work invisibly while you surf, collecting the addresses of sites you visit or displaying irritating banners. (Some spyware programs even go so far as to change your browser's home page to a sponsor site!) All spyware has one thing in common, though: these programs slow down your PC, so they should be eradicated. I recommend two free spyware removal applications: Patrick Kolla's SpyBot Search & Destroy (www.spybot.info) and LavaSoft's Ad-Aware SE (www.lavasoftusa.com).

Organize Your Software

Floppy disks, backup tape cartridges, CD and DVD discs, and Zip disks . . . where do you put all this stuff? It's easy to throw everything into a shoebox, but can you find a particular disc when you need it?

A power user keeps software organized and within easy reach. For CD and DVD-ROMs, I suggest an audio CD rack that stands on the floor or mounts on the wall. (Another good choice for discs that you've burned is a *CD binder*, which allows you to carry your gaggle of discs easily while protecting them from scratches and dirt.) You should keep floppy disks and Zip disks in a disk case, preferably with dividers that can help keep your games separate from that spreadsheet work you brought home from the office. If you need a little extra security, look for a disk case with a lock. You can also store backup tape cartridges in a special tape case. Although tape cases are a little harder to find, you should be able to buy one at your local office supply store.

Use the Power of Your Voice

Does the idea of controlling your computer with your voice seem like science fiction? How would you like to dictate your next report or memo to your computer — without typing a single character of the text? Thanks to programs such as NaturallySpeaking from ScanSoft (www.dragonsys.com) and ViaVoice from IBM (www.ibm.com), you can dictate text without adding artificial pauses between words. These programs understand your normal speaking voice, and they can handle more than one hundred words a minute (which beats touch typing).

Although this technology has come a long way, you still have to "train" the computer to recognize your speech patterns, and voice dictation on a computer is still nowhere near 100 percent accurate. Unfortunately, using voice-recognition software doesn't get you out of proofreading your text. If you use a word that your computer doesn't recognize (such as a technical term or a phrase from a foreign language), it takes only a second to add that word to the computer's dictionary; after you save the updated dictionary to the hard drive, your computer recognizes and types the new word in future sessions.

At a minimum, your PC needs a 16-bit sound card and a microphone to use a voice-recognition program, or a USB headset and microphone combo. However, the more system RAM you have, the better.

Everyone Needs a Good Image Editor

"A picture is worth a thousand words." That adage is the foundation of today's World Wide Web as well as graphical operating systems such as Windows. Power users add graphics to their documents, use images as a background for their operating system or their Web pages, build animated GIFs (*graphic interchange format,* one of the popular image formats on the Web), and demand high-resolution digital cameras for taking pictures of everything from the family dog to Stonehenge.

Because images are so important to today's computer power user, it's no accident that graphics editors such as Paint Shop Pro, from Jasc (www.jasc.com), and Photoshop Elements, from Adobe (www.adobe.com), are some of the most popular applications available today. With an image editor, you can alter the size and shape of an image, crop it to enhance a particular element, and rotate it as you please. It's easy to add text or paste another image on top of an original. You can even edit the individual dots (*pixels*) in an image or draw on an image with a virtual paintbrush or spray can.

Keep It Clean!

What power user wants to sit at a dirty keyboard? After you've spent time and money building your own computer, it makes sense to clean the case, monitor screen, keyboard, floppy drive, and pointing device from time to time (as well as your scanner and printer, if you have them). Dust and grime can interfere with the proper operation of your mouse or trackball. And if you don't clean the heads on your floppy drive and tape backup, they start losing data!

Here are a few tips for keeping your hardware squeaky clean:

- **Case:** I recommend using a sponge dampened with mild soap and water to clean the outside of your computer case; others have told me that they use an antistatic surface cleaner, which you can find at an office supply store.

✔ **Monitor:** For your monitor, use a lens-cleaning solution and a soft lens-polishing cloth, both of which you'll find at your local computer store, eyeglass shop, or camera store. Avoid using plain old window cleaner like you would avoid a case of pneumonia.

✔ **Keyboard:** For your keyboard, nothing is better than using a can of compressed air; it's great at cleaning hard-to-reach crevices. I've also used a cotton swab (sometimes soaked with a little alcohol-based cleaning solution) to clean the ridges on my keyboard.

✔ **Floppy/tape backup drives:** For your floppy drive and tape backup drive, visit your local computer store and pick up the appropriate head cleaner. These cleaning systems typically use some sort of cloth pad, which you soak in alcohol and then load into the drive.

✔ **Mouse/trackball:** To clean your mouse or trackball, remove the retaining ring around the ball — usually you twist it in the direction indicated on the bottom of the mouse — and clean the contact points and rollers inside the mouse with a cotton swab soaked in alcohol. (Optical pointing devices don't need this kind of maintenance.)

Chapter 18

Ten Important Assembly Tips

Assembling your own computer is a simple job if you're handy with a screwdriver — but, like just about every other human endeavor, you gain experience each time you build another PC. In this chapter, I present a list of tips and tricks that I've learned over the years that can help speed up the entire assembly process, help prevent accidents and mistakes, and generally make the assembly process more enjoyable.

Read the Instructions First! (Rule Number One)

I know, I know . . . *nothing* is more boring than reading the instructions for installing a hard drive or a video card; even techno-nerds dislike reading hardware and software documentation. However, every second that you spend reading about and familiarizing yourself with the installation process for a computer component will save you hours of frustration when you're knee-deep in your computer, trying to get that new part to work. It doesn't matter whether you read the instructions fifteen minutes before you start installation or three days ahead of time, just *read them completely* first. Trust me on this one — even the folks at NASA (and the techs in nuclear submarines) read instructions. If you don't have a manual for a scavenged component, check the manufacturer's Web site — often, you'll find a documentation archive for discontinued products.

Build the Perfect Workspace

Your kitchen table might be the most convenient place to assemble your computer, but is it truly the best workspace? Your work area must be large and sturdy enough to hold your computer's chassis and parts and your tools — and secure and quiet (think kids and furry beasts). A well-equipped workspace also has these features:

- ✔ **Access to at least two or three power plugs:** During testing, you have to at least provide power to your computer and the monitor, but it never hurts to have a spare plug available in case you need to add and test an external device, such as a DVD recorder or tape backup unit.

- ✔ **An adjustable lighting source:** If you can't see it, you can't tighten it! I use an adjustable extension lamp. (The gooseneck variety can be positioned perfectly.)

- ✔ **A smooth surface that won't scratch or mar your computer case:** Because the paint on a PC's case — especially a fancy neon green mod case — is easily scratched, it pays to cover your workspace with a few sheets of newspaper to keep your case looking new. And unlike a tablecloth, that newspaper won't build up static electricity.

Keep Track of UTOs (Unidentified Tiny Objects)

Why do some pieces of computer hardware have to be so doggone small? I'm talking about screws, jumpers, terminators, and other assorted tiny objects that you need to keep track of while you're assembling your computer.

Here's how you can make the perfect receptacle for these diminutive troublemakers: Glue a small magnet into the center of an old ashtray or ceramic bowl with a broad base and then keep this "parts basket" handy and near to you while you're assembling your computer. (Or, if you like, fasten it to your worktable.) The magnet will hold small screws, slot covers, and the like — and you won't be constantly digging in your pockets for small parts. (Don't permanently park a floppy disk in your bowl.)

Make Sure That You Have Everything You Need

Before you start the installation of a new component, make sure that you have all the cables, screws, and connectors required for finishing the job. When you open your new part, check that the box contains everything it should; if you're scavenging a part from an older PC, you should also take any screws, cables, or wires that connect it or hold it in place.

Similarly, it always pays to identify the requirements for a new part before you add it. For example, if you're going to install a new internal DVD recorder, does your power supply still have an unused power cable and connector of the right size? If not, you'll need a *Y power cable adapter,* which transforms a single power cable into two cables and connectors. If you're buying a parallel port printer, do you have a bidirectional printer cable with the right gender connectors handy, or will you have to buy one? If you're buying an internal component, does your PC's chassis still have an open bay of the right height?

A little preparation goes a long way toward avoiding simple frustrations (for example, suddenly realizing that you don't have the required batteries for your new multimedia speakers) as well as big headaches (such as discovering that you don't have a spare PCI adapter card slot for your new internal modem).

Yell for Help If Necessary

Some of the assembly steps that you encounter when building your own PC might make you nervous — for example, installing a CPU or a memory module — whereas others might require additional configuration, such as fine-tuning your computer for use with a new DVD recorder or adding drivers for a new network card. Always keep in mind that several sources of assistance are available and that there's no reason to be embarrassed about asking for help.

If you can't find the answers that you're looking for in the documentation that accompanied the new part, try these resources:

✔ **Query the manufacturer:** Most hardware manufacturers offer technical support over the telephone and also provide FAQs (lists of *frequently asked questions*) about their products on their Web sites.

✔ **Ask someone:** A friend, family member, or fellow computer club member with experience in computer hardware can come in very handy. (Don't forget to pick up the check the next time you have lunch together.)

> ✔ **Find a computer store/tech:** Most computer repair shops are happy to answer a few questions for free. If you find yourself completely unable to install a particular component, it's likely (of course) that you can pay one of the store's techs to install the part for you. (Hey, techno-types need new hard drives, too.)

Use a Magnetic Screwdriver

Carpenters have their hammers, woodsmen are skilled with an ax, but the computer technician's tool of choice is a trusty magnetized screwdriver. Look for a reversible model that has both standard (straight) and Phillips (star) tips. With your magnetized screwdriver by your side, you won't panic when you inevitably drop a screw deep within the guts of your new PC. Just poke around in the general area and let magnetism do the rest for you.

Don't worry that the screwdriver will wreak magnetic havoc on floppy disks or backup tapes: The magnetic field from a screwdriver isn't powerful enough to damage disks or tapes unless you park your screwdriver on top of them for at least a weekend. Therefore, when your screwdriver is not in use, keep it in a drawer or on the wall. Some true techno-wizards keep their screwdrivers in a belt holder. Thankfully, a screwdriver or all-purpose, multifunction-style tool slung on your belt has replaced the pocket protector as the status symbol of the uber-tech.

Start Your Own Parts Box

The last time that you installed a computer component, did you find yourself with an extra unneeded screw, adapter card slot cover, cable, or connector? If so, don't throw away those extras. Instead, grab an empty cardboard box and throw all your unneeded computer parts in there (except for circuit boards and larger components, which should be stored separately in static-free plastic bags). Voilà! You've created your own parts box. The next time you suddenly find yourself one screw short or you need an extra jumper block, check your parts box before you take off to your local Maze o' Wires electronics store. The more that you work with computer hardware, the more this box will grow. You'll soon have a comprehensive treasure chest of small computer parts.

When you upgrade parts of your computer, you can always keep the older components as backup hardware in case of failure; as a general rule, however, I try to sell older components (or donate them to my local school or church if I can't sell them). Unlike the small parts in your parts box, older components that you've outgrown end up taking up too much room in your closet or garage.

Take Your Time: The Zen of Assembly

You might be excited about building your own PC, but rushing through an assembly step can lead to frustrating mistakes, such as mismatched cables and upside-down components. Follow the step-by-step instructions in this book and the documentation that comes with your hardware — and don't move to the next step until you've completely finished every task in the current step.

If you're working on a particularly delicate assembly step (such as adding a CPU or a memory module to your motherboard) and it's not going well, take a deep breath or two. Then verify that you're trying to do the right thing. A friend of mine has a big sign above his workbench that reads "This isn't a race!" (That's good advice for any craftsperson.)

No one is timing you, so move at your own speed.

Don't Cover Up Too Quickly

I would never use a computer on a day-to-day basis without its case; the components would get far too dirty too quickly, and there would always be a danger of spilling liquids on exposed components or touching a circuit board while the computer is on.

However, because everything changes when you're installing a new internal part in your computer, keep the case off until you're certain that the new component is working properly. Nothing is more irritating than attaching the case on a computer and then finding that you forgot to connect the power cable to your new DVD recorder or hard drive. Before I learned this important rule, I would sometimes remove the case on my PC three or four times until everything finally worked. As long as you keep liquids away from your computer and don't touch any internal components while it's on, you're in no danger. Save time and trouble by leaving the case off until you're sure that your computer is working.

The Cable Rule: Check and Double-Check

I've spoken to many computer technicians and hardware techno-wizards, and every one of them agrees: The number-one error that crops up while installing a new part in your computer is mismatched or disconnected cabling. Problems can even crop up with cables that are supposed to be foolproof. Although internal power cables are designed to fit only one way, you have to remember to connect them in the first place. (This oversight is typically the cause of the classic line "Hey, it doesn't act like it's getting power at all!" That's because it *isn't*. Around my shop, this discovery is typically followed by the sound of my palm hitting my forehead.)

On the other hand, many internal EIDE and SCSI cables can be connected upside down, so remember the pin 1 rule: Pin 1 of the male connector on the component should always align with the marked wire on the cable (which is the cable manufacturer's way of identifying which wire on the cable is wire 1).

Although it might take a few seconds extra when you install a new part, I recommend that you check each cable connection — including cables leading to other parts — before you test the new component. You can easily and accidentally unplug an existing connection while you're routing wires and moving things around inside your computer's chassis. If you install a new part and another part suddenly refuses to work properly, there's a good chance that you accidentally unplugged something.

Chapter 19

Ten Ways to Speed Up Your PC

*I*f computer owners have one universal desire, it's more speed. In this chapter, I outline several tricks that you can use to improve the overall performance of your computer. Some of these tips cost money (such as adding memory modules or selecting faster hardware), but others won't cost you a cent. Go, Speed Racer, go!

Defragment Your Hard Drive

Over weeks and months of use, computers running any version of Windows (including XP and 2000) will invariably slow down significantly because of hard drive fragmentation.

First, a quick explanation: When you delete a file from your hard drive, that area of your hard drive can then accept data from another file. If the file to be saved is larger than this open area, however, Windows must split the file into fragments. When your computer needs to load a file, Windows automatically (and invisibly) reassembles these fragments back into the complete file. However, the more fragmented the files are on your hard drive, the longer this step takes and the slower your PC becomes.

How can you defragment your hard drive? If you're running Windows XP or Windows 2000, click the Start button, and then choose Programs⇨ Accessories⇨System Tools⇨Disk Defragmenter.

My defragmenting program of choice for Windows XP is the Speed Disk program included with the Norton SystemWorks package (www.norton.com), which you can find online for around $70.

Get Connected with the Speediest Interfaces

If you're interested in the fastest possible throughput from your internal hard drives and CD-ROM/DVD drives, your computer cries out for a serial ATA or SCSI connection — for plugging in external devices, demand FireWire or USB 2.0 connections.

If your PC came with an enhanced integrated drive electronics (EIDE) hard drive, you can still add any of these connections (either by using your motherboard's built-in hardware or by buying a PCI adapter with the correct connectors). However, if you've done your homework and you're looking for a power user PC, it pays to build your computer around a motherboard with serial ATA (or SCSI), FireWire, and USB 2.0 built-in. "Just say *no* to EIDE and USB 1.1!"

I recommend an AGP or a PCI-Express video card as well — especially if gaming is high on your list of applications!

Install More RAM

Friends, installing more RAM (*random access memory)* is the big one! Any 32- or 64-bit operating system — including all breeds of Windows, Linux, and UNIX — benefits from more system RAM. And with RAM prices free-falling over the past few years, most PC owners can afford to bulk up to a gigabyte or two of RAM. Here's the skinny: If a program and its data don't fit in RAM, your operating system must save that data to and read it from a temporary file (or *virtual memory*) on your hard drive. This process, called *swapping,* can slow everything down to a crawl while your PC juggles data back and forth.

With at least 512MB of memory or more, your operating system will have more elbow room, and it will have to swap less data to disk — which means that you can open more applications at one time and your entire computer will run faster overall.

Crank Up the CPU Steam

If you've already traversed Chapter 3, you're familiar with processors and motherboards. Armed with this knowledge, you can consider an upgrade to your existing CPU — if your motherboard can accept a faster CPU. You reap the benefits while you're using processor-intensive applications such as graphics programs, spreadsheets, and the latest games. The old CPU can be stored as a backup, sold to friends or family, or donated. (Science teachers love 'em!)

As a rule, I don't go through the trouble of upgrading a CPU just one grade. In other words, you probably won't see a dramatic increase in performance when you upgrade from a Pentium 4 running at 2.4 GHz to a Pentium 4 running at 2.8 GHz. On the other hand, if your motherboard can "jump" at least two steps — from 2.4 GHz to 3 GHz, for example — you'll be extending the life of your existing motherboard, and you'll *really* notice the difference.

 Some Web sites will advise you to *overclock* your processor: In other words, configure the motherboard settings so that the CPU runs faster than its rated speed. I do *not* recommend overclocking for several good reasons: It shortens the life of the CPU, and you have to use one or two fans on the chip to keep it cool. Overclocking is not an easy task, and it doesn't work as often as it does work. You can end up locking up your PC as tight as Fort Knox while you're monkeying with different clock speeds and bus speed settings. Overclocking just isn't worth the effort!

Keep Your Backgrounds Plain

Graphical operating systems such as Windows XP and Linux can be dressed up with 16-million-color photographs as backgrounds, animated icons, and other exotic eye candy. If you want your PC to run faster under one of these operating systems, however, select a simple, single-color background. Why? Your PC must use extra RAM to display true-color images or animated icons. Some full-screen background pictures that I've seen are nearly 6 megabytes in size — they're meant for resolutions of 1600 x 1200 (and even higher), and they're 16-million-color bitmaps! If you use a high-resolution, full-screen bitmap with 16 million colors as your background, you may notice that your PC slows down significantly when it's loading the background image (or redrawing it after you've closed a window or quit a game).

Install a Fast CD-ROM or DVD Drive

Paying for a higher X factor is worth the money when you're shopping for your CD-ROM or DVD drive. This *X factor* is a method of describing the speed of the drive's throughput as a multiple of the original single-speed drive, which (in the case of CD-ROM drives) delivered 150 Kbps.

The higher the X factor of your CD-ROM or DVD drive, the faster the drive can deliver data to your computer. You especially notice a faster drive when you're installing a new program, watching a DVD movie, or playing a game and the drive is reading digital video. For complete details on adding a CD-ROM or DVD drive to your PC, visit Chapter 8.

Remove Resident Programs

Beware! Your computer might be harboring hidden programs that are sucking power and resources from your applications. No, I'm not talking about viruses; these programs, called *resident programs,* have been around since the days of DOS. A resident program is loaded automatically when you boot your computer, and the program continues to work in the background while you run the applications that you want. Unlike a virus, a resident program is usually doing something you want, such as checking the status of your disk drive, polling your Internet service provider for your e-mail, or displaying stock quotes.

Unfortunately, if you load down your computer with too many resident programs, your PC has to devote too much processor time and RAM to maintain them; thus, your applications will slow down accordingly. To make sure that this slowdown doesn't happen, don't load more than two or three resident tasks. Also avoid installing programs that automatically start each time that you boot your PC unless you really need them to.

Under Windows XP and 2000, you can recognize most resident programs by their icons in the system tray, which occupies the far-right side of the status bar opposite from the Start button. To determine what each of these icons does, you can usually left- or right-click the icon to display a menu. (And most resident tasks have a menu item that you can select to shut them down.) If you don't need a program and it keeps loading a system tray icon, feel free to choose Start➪Control Panel➪Add or Remove Programs. This will take you to the Add or Remove Programs dialog box, where you can click the offending application and then click Change/Remove to delete it. Hurrah!

Under UNIX, Linux, or Windows NT, display your list of applications that are running and look for resident programs that might have been loaded during the boot process.

Although uninstalling a resident program is always the best way to banish it from your system, you can also stop a specific program from loading during startup under Windows XP. Choose Start⇨Run to display the Run dialog box, type **MSCONFIG** in the Open box, and then click OK. This runs the System Configuration Utility Windows XP application, where you can make changes to the behavior of XP during the boot process. Click the Startup tab, and you'll see a list of the applications that Windows XP automatically runs during startup; locate the program that you want to disable in the list, clear the check box next to the program, and then click OK.

Accelerate Windows with Your Video Card

If you're scavenging parts from an older computer for use with a new Pentium 4 PC that you're building and you're interested in the best video performance, buy a new accelerated graphics port (AGP) or PCI-Express video card instead of using an older PCI video card. Most video adapter cards sold a few years ago don't provide high-performance hardware acceleration support or efficient 3-D support for Windows. A modern Windows 3-D accelerated card made with an NVIDIA or an ATI graphics chip speeds up your entire PC because it takes over most video-related tasks from your computer's CPU (which can then turn its attention to other, more important CPU stuff). The speed increase is most apparent when you're playing games and when you're opening and closing several application windows on your PC. Naturally, the heavier the graphical load on your PC, the more you benefit from an accelerated video card. Chapter 4 provides more detail on the different types of slots and adapter cards.

Use a Native File System

Traditionally, PC data storage has been formatted under the *DOS file system,* which is essentially a road map that your computer uses to store and retrieve files on your hard drive. Although the DOS file system has been used for many, many years, it isn't the most efficient design, and it doesn't directly support neat features such as long filenames.

If you've decided to use Windows XP, Windows 2000, Linux, or UNIX, you'll find that you have at least one alternative format for storing and retrieving files: Each of these operating systems has a *native file system* that improves on the DOS file system. In every case, your operating system can save and load data faster from its native file system, which was designed for use in a 32- or 64-bit multitasking environment. I especially recommend using the NT file system (NTFS) if you're running Windows XP or Windows 2000.

When you install Windows, Linux, or UNIX on a new hard drive, you're given the chance to reformat your hard drive for native file system support. I recommend that you use the native file system. If you still need DOS partitions on your computer — for example, if you've decided to run multiple operating systems — they should be formatted separately, and you should use a multiple-boot utility, such as System Commander, from Avanquest Publishing (www.v-com.com).

Don't Forget That Turbo Button!

Does your older PC with a scavenged case have a Turbo button? (The computer cases manufactured today no longer carry this switch — and even if your case has this switch, it might not be connected.) If your PC does have a Turbo button, you might boot your computer one day and find that everything suddenly seems to run slower, as though the CPU has been dipped in concrete. If so, your first suspect should be that doggone Turbo button; if your PC isn't running in Turbo mode, it's forced to run more slowly.

Try punching the Turbo button and see whether your PC speeds up dramatically; if so, grab a piece of tape and a marking pen and cover the button with a barrier that reads *Hands Off!* (In fact, the owners of some computers that I've built have requested that I disconnect the Turbo switch wire from the motherboard, which usually defaults to normal Turbo mode.)

Chapter 20

Ten Things to Avoid Like the Plague

● ●

In This Chapter

▶ Avoiding refurbished hardware

▶ Saying, "No" to the Pentium III chip

▶ Averting disaster from lost data on floppies

▶ Turning off unnecessary passwords

▶ Making sure that you don't violate a copyright

▶ Keeping small children away from the keyboard

▶ Giving pirated software a wide berth

▶ Leaving monitors and power supplies closed

▶ Avoiding a long-term lease on a computer

▶ Watching version numbers when buying software

● ●

In this chapter, I name a number of computer-related things that can lead to lost data, hardware headaches, legal hassles, and even physical injury — in other words, things that you should shun at all costs! Some things on this list should be avoided while you're building your PC, and others are dangerous practices that some people engage in with their computer after it's up and running. I recommend that you keep the following three sayings in mind; they seem to cover most situations in this chapter:

✔ If it seems too good to be true, it probably *is*.

✔ Let the buyer beware.

✔ Warning labels are there for a reason.

(That last one is a Mark's Maxim, but it ought to be just as famous as the others.)

It's "Refurbished" for a Reason

The word *refurbished* seems to be appearing more and more often in computer hardware magazines, computer stores on the Web, and catalogs for discount computers. *Refurbished hardware* is hardware that was returned for some reason to the manufacturer (usually because it was defective). The company fixes the defect and then resells the hardware to another distributor.

By law, refurbished computers and hardware components must be identified as such in any advertising. The distributor usually trumpets the features offered on the computer, the fact that you get a warranty, and perhaps even that the merchandise is "like new." Usually, you do save a significant amount on refurbished hardware, so the prices that these companies advertise will indeed catch your eye.

However, I recommend that you give refurbished components a wide berth and buy only new parts (or scavenge working parts from an existing computer). Personally, I would *never* purchase a refurbished computer or refurbished component, and here are the reasons why:

✔ You have no idea why the item was returned — but you can usually safely assume that it wasn't working properly.

✔ You have no way of knowing how the former owner treated the item.

✔ The manufacturer's warranty is typically less than 90 days, which is usually a much shorter length of time than the warranty on a new item.

✔ Many refurbished parts are not completely retested before they are shipped back to the store.

✔ The sale is usually final, so if it breaks, you're stuck with it.

If you do decide to buy a refurbished item, here's another Mark's Maxim for you:

Always find out all you can about that refurbished bargain before you spend your money!

Looking for an Antique? Buy a Pentium III CPU

Many stores and mail-order companies that sell computer hardware are still selling CPU chips and motherboards based on the Pentium III design. The Pentium III was a grand chip, and many of us techno-types with several computers in the house can point to at least one, but the days of the Pentium III are past us now. If you're building a new computer to run any operating system other than Windows 98 or Windows ME, take my advice and buy a Pentium 4 CPU and motherboard.

Although the Pentium III CPU can indeed run Windows XP, the older architecture simply isn't fast enough or advanced enough to offer anywhere near the performance of a Pentium 4 computer. Sure, these older components are much cheaper now, and you can save a considerable amount of money. However, you'll likely start looking for an upgrade CPU soon, and a Pentium III-socketed motherboard doesn't accept a Pentium 4 CPU.

If you're building a computer from the ground up, buy a Pentium 4 processor; you'll thank yourself for many months to come!

Never Depend on Floppies

Floppy disks and important data just don't mix. Floppies are susceptible to magnetic fields (*never* store them on top of a speaker or your PC's case); they have a low *shelf life* (the amount of time you can reliably store a floppy disk and then retrieve data from it); the exchange of floppies can spread viruses; they're easily mixed up or mislaid (even if you label them); and occasionally one computer can't read floppy disks formatted on another computer. In my years as a consultant and computer technician, I've felt the pain of literally dozens of folks who lost valuable data by trusting those familiar floppies.

Don't get me wrong: Floppies are fine for carrying a document or two in your pocket or sending a document through the mail — as long as you have a backup copy of that data on your hard drive. From time to time, I even save a document on a floppy as a simple backup for a day or so, but I don't expect with absolute certainty to be able to read that document after six months.

If you need to store your data away from your computer or send it to someone else, *please* consider something more reliable, such as a Zip drive, or back up that information to digital audio tape (DAT). The best solution, however, is a favorite of mine: A CD recorder can archive information for more than ten years at 700MB on each disc, and CD-R discs are a much more permanent data-retrieval system than any magnetic method. If you opt for DVD, you can store 4 to almost 9GB of data, with the same reliability. (I discuss CD and DVD recorders in Chapter 8, and Chapter 7 contains more information about Zip drives and DAT backup.) Of course, the person who receives your nomadic data will need the same type of hardware to read the media you send.

Another removable storage device that's sweeping the PC world is the USB Flash drive, which plugs directly into your PC's universal serial bus (USB) port and provides 32MB to a whopping 2GB of storage!

Under Windows 2003 Server or Windows XP, a Flash drive requires no drivers or special software. Just plug it in, and your PC will recognize it as a removable media drive. The USB connection means that it's universally compatible with any late-model PC or Macintosh and that it transfers data much faster (and more reliably) than a floppy drive. Plus, these convenient solid-state drives aren't much bigger than a ballpoint pen. Also, because there are no moving parts, they'll last practically forever. Prices range from $50 to $300 for Flash drives.

Help Stamp Out Unnecessary Passwords!

Password protection is appropriate for sensitive files stored in an office network environment or connecting with your Internet service provider. But passwords that you've assigned to Zip disks, backup tapes, screen savers, archived files in .zip format, and even basic input/output system (BIOS) passwords that don't allow your PC to boot are nothing but trouble for the typical home computer owner. If you have no reason to be overly cautious about your computer and its data, for heaven's sake, *don't assign passwords that you don't need!*

Why do I despise unnecessary passwords? I've received countless calls from friends, family members, and clients who can't retrieve data from a disk or an archive file (or even log on to their own computer) because they've forgotten the password or typed it incorrectly. In effect, you're locked out from accessing your own data. In the worst-case scenario, all you can do is reformat that backup tape or that Zip disk and bid that data good-bye. (And I can tell you that your memories of lost data will last a long, long time.)

Honor Thy Friend's Copyright

Computers and the Internet are the best tools ever invented for accessing and sharing information across the entire globe, and this dynamic duo also makes it extremely easy to cut and paste your way to plagiarism and copyright violations. If an image or a document is not your original work, you *must* be careful (and that includes quoting — even simple phrases).

For a quick rundown on the basics of copyrights, jump to Chapter 14.

Your PC Is Not a Kindergarten

If you're a parent, you probably want your children to be computer literate by the time they graduate from elementary school. And it's true that the earlier your children are exposed to a computer, the more comfortable they will be with a computer later in life.

However, I recommend that you keep very small children away from your computer until they're older; a good minimum age is about four years old. An active toddler can do a surprising amount of damage to a typical PC: jamming floppies the wrong way (or jamming toaster pastries any way) into drives, spilling juice or milk on the keyboard or the case, yanking on wires and cords, and slapping the monitor. I've even seen a CD-ROM drive with peanut butter inside. To a one- or two-year-old, your PC is just another interesting toy with lights, and that child won't be learning anything useful about the computer for a while. Keep your computer safe until the kids are ready at three or four years old.

Don't Jump on the Pirate Ship

Programs illegally copied or distributed are referred to as *pirated* software. You can download such illicit commercial software — such as games, applications, and utilities — from a large network of Web sites and Internet newsgroups.

Besides being illegal, pirated software is an invitation for disaster; many renegade computer programmers use pirated software to distribute viruses and Trojan horse programs. Although a Trojan horse program is described as a useful application and might even look like one while it's running, it destroys data on your computer — or, in the worst case scenario, even allows a hacker to remotely gain control of your PC over the Internet!

Support the authors of shareware and the companies that produce the best commercial software: Buy their products and *don't pirate them!*

Keep Out of Monitors and Power Supplies

Most of the components used in your computer, such as the hard drive, are sealed; even if you could open them, you'd never be able to repair them. Building a computer is a task of assembly, and you should never have to disassemble anything — except for removing components that you're scavenging from an older computer.

Two sealed components deserve an even wider berth: your computer's power supply and your computer monitor. *Never attempt to open the case on either of these parts.* They can be repaired only by computer technicians or if sent back to the factory. They can also be quite dangerous if plugged in while uncovered.

Don't Lease a PC for the Long Haul

Are you considering leasing a PC instead of building your own system? Leasing sometimes seems like a better deal; after all, you can start using the PC immediately, and if something breaks it generally gets fixed for free. Some mail-order companies and larger computer chain stores allow you to lease a computer for a monthly fee. If you need a computer for only a couple of months, leasing is fine. However, leasing a computer for more than six months is not a very good idea. PCs depreciate in value so quickly and advance in technology so fast that your leased computer will be significantly less powerful and worth less within just a year or two.

By building your own computer, you end up with the most power for the money, and you can continue to upgrade your PC to stretch its useful life over many years.

Avoid Older Versions of PC Software

If you're a novice at buying computer software for your new PC, pay close attention to the version numbers of the software you're buying. Often, you see expensive applications being sold for far less than the going rate in a catalog or on a Web site. For example, an integrated suite of office applications might be advertised at $500 at one store but only $250 at another. Usually, the store selling the software for much less is selling an older version. For example, the more expensive office suite might be Version 7.0, and the cheaper version might be Version 6.0. The version number is usually listed in the advertisement, but it might be stuck down at the bottom of the ad.

If you're unsure about the latest version number of a particular program, call the store or connect to the manufacturer's Web site.

Part VI
Appendixes

The 5th Wave   By Rich Tennant

"Can't I just give you riches or something?"

In this part . . .

Here you can find two helpful appendixes: a comparison of the popular operating systems now available for the PC and a glossary of all those awful computer acronyms, abbreviations, part names, and terms that you don't want to memorize.

Appendix A

Choosing Your Operating System

● ●

*M*ost computer owners run whatever operating system came with their computer or whatever's the hot topic in this month's *CompuSmarts* magazine — whether it's right for them or not. Running under the wrong operating system is as bad as using the wrong workbench to build a piece of furniture: You'll probably finish the job eventually, but it will take much longer than it should and your finished work won't look as good.

How do you determine which operating system is right for you? In this appendix, I show you the good points and bad points of each major operating system used on PCs today: Is it fast enough? Stable enough? Does it support the applications that you want? Most important, does it make life on the computer easier for you?

Become Your Own Consultant!

You might be asking yourself, "Why don't I just run what everyone else runs?" True, today's common PC operating system of choice is Windows XP, and it does a great job for 70 percent or so of all the PCs around the world. But what if your needs fit in the *other* 30 percent? That's why you need to become your own consultant to choose an operating system. Heck, if you want to make things as authentic as possible, you can even charge yourself a tremendous amount of money. (Just don't try claiming it on your taxes.)

Consider these points when you're choosing an operating system:

> ✔ **Speed:** Are you looking for the fastest operating system? If so, score one point for the more popular 32- and 64-bit operating systems on your list: Windows XP and XP x64, Windows 2003 Server, UNIX, and Linux. These platforms load programs and data faster because they improve many of the shortcomings of older operating systems, provide native file systems (more on this later), and were designed for today's faster CPUs.

✔ **GUI:** Do you want a *graphical user interface?* In terms that mere techno-mortals can understand, do you want to use a mouse and icons to run programs or drag and drop a file on your printer? If so, you should lean toward Windows 2003 Server, Windows XP, or Linux (with a graphical shell). However, don't automatically assume that a graphical user interface is faster and easier for everything you do on a computer. Those of us who have been working with computers for many years often find the DOS command line better for many tasks. For example, you can open a DOS command line box from within Windows XP to move files from one directory to another.

✔ **Stability:** Is stability a factor? Does your application need to keep running day after day, solid as a rock? If so, consider Windows XP, Windows 2003 Server, Linux, and UNIX, which are the most stable platforms. They're least likely to lock up (or, as computer types like to say, *crash*). DOS and the remaining Windows platforms (Windows 98 and Me) unfortunately hit the finish line in last place.

✔ **Legacy applications:** Will your new computer be running an older DOS program as its primary application? If so, consider leaving DOS as your operating system and don't upgrade (especially if the program will be controlling any special hardware, such as a light pen, cash drawer, or digital sensor). Although all versions of Windows enable you to access DOS through a special window, none of these newer platforms is as completely compatible as the real McCoy! This is the reason why many small businesses are still running PCs with DOS: The application that they're running was written in the early 1990s, and because the computer is used for only that one application, there's no need for an upgrade to another operating system. (That's if the program recognizes that you've crossed into Y2K, of course — thank goodness *that* whole thing is behind us!)

Programs that were written years ago and are bug-free and dependable are *legacy applications.* For instance, a movie rental shop might be using a checkout program and database written for DOS several years ago. Sure, you could buy all-new Windows-based checkout and database software — if you can afford new tools, that's certainly a good decision. But what if business hasn't been that good recently? Or what if your corporate bigwigs demand that you use their system? Sometimes it's better to follow the programmer's adage: "If it ain't broke, don't mess with it!"

✔ **Hardware auto configuration:** Do you want your operating system to automatically configure new hardware whenever possible? If so, Windows XP and Windows 2003 Server easily win the race. DOS and UNIX don't finish at all because they offer no automatic configuration. (Linux, however, is becoming more hardware-friendly with each new version.)

✔ **Software compatibility:** Are you looking for the operating system offering the most applications and software? In that case, the definite winners are Windows 98 and Windows Me, which can run programs written for Windows 95 and Windows 3.1 as well as most DOS programs. Windows XP and Windows 2003 Server can run most Windows 95 software, but they have more compatibility problems with DOS and Windows 3.1 applications. At the end of the line are DOS, Linux, and UNIX, which can run only applications written especially for them, although both Linux and UNIX can run *emulators* — programs that allow one operating system to run programs written for another operating system.

✔ **Security:** Will your new computer be used as a Web server, an intranet machine, or an Internet firewall? The platforms to watch are Linux, UNIX, and Windows Server 2003. These operating systems include the low-level security features needed for an Internet server; in fact, the Internet was built on a backbone of UNIX computers, and most machines carrying the Internet's digital traffic still use Linux or UNIX. (This explains why Internet old-timers know all those cryptic Archie, Gopher, and FTP commands by heart!) If you prefer a graphical Internet platform, Windows 2003 Server has Internet applications built in for the network administrator.

✔ **Networking:** Will your new computer need to run on an office network? Give the nod to all versions of Windows; all these platforms have built-in networking capabilities with automatic configuration. Linux, UNIX, and DOS can also network, although they require more work — and DOS needs additional software to run a network as well.

"But, Wait — 1 Collect Operating Systems!"

Many computer owners don't fit into one of those nice, neat slots that indicate precisely which operating system is the right one. I should know — I'm one myself. Because you can run only one operating system on a PC, does that mean that you need more than one computer? Perhaps more than one of *everything?* (Hey, this could cost you a million dollars by the time that you're through!)

Back up a second there. You *can* actually run more than one operating system on a single computer. Windows XP, Windows 2003 Server, UNIX, and Linux all have a basic *multiboot* feature, which, in plain English, means that you can select from multiple operating systems when you turn on your PC. For example, you can select whether you want to run Linux or Windows XP. This is the way to go if you sometimes need to run a particular application available only under Linux, but you'd rather run Windows XP most of the time.

There's an even better way to take care of a multiboot computer, though. To choose an operating system at startup, use a commercial multiboot utility, such as System Commander 8, from V Communications (www.v-com.com). This type of program keeps track of all the files that you need for maintaining each operating system. You can even set up your hard drive with partitions for each platform. If you boot into one particular platform more than the others, you can set up a default operating system that loads automatically after a certain number of seconds have elapsed. You can add or delete operating systems at any time, and the better multiboot programs are easy to use.

If you've decided to run a multiboot configuration, make sure that you have more than enough hard drive real estate to comfortably hold all the operating systems that you'll use (as well as the applications and assorted other junk that normally fill up a hard drive). For example, if you want to run a computer with both Windows XP and Linux or UNIX, you need a minimum of 5 or 6GB for an average installation. Check the system requirements listed in the manual for each operating system that you plan to run, add them together, and then add an extra gigabyte for *lagniappe* (a Cajun word that means *something extra*)!

DOS: The Old Workhorse Lives On

Name: DOS
Aliases: PC-DOS, MS-DOS, Pokey, Dinosaur
Learning curve: Novice to intermediate
Architecture: 16-bit, character-based, limited graphics

Sure, the guy at the computer store says, "DOS is dead." However, don't forget that DOS was around for many, many years before Windows arrived on the scene, and a mind-boggling number of freeware, shareware, and commercial programs have been written for DOS. Those applications still do the job — they just don't look as pretty, and they don't have the icon-encrusted, drag-and-drop visual controls of a Windows program. Figure A-1 illustrates a common DOS application. Okay, I'll admit it: That's a great old DOS game called DND that I still play.

DOS has one or two other advantages: As I mentioned earlier in this chapter, many computer techie types who have been around for years find it faster to type commands than to select them from a menu. DOS doesn't take up acres of hard drive territory, so you don't lose 350MB of space on your drive just to hold the operating system. Because it's not a multitasking system, DOS is inherently more stable than Windows (as long as the program you're running doesn't lock up). However, you can run only a single program at one time, so don't expect to handle your finances while you're e-mailing Uncle Milton. (Actually, because very few DOS applications are designed for the Internet, you should forget about e-mail.)

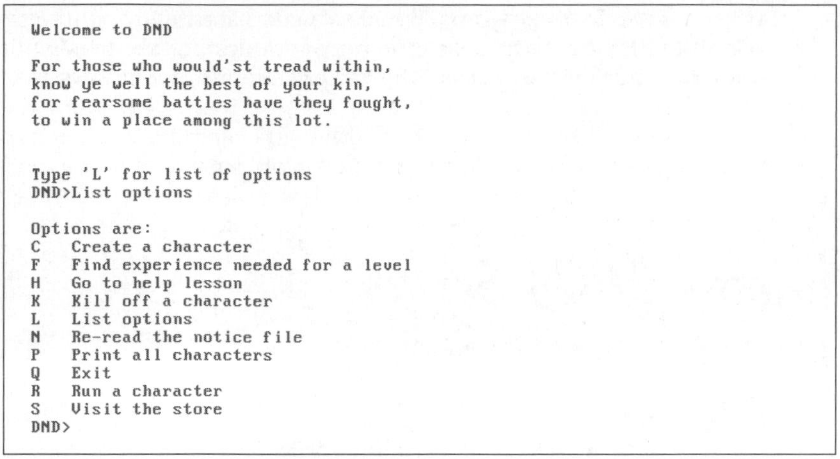

```
Welcome to DND

For those who would'st tread within,
know ye well the best of your kin,
for fearsome battles have they fought,
to win a place among this lot.


Type 'L' for list of options
DND>List options

Options are:
C    Create a character
F    Find experience needed for a level
H    Go to help lesson
K    Kill off a character
L    List options
N    Re-read the notice file
P    Print all characters
Q    Exit
R    Run a character
S    Visit the store
DND>
```

Figure A-1: DOS may be old, but it ain't dead yet, pardner.

DOS summary: At this time, the only major continuing development of DOS software is for specialized hardware such as point-of-sale terminals and scientific devices, and even that is fading away. Time to wave farewell to DOS. I'm certainly not advocating that you run DOS on a new PC. But DOS will probably continue as the least-common-denominator operating system for a while, so it deserves at least a mention in passing.

Windows 95, 98, and Me: Thanks for the Memories

Name: Windows 95, Windows 98, and Windows Me
Aliases: Win95, WinDoze, the Mac lookalike
Learning curve: Novice to intermediate
Architecture: 16-bit/32-bit graphical user interface

The legacy DOS-based versions of Windows have finally passed the crown to their more stable offspring, Windows XP and Windows 2003 Server, so I don't go into great detail here. Suffice it to say that these older versions of Windows might not have the driver support for today's hardware (majorly important), they lack the robust Internet and multimedia support of

Windows XP (majorly important), and they don't have many minor perks that have been added to more recent releases of Windows (minorly important).

However, if you've been given a copy of Windows 95 or 98, you can upgrade to Windows XP in the future, and virtually all Windows software still runs on Windows Me. In other words, it makes a good start while you're saving up for Windows XP. (And yes, these crotchety antiques do take up significantly less room on your hard drive than the newer versions of Windows.)

Windows 95, 98, and Me summary: Although I can't believe it, it's finally time to wave goodbye to Windows 98. Thanks, old friend.

Windows 2003 Server: Microsoft's First String

Name: Windows 2003 Server
Aliases: Windows 2K3, Neat, Windows with Teeth
Learning curve: Intermediate to advanced
Architecture: 32-bit graphical user interface

Windows 2003 Server is the preferred networking platform for the PC, although it demands the best of everything to run at thoroughbred speed: A typical 2003 Server machine has a minimum of 512MB RAM, the fastest possible processor, and as many gigabytes of hard drive space as you can pack into your case. Windows 2003 Server is also considerably more expensive than the Home Edition of Windows XP.

Windows 2003 Server supports multiple CPUs with SMP (short for *symmetric multiprocessing,* if you hadn't guessed). In English, this means that you can put more than one Pentium processor to work in the same machine! (Of course, your motherboard has to support SMP.)

Windows 2003 Server comes in a Small Business Edition as well, which features extra components such as a shared fax service and enhanced firewall. Windows 2003 Server features a user interface that's quite close to Windows XP, so if you're familiar with Windows XP, you need to educate yourself only on the Internet applications within Windows 2003 Server.

Windows 2003 Server summary: If you can afford the high price, if your computer is powerful enough to keep up with the requirements of Windows 2003 Server, and if you don't need to run any DOS applications, Windows 2003 Server is hard to beat for the PC power user, programmer, hardware technician, or network administrator.

Windows XP: The King of the Hill

Name: Windows XP
Aliases: WinXP, WinDoze: The Next Generation, Microsoft Bob II
Learning curve: Novice to intermediate
Architecture: 32-bit graphical user interface

There's no doubt about it: Windows XP is now the top dog at Microsoft. Why mess with success? Like Windows 98 before it, Windows XP is universally supported, runs 32-bit software, and can still run many older 16-bit applications. So what improvements have been added by the Microsoft crew to Windows XP over Windows 98? The major change is in the addition of new Internet technologies, such as the built-in Internet firewall and the ability to share a broadband Internet connection across a home or small office network. XP is far more stable than Windows 98 or Me because it has forever cast off the remnants of DOS that continued to cling to the operating system. XP also has the best support for recent multimedia arrivals, such as your MP3 player and your digital camera. Figure A-2 is a typical Windows XP screen shot, illustrating the screen effects, 3-D objects, and all-around high-tech look befitting our Matrix world.

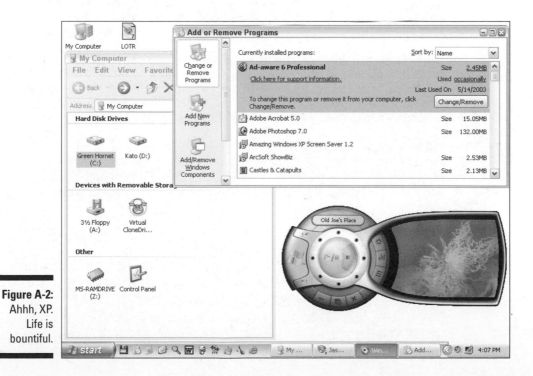

Figure A-2: Ahhh, XP. Life is bountiful.

If you are accustomed to Windows 98 and are stubborn, you can turn off certain parts of the new interface (or all of it, if you want to keep your Windows 98 functionality).

Even novices find that Windows XP is easy to learn. Online help is plentiful and easy to access, including the ability to retrieve the latest help from the Internet.

Conveniences abound within Windows XP. For example, the automatic hardware detection that it provides makes adding a new modem, printer, or scanner to your system much easier. Plug in the new device or install it within your computer's case, reboot, and Windows XP will likely recognize the device automatically.

Windows XP also includes built-in support for TCP/IP (*transfer control protocol/Internet protocol*), which is the communications protocol used to connect to the Web and the Internet, as well as excellent all-around support for LAN (local area network) connections. (For more about networking, see Chapter 12.) Game players will enjoy *DirectX,* which is the graphics engine that enables Windows games to use all the fancy features of your 3-D video card. (Chapter 6 tells you all about video cards.) If you're interested in multimedia, Windows XP includes support for digital video (in AVI and MPEG format) and digital audio (in MP3 and WAV format). You can now import pictures directly into your applications, including e-mail, word processing, and printing software.

You also get a number of utilities and tools that help you keep your computer running in top shape, including a disk defragmenter, a scanning program that can check your computer's hard drive for errors, a scheduler that can automatically launch programs whenever you specify, and (with the Professional version) a backup program that helps you back up the data on your computer.

The downside? Although Windows XP can run all the same 32-bit applications as Windows 2003 Server, it doesn't have many of Windows 2003 Server's server-level security features or built-in network support applications. And there have been a number of well-publicized loopholes in Windows XP security.

Just like its ancestors, Windows XP is a drive hog: Expect it to gobble up at least 4GB of your hard drive for a full installation, and that figure rises exponentially when you add programs and features. Whatever happened to the days when you could comfortably fit everything on a 40MB drive? (Oh, I remember — see the section entitled "DOS: The Old Workhorse Lives On," earlier in this appendix.)

Windows XP summary: XP has taken the place of Windows 98 and Me because it is bundled with new computers and is a great operating system for novices.

Truly, this is the version of Windows that most home PC owners have deserved for many years now (and Macintosh owners have *had* for several years now, but that's another story). (Now I'm going to catch all sorts of bad karma.)

I think this is a good time to mention my book *PCs All-in-One Desk Reference For Dummies,* 3rd Edition (Wiley). If you need a complete introduction to Windows XP, you'll find it there, along with coverage of all of today's hottest PC technologies, such as wireless networking, digital cameras, DVD recording, and Microsoft's Office 2003 suite. This is truly the one book that takes a snapshot of the entire PC world, and I'm particularly proud of it!

Linux: It's Not Just for Techno-nerds!

Name: Linux
Aliases: Freedom, The Power Box, Pain, Torture
Learning curve: Intermediate to advanced
Architecture: 32- and 64-bit character-based interface (graphical shell available)

You can't discuss Linux without mentioning its roots: the commercial UNIX operating system. UNIX has a long history as an unbreakable and robust multitasking platform dating back before a mouse was even imagined. In their pure form, both Linux and UNIX are character-based like DOS, and their command language has inspired many a college computer student to change majors within minutes of first exposure. (However, both Linux and UNIX can take advantage of graphical shells that can transform them into graphical operating systems that rival XP in sheer beauty.) UNIX has airtight security features, and it's a highly efficient operating system that can even run on older and slower Pentium II and Pentium III computers with as little as 16MB of RAM.

Before the arrival of Windows NT (and its successors, Windows 2000 and Windows 2003 Server), UNIX machines were used as network servers, dial-up servers for modems, and other applications that required security, multitasking, and stability. And one of the primary uses of UNIX over the past decade or so has been on the Internet. Many Internet functions familiar to researchers, scientists, and students today have their basis in UNIX commands. Like Windows NT, UNIX supports SMP (which I explain in the "Windows 2003 Server: Microsoft's First String" section), so you can put more than one CPU in your computer for extra processing power.

Now that you're more familiar with the history, let's talk about Linux. Why is it such a hot topic these days? A direct competitor of Windows XP and

Windows 2003 Server, Linux is basically a rewrite of UNIX created by programmers from around the world, working almost exclusively on the Internet to share code, specifications, and ideas. Linux is copyrighted, but it's free of charge for personal use. (That's one of the reasons for its success right there!) It runs virtually all UNIX software, and emulators that run most popular DOS and Windows programs are available for it. Linux can talk shop with most of the popular DOS, Windows, and Apple Mac OS X networking protocols.

Linux is an Internet nut's dream. It provides built-in support for TCP/IP (the communications protocol used on the Internet), Ethernet networking (see Chapter 12 for networking details), and multiple modems, so it's no surprise that many Internet service providers and small businesses choose Linux to power their Internet and intranet servers. Linux handles FTP, Internet e-mail, the Web, and Telnet with ease. Figure A-3 illustrates a typical Linux session; Note, however, that this is pure Linux, without a graphical user interface (GUI) shell.

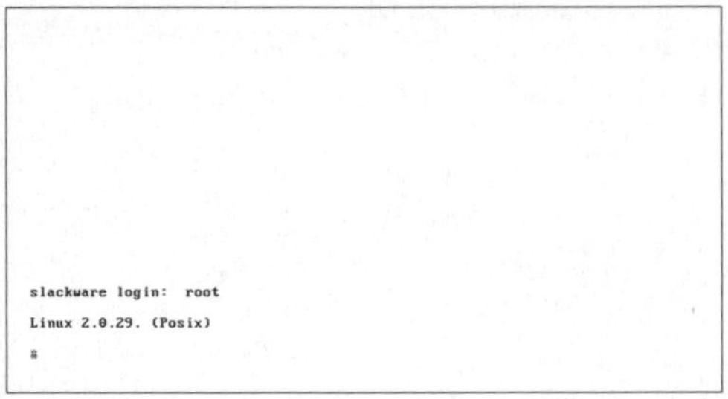

Figure A-3:
Without a
pretty GUI,
Linux is
character-
based
power.

```
slackware login:  root
Linux 2.0.29. (Posix)
#
```

With a graphical shell, Linux suddenly blooms into a beautiful butterfly — figuratively, anyway — featuring a design similar to Windows XP. Unlike with Windows, though, you can literally choose your own interface. A rapidly growing number of shells are available, each handling appearance and functionality differently (with variations both subtle and outrageous). For example, your icons can rotate, your windows can shimmer in and out of existence, and menus can be rearranged at will. In my opinion, the most popular Linux GUI, X, is practically as easy to use as Windows XP.

Linux has also proved popular because of its broad support and development among programmers. New hardware support is added constantly, and new technologies are often implemented within a few months. Linux is as well documented as UNIX or Windows 2003 Server, and programmers are constantly writing applications and utilities that run under Linux. In fact, the full source code package for the entire Linux operating system is available for the asking. (On the Web, you can download the source from the Linux Kernel Archives, at www.kernel.org).

In the early years of its growth, Linux was criticized for a lack of commercial programs. Where were the applications and games that have built the Microsoft kingdom? Linux could never enter the mainstream of the home computer world without these programs. Slowly, the times are a 'changin' as evidenced by commercial-quality multimedia applications such as MusicMatch Jukebox and games such as Doom 3 now on the Linux shelves at your local computer store (or available free for the downloading). Heck, I can remember when a store manager would have busted out laughing if you had even suggested a shelf dedicated to Linux.

Even with the appearance of mainstream applications, however, I can't say that Linux has reached the home market quite yet. Although new user-friendly commercial versions of Linux, such as Red Hat and Caldera OpenLinux, now ship with simpler installation programs and automated setup and configuration utilities, the character-based behemoth that is Linux still hides underneath. If you're going to use the full power of Linux — for example, by setting up the Apache Web server or an e-mail listserver or by building your own network around Linux — prepare to buy a shelf full of reference manuals. As a C programmer once told me, "It's not impossible to become a Linux guru, but you're going to gain weight with all that reading!"

UNIX and Linux summary: Linux is definitely not for the computer novice, but if you've had experience with DOS, networking, or the character-based tools on the Internet — or if you've ever used UNIX — it's certainly not impossible to figure out how to use it. Add to that factor the nonexistent price tag, the reduced system requirements, the arrival of new GUIs and commercial programs, performance that beats Windows 2003 Server, and the constant development, and you can see why Linux is giving Windows XP and Windows 2003 Server stiff competition.

Before You Install Your Operating System

Because all these operating systems are installed differently, I can't give you one comprehensive set of instructions. However, here's a checklist of preparations that should make your installation run more smoothly, no matter which platform you choose:

- ✔ **Back up your hard drive:** If you've saved any data or created any documents that you'd hate to lose, back up your computer completely before installing your operating system.

✔ **Defragment your hard drive:** Many operating systems need to create large temporary disk files, and it's easier to create these huge files on a defragmented hard drive. Defragmenting optimizes all the files on a hard drive so that your computer can read them faster. If you're running MS-DOS 6.22, you can use the DEFRAG utility to defragment your drive. If you're running Windows 98, Me or 2000, click the Start button and then choose Programs➪Accessories➪System Tools➪Disk Defragmenter. Under Windows XP, click the Start button and then choose All Programs➪ Accessories➪System Tools➪Disk Defragmenter.

✔ **Read the installation instructions:** Sure, your new operating system is designed to be installed by a kindergarten kid who's half asleep, but that doesn't excuse you from at least scanning the installation instructions.

✔ **Read the README file:** If something is important enough to include in a README file on the distribution disks (or CD-ROM), it might affect your installation.

✔ **Keep your driver disks handy:** Although you've installed parts under your previous operating system, you might need the specific drivers that came with your parts for your new operating system.

✔ **Impose on a friend:** Do you have a computer guru for a friend or a relative? Enlist an expert's help if you need it, especially if that person runs the same operating system that you're installing.

✔ **Yell for the cavalry:** What do you do if something goes horribly wrong and you can't find anything about it in the installation guide? Don't panic! Keep the tech support number for the operating system close at hand; it should be located in the manual or the additional literature that accompanied your operating system.

Before calling for tech support: Have your serial number handy and be prepared to answer questions about what type of computer you have and the parts you've installed. Be patient, too — tech support representatives for major software developers answer literally hundreds of calls per day, and you'll probably have to wait for at least five minutes before you speak to a human voice.

Appendix B

Glossary

- -

access time: The amount of time that a hard drive, CD-ROM drive, DVD drive, or memory module takes to read data. The faster the access time, the better.

adapter card: A circuit board that plugs into your motherboard to provide your computer with additional functionality. For example, a video adapter card plugs into your motherboard and enables your computer to display text and graphics on your monitor.

AGP (accelerated graphics port): A bus standard for many of today's fastest 3-D video cards that offers graphics performance even better than "ancient" video cards that use the PCI bus. AGP slots are rated by 2x, 4x, and 8x speeds — as you might guess, the higher the X factor in the speed rating, the faster the data flows to and from your video card. **See also** PCI.

application: A program that performs a task on your computer. For example, an Internet application is a program that performs some useful function while your computer is connected to the Internet.

AT-class: An older, standard set of dimensions for a PC's motherboard and case derived from the original IBM AT-class computer. If your PC used an AT-class motherboard, you must also have an AT-class case. AT-class cases and hardware are practically extinct (except to scavengers) because ATX-class cases and hardware have taken over the PC market.

Athlon Sempron: A lower-cost version of the Athlon XP processor, designed for the least-expensive entry PCs (like the kind you see offered by mail-order and department stores). The Sempron is not recommended for gaming or power user PCs.

Athlon 64: A new 64-bit Athlon processor. At the time of this writing, the Athlon 64 CPU is the most popular midrange processor offered by AMD and is a good choice for all but hard-core gamers and those looking for the absolute fastest PC.

Athlon 64 FX: A version of the Athlon 64 processor designed for delivering the best performance in games and high-end 3-D rendering applications. The FX series is significantly faster than a standard Athlon 64 (and quite a bit more expensive).

Athlon 64 X2 Dual-Core: The latest and fastest version of the Athlon 64 processor, utilizing two CPU cores that allow far superior efficiency and speed (especially when multitasking among more than one application). As you might have guessed, the X2 Dual-Core is one of the most expensive CPUs in the AMD lineup.

Athlon XP: An older processor series from Advanced Micro Devices (more popularly called AMD). The Athlon XP is a good choice for an inexpensive PC, but it is rapidly disappearing from the market and no longer offers the best performance for power user applications and computer games.

ATX-class: Today's standard set of dimensions and features for a PC's motherboard and case, with support for standard built-in ports on the motherboard and simpler connectors for power, case switches, and case lights. If you buy an ATX-class motherboard for your computer, you must also use an ATX-class case.

bank: Another term for a RAM module socket on your motherboard. Most motherboards have at least two RAM banks.

BIOS (basic input/output system): Your PC's BIOS software controls many low-level functions of your computer, such as keeping track of your hard drive's characteristics and what type of monitor you're using. The BIOS resides on one or two computer chips on your motherboard.

bit: The smallest unit of information used by a computer. It can have a value of either 1 or 0.

bonding: A technique for combining two analog or DSL modem connections to double the throughput (as a single connection).

bps (bits per second): A common method of measuring the speed of a modem. Today's high-speed modems are usually measured in kilobits per second (Kbps), as in 56 Kbps.

broadband: A high-speed Internet connection that delivers data much faster than a traditional dial-up analog modem connection. Common Internet broadband connections include DSL, cable, and satellite. **See also** DSL.

bus: A slot on your motherboard that accepts adapter cards. Bus slots on Pentium motherboards are generally 16-bit ISA slots, 32-bit PCI slots, AGP slots, or PCI-Express slots. **See also** AGP, ISA, PCI, and PCI-Express.

byte: A group of eight bits that represents a single character of text or data stored in your computer's RAM.

CA (commonsense assembly): The technique of preventing mistakes during the assembly of a computer by using your common sense. First postulated by the author of this book.

cable modem: An external device that connects your computer to your cable TV company's coaxial cable. A cable modem is a requirement for connecting to the Internet through cable access. Although a cable modem really isn't anything like a traditional analog modem, it looks like one.

cache: A special bank of memory that holds data that is often used or that will be required in a few nanoseconds. Storing data in a cache speeds up the operation of your PC because the data doesn't have to be retrieved from RAM or your hard drive. Many components have a cache, including your CPU, your hard drive, and your CD/DVD recorder.

case: The metal enclosure that surrounds your computer and holds all its parts. The case, typically held on with screws or thumbwheels, might have a separate cover that you can remove to add or remove parts; other cases are one piece and simply open up.

CD-ROM drive: An internal device that can read both CD-ROMs (which store computer programs and files) and audio CDs (which store music). A typical CD-ROM can hold as much as 700MB of data. CD-ROM drives cannot write to the disc; they can only read data.

CD-RW drive: Also called a CD recorder. Enables you to record (and re-record) CDs. Discs made with a CD-RW drive can hold computer data and music. CD-Rs can be read on any CD-ROM drive but can be recorded only once. CD-RWs can be read on most CD-ROM drives and can be re-recorded.

Celeron: A less expensive version of the Pentium 4 CPU produced by Intel for the home market. Although a Celeron chip lacks the performance of a full Pentium 4-class CPU of the same speed, it's still a popular processor for low-end PCs.

CGA (color graphics adapter): The original IBM PC color standard. Programs with CGA support could display a stunning four colors at a time.

client-server: A network in which computers act as clients and retrieve information or services from a central server computer. Server computers can also hold common shared resources, such as modems or CD-ROM drives, or provide shared access to Internet services such as e-mail and a Web site.

CMOS (complementary metal-oxide semiconductor): CMOS RAM stores configuration data about your PC's hardware even after your PC is turned off.

coax: Standard Ethernet cable (also called 10Base2 or 10Base5); commonly used on simple peer-to-peer networks.

color depth: A reference to the number of colors in an image. Popular color depths are 256 colors, 64,000 colors, and 16 million colors.

COM port: A numeric designator for a serial port that uses standard hardware settings. Most PC serial ports can be set to one of four COM ports: COM1 through COM4.

component: The technoid word for a piece of computer hardware; a computer part.

compression: The use of a mathematical formula to reduce the amount of disk space taken up by a file, a video clip, or an image. Some compression schemes can reproduce the original exactly; other compression schemes lose some detail from the original. Modems also use compression to reduce the time necessary to transfer a file.

CPU (central processing unit): The chip that acts as your computer's brain. The CPU performs the commands provided by the programs that you run.

DAT (digital audio tape): A high-speed tape drive used to back up the data on your hard drive. DAT backups, which can hold 4 to 80GB or more of data on a single tape, are the most reliable backup drives on the market. Most companies with networks use DAT drives to safeguard their data by backing up nightly — and you, too, should back up the data on your hard drive regularly.

DDR (double data rate): The standard RAM module used on Pentium 4 computers. A DDR memory module is effectively twice as fast as an older SDRAM module of the same speed. **See also** SDRAM.

DDR2: A faster standard for RAM modules developed by Intel, offering increased bandwidth and better performance with upcoming hardware. At the time of this writing, however, DDR2 modules still perform at about the same speed as DDR memory modules.

digital camera: A camera that looks and operates much like a traditional film camera, except that its finished images are uploaded directly to a computer rather than processed into photographs. Digital cameras are more expensive than their film cousins.

DIMM (dual inline memory module): A specific type of RAM module usually used with Pentium 4 and Athlon computers.

DIP (dual inline packaging) switches: A bank of tiny, sliding (or rocker) switches that enables you to set different features on your motherboard, some components, and many adapter cards. Use the tip of a pen to slide or push the switches into their proper sequence.

DirectX: An extension to Windows XP and Windows 2003 Server that enables fast animation and graphics display in game and multimedia programs.

distinctive ring: A service from your telephone company that enables more than one telephone number to use the same physical telephone line.

DOS (disk operating system): One of the oldest operating systems still in use on PCs. This character-based operating system requires you to type commands to run programs.

dot pitch: The amount of space between pixels on a monitor. The smaller the dot pitch, the clearer and more detailed the display.

DPMS (display power management signaling): A feature that enables your computer to power down your monitor after a specified period of inactivity. This feature helps save energy and money.

drawing tablet: An input device that looks like a larger version of a touchpad. Although the drawing tablet can be used as a pointing device, it is typically used by graphic artists for freehand drawing in graphics applications.

DSL (digital subscriber line): A high-speed connection to the Internet offering top speeds of around 4 to 8 Mbps. Although DSL uses regular copper telephone line and is always on, it's still not available in some rural areas of the country.

DSL modem: An external device that connects your computer to a DSL line. The modem looks like a traditional analog telephone modem but delivers data much faster.

DVD (digital video disc or digital versatile disc): The replacement for the older CD-ROM format. A single DVD can hold from 4.7 to 17GB. DVDs can hold computer data, full-length movies, and several hours of audio in MPEG format.

DVD-RW/DVD+RW drive: A DVD recorder that enables you to record (and re-record) DVDs. DVD-Rs and DVD+Rs can be read on any DVD drive (and virtually all DVD players designed for use with your TV set), but they can be recorded only once. DVD-RWs and DVD+RWs are not as compatible as DVD-R and DVD+R discs, but they can be re-recorded.

DVI (digital visual interface or digital video interface): A high-performance port that connects your video card to the latest flat-panel LCD and CRT monitors. A DVI connection provides the best-quality video signal and the fastest data transfer between your PC and your monitor — digital end-to-end, as the techs say.

EDO (extended data output): A standard type of RAM module used on older 486 and Pentium-class computers that provides faster operation than earlier types of RAM.

EIDE (enhanced integrated drive electronics): The standard hard drive and device interface technology in use on PCs. Standard EIDE controllers (which are built into today's motherboards) can handle as many as four EIDE devices, which can include additional hard drives, tape backup drives, and DVD drives.

Ethernet: A network topology in which data is broadcast across the network between computers. Although Ethernet is generally less efficient than other network architectures, it's less complex and less expensive to maintain.

external peripheral: A type of peripheral or device that sits outside your computer's case and is connected by a cable — for example, an external modem.

fax modem: A type of modem that has all the functionality of a standard modem but can also exchange faxes with either another fax modem or a standard fax machine.

female connector: A cable connector with holes that accept the pins on a male connector.

fingertip mouse: A pointing device that uses a small button. To move objects onscreen, you push the button in the direction that you want. Fingertip mice are common on laptop computers.

firewall: A program or device designed to protect network data from being accessed by a computer hacker. Most Internet and Web sites use a firewall to provide security for company data.

FireWire: The popular name for the IEEE 1394 high-performance serial bus connection standard; developed by Apple. A FireWire connection is similar to a USB connection. Devices can be added or removed without rebooting the computer, and you can daisy chain as many as 63 FireWire devices from a single port. Because of a FireWire port's high data-transfer rate of 400 Mbps and ability to control digital devices, it is especially well suited for connecting digital camcorders and external hard drives to your PC. The latest FireWire 800 standard (which is now available for PCs) can transfer data at a mind-boggling 800 Mbps.

Flash BIOS: An advanced BIOS chipset that can be updated with new features by running an upgrade program (usually available from the manufacturer of your motherboard).

Flash drive: An external solid-state removable storage drive that connects to your USB port. These drives store data using the same technology as the memory cards that you find in digital cameras.

flat-panel monitor: A monitor that uses LCD technology instead of a traditional tube. LCD monitors have been used on laptop computers for years and are now just as popular for full-size desktop computers. A flat panel is much thinner than a traditional tube monitor and uses less electricity and emits very little radiation.

floppy drive: A component housed inside your computer; can save program and data files to floppy disks, which can be stored as backups or loaded on other PCs. Computers use 3½-inch floppy disks that can store as much as 1.44MB of data on a single disk. However, floppies are unreliable and might not be readable on other PCs.

game port: A port for connecting joysticks and game peripherals. Game ports can be installed separately, although most sound cards have a game port built in.

GB (gigabyte): A unit of data equal to 1024MB (megabytes).

GHz (gigahertz): The frequency (or speed) of a CPU as measured in billions of cycles per second.

hacker: A computer user who attempts to access confidential information or steal data across the Internet or a network without authorization. Hacking is a criminal offense.

hard drive (or hard disk): A component that usually fits inside your case. Your hard drive acts as permanent storage for your programs and data, enabling you to save and delete files. Unlike the RAM in your computer, your hard drive does not lose data when you turn off your PC.

infrared port: An external optical port that allows fast, wireless transfer of data between your PC and another computer equipped with a compatible infrared port.

inkjet: A method of printing in which ink is injected from a cartridge onto paper to create text and graphics on the page. Color inkjet printers are relatively inexpensive but take longer to print a page than a comparable laser printer.

interface: A technoid term that refers to the method of connecting a peripheral to your computer. For example, printers use a parallel port interface or a USB interface; hard drives use EIDE, FireWire, SATA, or SCSI interfaces. Some interface types refer to adapter cards; others refer to ports and cables. **See also** EIDE, FireWire, SCSI, and USB.

internal component: A component that you install inside your computer's case — for example, a hard drive or an internal modem.

ISA (industry standard architecture): ISA bus slots accept 16-bit adapter cards to add functionality to your computer. ISA cards are typically slower than PCI adapter cards, and many motherboards no longer include an ISA slot.

joystick: An input device (for games) that's similar to the control stick used by an airplane pilot. Predictably, joysticks are usually used by game players who enjoy flight simulators.

jumper: A set of two or more pins that can be shorted with a tiny plastic-and-metal crossover. Jumpers are commonly found on motherboards, components such as hard drives, and adapter cards.

KB (kilobyte): A unit equal to 1024 bytes.

keyboard port: Where the cable from your keyboard connects to your computer. Keyboard ports come in two sizes: the older, larger port and today's standard PS/2 smaller port. You can buy an adapter to make any keyboard fit either size of keyboard port.

LAN (local area network): See network.

laser: A printer technology in which a powder is bonded to paper to create text and graphics. Laser printers are fast and produce excellent print quality but are typically more expensive than inkjet printers.

Linux: A 32-bit (or 64-bit) operating system similar to UNIX and popular on the Internet for use with Web servers. Unlike UNIX, Linux is freeware and its source code is available. **See also** UNIX.

male connector: A cable connector with pins that fit into the holes on a female connector.

MB (megabyte): A unit equal to 1024KB.

MHz (megahertz): The frequency (or speed) of an older CPU as measured in millions of cycles per second.

MIDI (musical instrument digital interface): The MIDI hardware standard enables computers of all types to play MIDI music and enables interaction between the computer and the instrument. MIDI music files are common on the Internet.

MIDI port: Enables you to connect a MIDI-compatible musical instrument to your computer. Notes that you play on the instrument can be recorded on your PC, or your PC can be set to play the instrument all by itself.

modem: A computer device that converts digital data from one computer to an analog signal that can be sent over a telephone line. On the opposite end, the analog signal is converted back to digital data. Modems are widely used to access the Internet, online services, and computer bulletin board systems.

monitor: An external component that looks something like a TV screen. Your computer's monitor displays all the graphics generated by your PC.

motherboard: Your computer's main circuit board. It holds the CPU, RAM modules, and most of the circuitry. Adapter cards plug into your motherboard.

mouse: The standard computer pointing device. You hold the mouse in your hand and move it in the desired direction to create movement on your screen. A mouse also has buttons that you can press to select items or run a program.

Mozart, Wolfgang Amadeus: My favorite classical composer, and a doggone good piano player to boot. He created the world's most beautiful music, and I'm happy to say that I now have a complete audio CD collection of every single note that he ever composed.

MP3: A popular digital sound format used to download CD-quality music from the Internet. Your computer can play MP3 files through its speaker system, you can listen to them with a portable MP3 player, or you can record MP3 files to a CD-ROM and play them in any standard audio CD player.

MPEG (Moving Pictures Expert Group): A popular digital video format and compression scheme often found on the Web. MPEG-format video is used on commercial DVD movies.

network: A system of computers connected to each other. Each computer can share data with other computers in the network, and all computers connected to the network can use common resources such as printers and modems.

newsgroups: Also called Usenet. International Internet message areas, each of which is usually dedicated to a special interest. Reading and posting questions in these newsgroups is a fun way to find out more about a subject (as well as receive tons of unwanted Internet e-mail, which is lovingly termed **spam**).

OCR (optical character recognition): OCR software can "read" the text from a fax or a document scanned by a digital scanner and "type" that text into your computer word processing program.

parallel port: A standard connector on most PCs that enables you to add peripherals. Parallel ports are generally used to connect printers to PCs, although other devices, such as Zip drives and digital scanners, are available with parallel port connections.

PC card (or PCMCIA card): A device resembling a fat business card that plugs directly into most laptops. The card can perform the same function as a full-size adapter card, such as a modem, a network interface card, a SCSI adapter, or even a hard drive. A PC card can also be used on a desktop computer equipped with a PC card slot.

PCI (peripheral component interconnect): A PCI bus slot can hold a 32-bit adapter card to add functionality to your computer. PCI slots are faster than older ISA slots, so they're used for everything these days: for example, Ethernet cards, sound cards, and SCSI adapter cards. **See also** ISA and SCSI.

PCI-Express: The high-performance successor for a standard PCI slot, the PCI-Express bus is most commonly used these days for adding the latest and fastest video card to your PC.

peer-to-peer: A type of network in which every computer is connected to every other computer, and no server computer is required.

Pentium: The original Pentium CPU; the successor to the 486 series of processors. It was manufactured by Intel — successive versions included the Pentium II and Pentium III.

Pentium 4: The fourth version of the Pentium CPU from Intel. At the time this book was written, the Pentium 4 is the most popular CPU chip made for IBM-compatible personal computers.

Pentium Extreme Edition: The latest (and most expensive) Pentium CPU from Intel, offering dual-core architecture that delivers better performance while multitasking applications or playing games.

Pentium Xeon: A version of the Pentium 4 CPU designed for network server computers and high-powered workstation PCs. It's considerably more expensive than the standard Pentium 4 CPU.

pixel: A single dot on your monitor. Text and graphics displayed by a computer on a monitor are made up of pixels.

plug and play: A type of adapter card or external device that can be automatically configured by Windows. If your hardware device offers plug and play, the chances are greatly reduced that you have to manually configure the settings for it.

port: A fancy name for a connector that you plug something into. For example, your keyboard plugs into a keyboard port, and your USB scanner plugs into a USB port.

power supply: The box that carries electricity to your PC's devices. Your computer's power supply provides a number of separate power cables; each cable is connected to one of the various devices inside your computer that need electricity. A power supply also has a fan that helps to cool the interior of your computer. **Never attempt to open or repair a power supply!**

printer: An external device that can print text, graphics, and documents from your computer on paper. Most printers sold these days use inkjet or laser technology.

PS/2 mouse port: A special port that first appeared on the IBM PS/2 computer (hence the name). Most Pentium and Athlon-class motherboards feature a port reserved especially for your mouse or pointing device.

RAM (random access memory): The type of chip that acts as your computer's short-term memory. This memory chip holds programs and data until you turn off your computer.

RDRAM (Rambus dynamic RAM): An older design for RAM modules that delivered better performance than DDR RAM but is now being phased out in favor of DDR2 memory.

refresh: The number of times per second that your video adapter card redraws the image on your PC's monitor. Higher refresh rates are easier on the eyes.

rendering: A technoid term for creating 3-D objects and full 3-D scenes on your computer. The classic films **Toy Story, Finding Nemo,** and **A Bug's Life** feature rendered 3-D characters.

resolution: The number of pixels on your screen measured as horizontal by vertical. For example, a resolution of 1024 x 768 means that there are 1024 pixels across your screen and 768 lines down the side of the screen.

rpm (revolutions per minute): The speed of the platters in a hard drive. The faster the RPM, the faster the drive can access your data.

SATA (serial ATA) interface: A popular hard drive and device interface technology that is easier to configure and faster than EIDE, but SATA hardware typically costs somewhat more.

scanner: A device that converts (or captures) text and graphics from a printed page into a digital image. Scanners are often used to "read" pictures from books and magazines; the digital version of the picture can be edited and used in documents or placed on a Web page.

SCSI (small computer system interface): A popular hard drive and device interface technology that is faster and supports more devices than EIDE but costs more. **See also** EIDE.

SCSI ID: A numeric identifier assigned to each device in a SCSI chain. Each device requires a unique SCSI ID for proper operation.

SCSI port: A connector built into most SCSI adapter cards that enables you to add external peripherals, such as CD recorders and scanners, to your SCSI device chain.

SDRAM (synchronous dynamic RAM): An older type of RAM module that was often used on Pentium II and Pentium III PCs. It offers faster performance than the standard EDO RAM modules used on 486 and original Pentium computers. **See also** RAM.

serial port: A standard connector on most PCs that transfers data to and from an external device. A serial port is generally used to connect an external modem to your computer.

SIMM (single inline memory module): A specific type of RAM chip usually used with older "antique" 486 and original Pentium-class computers.

slot 1: The motherboard slot designed to accept an older Pentium II (and some Pentium III) processors.

sound card: An adapter card that enables your computer to play music and sound effects for games and other programs. Sound cards can also record audio from a microphone or stereo system.

static electricity: The archenemy of all computer circuitry, especially computer chips. Before you install anything in your computer, you should touch the metal chassis of your computer to discharge any static electricity on your body.

subwoofer: A separate speaker that you can add to a standard two-speaker computer sound system. Subwoofers add deep bass response and can bring realistic depth to sound effects.

SVGA (super video graphics array): The most common graphics standard for PC video adapter cards and monitors now in use. The SVGA standard allows for more than 16 million colors (24-bit or true color).

tape backup drive: A type of drive that enables you to back up your computer's files to removable magnetic cartridges.

terminator: A switch or small resistor pack found on every SCSI device. (Each end of a SCSI device chain must be terminated for everything to work properly.) A different type of terminator is also required at each end of an Ethernet peer-to-peer network. **See also** SCSI.

token ring: A network topology in which data is attached to a token and circulated among computers on the network.

topology: The structure or design of a network.

touchpad: A pointing device that reads the movement of your finger across the surface of the pad. This movement is translated to cursor movement on your screen.

trackball: A pointing device that resembles an upside-down mouse. You move the cursor by rolling the trackball with your finger or thumb and clicking buttons.

twisted-pair cable: Also called 10BaseT, 100Base-T, and 1000Base-T, depending on the speed of the network. A form of network cable that looks much like telephone cord, twisted-pair cable is commonly used on Ethernet networks with a central hub or switch.

UNIX: A 32-bit, character-based operating system. Like DOS, UNIX is controlled from a command line, but graphical front ends are available. The UNIX commercial operating system is well known for security and speed, and UNIX computers have run servers on the Internet for many years. **See also** DOS.

USB (universal serial bus): A standard connector that enables you to daisy chain a whopping 127 devices, with data transfers at as much as 12 megabits per second for USB standard 1.1 (and a respectable 480 Mbps for USB standard 2.0). USB connectors have become the standard of choice for all sorts of computer peripherals, from computer videocameras and scanners to joysticks and speakers. (By the way, a USB 1.1 device works just fine when connected to a USB 2.0 port.)

VGA (video graphics array): The IBM PC graphics standard that featured 256 colors. Replaced on most of today's computers by the SVGA standard. **See also** SVGA.

video card: An adapter card that plugs into your motherboard and enables your computer to display text and graphics on your monitor. Advanced adapter cards can speed up the display of Windows programs and 3-D graphics.

voice modem: A computer modem that can also act as an answering machine and voice mail system. Voice modems typically have a speakerphone option as well.

WAV: The Microsoft standard format for a digital sound file. WAV files are common across the Internet and can be recorded in CD-quality stereo.

wavetable: A feature supported by all modern PC sound cards. A wavetable sound card produces more realistic instrument sounds (and therefore more realistic sounding music).

Windows 2003 Server: The latest advanced version of the Windows operating system from Microsoft. The direct descendant of Windows NT and Windows 2000, it comes in a number of flavors designed to appeal to small businesses. Windows 2000 makes a great network server or Internet server but, like NT before it, is much more expensive than Windows XP.

Windows Me (Millennium Edition): The last version of the Windows operating system to use a 16-bit DOS architecture (following in the footsteps of Windows 95 and Windows 98). Like Windows 98, Windows Me is no longer actively supported by Microsoft.

Windows NT: The predecessor to Windows 2000. In the days of Windows 98 and Windows Me, NT was the faster, more secure, more stable, and much more expensive version of Windows that was popular with power users and Web/Internet servers. NT is still popular as the backbone of some office networks.

Windows XP: The most popular 32-bit operating system for the PC. Windows is a multimedia, graphical operating system that relies heavily on a pointing device, such as a mouse. Windows 98, the predecessor to Windows XP, has fewer features and lacks support for the latest hardware. (On the other hand, it occupies less space on your hard drive than Windows XP.)

Windows XP 64: A new version of Windows XP that's designed to support the new generation of 64-bit processors from Intel and AMD. 64-bit functionality allows faster and more efficient multitasking, as well as faster hard drive performance.

wireless mouse: A pointing device similar to a standard mouse but without the cord that connects it to the computer. Wireless mice require batteries but are a little more convenient without the cord.

ZIF (zero insertion force) socket: A socket that makes it easy to upgrade your computer's CPU in the future. The lever unlatches the CPU so that you can easily remove it from the socket and then drop in a new CPU.

Zip drive: A type of drive that uses a removable cartridge about the size of a floppy disk. Each Zip disk stores anywhere from 100 to 750MB of data, and the data can be retrieved much faster from a Zip disk than from a floppy disk. Zip drives are available with USB, FireWire, and EIDE interfaces. **See also** FireWire, SCSI, and USB.

Index